AMIENS
1918

To Henry

AMIENS 1918

VICTORY FROM DISASTER

GREGORY BLAXLAND

Pen & Sword
MILITARY

AN IMPRINT OF PEN & SWORD BOOKS LTD.
YORKSHIRE - PHILADELPHIA

First published in Great Britain in 1968 by Frederick Muller Ltd.

Reprinted in this format in 2018 and 2020 by
Pen & Sword Military
An imprint of
Pen & Sword Books Ltd
Yorkshire – Philadelphia

ISBN 978 1 52679 646 2

A CIP catalogue record for this book is
available from the British Library.

Printed and bound in England by CPI Group (UK) Ltd, Croydon, CR0 4YY

Pen & Sword Books Limited incorporates the imprints of Atlas, Archaeology, Avia-tion,
Discovery, Family History, Fiction, History, Maritime, Military, Military Classics,
Politics, Select, Transport, True Crime, Air World, Frontline Publishing, Leo Cooper,
Remember When, Seaforth Publishing, The Praetorian Press, Wharncliffe Local
History, Wharncliffe Transport, Wharncliffe True Crime and White Owl.

For a complete list of Pen & Sword titles please contact

PEN & SWORD BOOKS LIMITED
47 Church Street, Barnsley, South Yorkshire, S70 2AS, England
E-mail: enquiries@pen-and-sword.co.uk
Website: www.pen-and-sword.co.uk

Or

PEN AND SWORD BOOKS
1950 Lawrence Rd, Havertown, PA 19083, USA
E-mail: Uspen-and-sword@casematepublishers.com
Website: www.penandswordbooks.com

CONTENTS

ILLUSTRATIONS

Gun teams move forward at Homiecourt (*Imperial War Museum*)

The 17th Northern Division in reserve after the retreat from the Flesquières salient (*Imperial War Museum*)

The 5th Gordon Highlanders at Nesle (*Imperial War Museum*)

German prisoners near Albert (*Imperial War Museum*)

British and French troops behind the lines near Boves (*Imperial War Museum*)

A scene in Amiens when the city was still in peril of capture (*Imperial War Museum*)

Villers Bretonneux and her Australian defenders (*Imperial War Museum*)

General Sir Hubert Gough (*Imperial War Museum*)

General Sir Henry Wilson, C.I.G.S. (*Paul Popper Ltd.*)

General Sir Henry Rawlinson at Fourth Army Headquarters (*Imperial War Museum*)

Lieut.-General Sir John Monash (*The Mansell Collection*)

Lieut.-General Sir Arthur Currie with General the Hon. Sir Julian Byng (*Imperial War Museum*)

Canadians en route to the front and German prisoners under escort from Hangard on August 8th (*Imperial War Museum*)

Headquarters 3rd Canadian Division as the attack was resumed on August 9th (*Imperial War Museum*)

A combined infantry and tank attack during the Australians' advance on Lihons, August 9th (*The Australian Government*)

A diminished Australian platoon being briefed for an attack (*The Australian Government*)

General Rawlinson and Field-Marshal Haig with King George V (*The Mansell Collection*)

Group at Fourth Army Headquarters, Flixécourt (*Imperial War Museum*)

Two men of the 5th Australian Division who did not get through the wire round Anvil Wood (*The Australian Government*)

Men of the 12th Division at Epéhy (*Imperial War Museum*)

Australians impeded near Bellicourt (*Imperial War Museum*)

The Band of the Staffordshire Brigade playing amid the ruins of Bellenglise

(*Imperial War Museum*)

Men of the Staffordshire Brigade at the St Quentin Canal (*Imperial War Museum*)

British troops were sent to Italy following the disaster the Italians suffered at Caporetto in October and November 1917

A small expeditionary force of two Portuguese divisions entered the line in French Flanders in late 1917

German prisoners

The allied powers launched a series of offensives on the Western Front in the summer and autumn of 1918

American troops during the Meuse-Argonne Offensive

An injured soldier being loaded into a first aid truck

Destruction caused in the historic city of Reims

Valenciennes, close to the French border with Belgium

MAPS

PREFACE

I feel I should make it clear from the start that I played no part in the events I have tried to describe. I was not in fact born until the ink had lain on the Armistice agreement for a month. This, as it turned out, was good timing for participation in the second term of World War, and like others of my generation I saw sufficient of it to marvel at the fortitude of those who endured the more intense, more harrowing, and infinitely more prolonged fury of the first. Endurance naturally was at its highest premium in the last year of war, and this was my main motive in making a study of 1918. Much has been written about the failures of the previous years. Here is a success story, and it is offered as a tribute from a member of a subsequent generation to his elders.

The most dramatic events of 1918, at any rate as far as the British are concerned, happened along a belt stretching due east from Amiens to a depth of some fifty miles, and I have therefore focused my spotlight on these events, without I hope obscuring those on other parts of the Western Front and such political developments as had bearing on the fighting, all of which have been sketched in as essential background scenery. Rawlinson emerges as the star actor on the Amiens front, and I have described the part he played in some detail for the example it affords of British generalship, as shaped by four years upon the anvil.

Deeds of valour by battalions and individuals have been picked out for description here and there. I make no claim that they were the best and the bravest. They have been chosen as samples and owe inclusion to the double chance of being on conspicuous record (usually as citations for the Victoria Cross in the case of individuals) and being pertinent to the story. For every V.C. won at least three hundred other acts of gallantry, trailing only slightly in degree, were recognised by decoration and many, many more escaped notice or acknowledgement. It is for what they represent, rather than for the glory of any individual, that the few have been picked from the many.

G. B.

SOURCES AND THANKS

The bones of this book have been provided by the British Official History, *Military Operations, France and Belgium, 1918* (Macmillan), edited by Brigadier-General Sir James Edmonds. It runs to five volumes, each over 500 pages long, and having not been completed until 1945 is well supplied with German information, which adds greatly to its interest. I am much indebted to this tome.

Meat has been added by the study of subsidiary histories, both for the particulars they give and the atmosphere they convey. Among them are Major-General Sir Archibald Montgomery's stodgy but splendidly illustrated *The Story of the Fourth Army* (Hodder and Stoughton, 1926), Captain G. H. F. Nichols's lively *The 18th Division in the Great War* (William Blackwood, 1922), Captain Cyril Falls's *History of the 36th (Ulster) Division* (Belfast, 1922), Major-General Sir Arthur Scott and P. Middleton Brumwell's *History of the 12th (Eastern) Division* (Nisbet, 1923), H. A. Jones's official *The War in the Air*, Volume VI (Oxford Clarendon Press, 1937), Colonel G. W. L. Nicholson's *The Canadian Expeditionary Force, 1914–19* (Canadian Ministry of Defence, 1962), and F. M. Cutlack's privately compiled and very entertaining *The Australians: Final Campaign, 1918* (Low, Marston, 1919). I have delved into a great number of regimental histories, of which the most valuable have been Captain B. H. Liddell Hart's *The Tanks* (Cassell, 1959), Lord Carnock's *History of the 15th The King's Hussars, 1914–22*, Colonel H. C. Wylly's *The History of The Queen's Royal Regiment, 1905–23*, Colonel R. S. H. Moody's *Historical Records of The Buffs, 1914–19*, Captain C. T. Atkinson's *The Queen's Own Royal West Kent Regiment, 1914–19*, Everard

Wyrall's *The Die-Hards in the Great War, 1916–19*, the anonymously written *The Sixteenth Battalion The Manchester Regiment*, Lieutenant-Colonel H. F. N. Jourdain's *The Connaught Rangers*, Volume III, and four from which extracts are quoted : Major W. E. Grey's *2nd City of London Regiment in the Great War*, G. D. Martineau's *A History of The Royal Sussex Regiment*, Captain S. McCance's *History of The Royal Munster Fusiliers*, and S. G. P. Ward's *Faithful: the Story of The Durham Light Infantry*. Two personal, more intimate accounts, both quoted, have been of great value : the Reverend R. W. Callin's *When the Lantern of Hope Burned Low* (1st/4th Northumberland Fusiliers) and Herbert Read's *In Retreat* (Hogarth Press, 1925).

I have obtained a few precious morsels in the form of eye-witness impressions by talking to veterans whenever opportunity arose and by consulting a selected few for whose help I am very grateful, namely Major-General A. L. Ransome and Major C. V. Wattenbach, late of the 18th Division, Mr. A. C. Piper, late of the 24th Division, Captain J. K. Wilson, late of the Tank Corps, Major R. J. Tuke, late of the 6th and 12th Divisions, and Mr. F. V. Lee, late of the 17th Division. During a trip to Amiens to see the ground I had the good fortune to meet an Australian, Mr. Roly Goddard, who had taken part in the recapture of Villers Bretonneux and settled in the neighbourhood, and I must also thank M. León Rinet, of Villers Bretonneux, for his assistance.

The accounts left by those in high places form, as it were, the book's nervous system. Diaries are the most valuable; they are bound to be slanted and may give distorted versions of conversations, but they throw vivid light on the outlook of the writer under the impact of events. Haig's diary, which seems to have been written with eventual publication in mind, is pre-eminent in this respect, and I have drawn widely on Robert Blake's *The Private Papers of Douglas Haig, 1914–19* (Eyre and Spottiswoode, 1952). Rawlinson was also a copious chronicler and correspondent. He not only kept a diary, which now resides at the National Army Museum with others of his papers, but also a journal, which was an enlargement on his diary, compiled every three or four days, and was the principal source for

Major-General Sir Frederick Maurice's *The Life of General Lord Rawlinson of Trent* (Cassell, 1928). Wilson's diary plays a similar part in Major-General Sir C. E. Callwell's *Field-Marshal Sir Henry Wilson* (Cassell, 1927). Of the auto-biographical histories, I have found them of value in the following order: General Sir Hubert Gough's *Fifth Army* (Hodder and Stoughton, 1931), General Sir John Monash's *The Australian Victories in France in 1918* (Angus and Robertson, Sydney, 1936), David Lloyd George's *War Memoirs*, Volume V (Nicholson and Watson, 1936), General Erich Ludendorff's *My War Memories* (Hutchinson, 1919), *The Memoirs of Marshal Foch* (Heinemann, 1931), and General John J. Pershing's *My Experiences in the World War* (Hodder and Stoughton, 1931). Use has also been made of a booklet of Sir Frederick Maurice's articles entitled *Intrigues of the War*.

As fluid for the joints I have relied on an old favourite issued as text-book at Sandhurst, Captain Liddell Hart's *A History of the World War* (Faber and Faber, 1934), also on General Sir Charles Harington's *Plumer of Messines* (Murray, 1935), Major-General Sir Edward Spears' *Prelude to Victory* (Jonathan Cape, 1939), Duff Cooper's *Haig* (Faber and Faber, 1936), John Terraine's *Douglas Haig, the Educated Soldier* (Hutchinson, 1963), Correlli Barnett's *The Sword Bearers* (Eyre and Spottiswoode, 1963), and the *Dictionary of National Biography*.

For their permission to reproduce extracts from books shown I am grateful to Mr. Robert Blake, Earl Haig and Eyre & Spottiswoode Ltd. (*The Private Papers of Douglas Haig*), to Beaverbrook Newspapers Ltd. (Lloyd George's *War Memoirs*), to Cassell and Company Ltd. (Callwell's *The Life of Field Marshal Sir Henry Wilson*), to Faber & Faber Ltd. (Read's *In Retreat*), to Hodder & Stoughton Ltd. (Gough's *Fifth Army*), to Hutchinson Ltd. (Ludendorff's *My War Memories*), to Low, Marston and Company (Cutlack's *The Australians: Final Campaign, 1918*), to Her Majesty's Stationery Office (*Military Operations, France and Belgium*), to Sir Edward Spears (*Prelude to Victory*), to Mrs. T. R. Slingluff (*The Memoirs of Marshal Foch*), to Captain G. D. Martineau and The Royal Sussex Association (*A History of The Royal Sussex Regiment*), to Lieutenant-Colonel W. E. Grey and The Royal Fusiliers (*2nd City of London Regiment in the Great War*), to The Durham Light Infantry (*Faithful*), and to Captain Cyril Falls (*History of the 36th (Ulster) Division*).

For their very helpful co-operation I am much indebted to the librarians of the Royal United Service Institution, the Ministry of Defence (Army and Central), the Imperial War Museum, and the Kent County Library, to the archivist of the National Army Museum, and the keeper of Public Records.

My grateful thanks also go to Mr. A. J. Smithers who very kindly and with great diligence read, checked, and by suggestion improved the manuscript.

1

THE DIMINISHED ARMY

(January)

The men of the London Regiment trudged on. It was dark, and the procession seemed endless as in single file and silence the blurred, stoic forms passed by, each huddled within a crust of moroseness and bent beneath the impedimenta of war. Greatcoats and jerkins were worn and, titled forward at the appropriate downcast angle, the squat steel helmets that had been laughed at as Chinese on their first appearance two years previously. Strapped to his chest, each soldier had a gasmask, unbuttoned for immediate use. Below it were his pouches, filled tight with .303 ammunition, with an extra bandolier carried slung; some also carried Mills grenades or a drum for a Lewis gun. On his back he carried a pack, with iron rations, socks, and shaving kit. Below it, making a mild clink at every stride, was his rounded mess tin, and below that, neatly rolled, was the groundsheet that did duty as bed, mattress and blanket, and below the groundsheet an entrenching tool. His bayonet bumped against his left hip, his water bottle against his right. His rifle was slung over one shoulder and on the other side he carried a shovel or pick. There were trenches to be taken over.

If the task was familiar and depressing, the surroundings were new and by comparison almost cheerful. For these men came from Ypres, where they had fought in the final battle for the Passchendaele ridge, and now they were in Picardy. The war appeared to have given this district little more than a pat, and although the ground was made slushy by thaw, there was nothing that these connoisseurs of the ghastly mixture would have reviled with the name of mud. Frogs croaked in the marshes, with only occasional interruptions from a falling shell, and a few

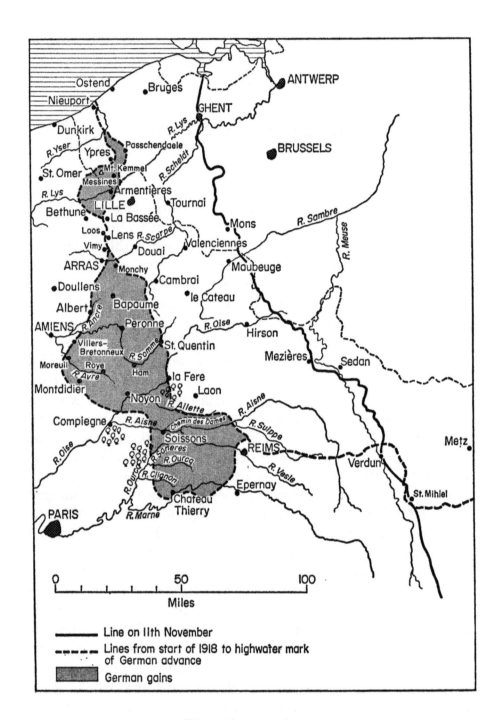

The Western Front

miles back peasants had been working with hoe and plough on land previously prepared for defence.

Further to alleviate the gloom, the outgoing troops were Frenchmen, and there was always a touch of pantomime in a relief between these volatile soldiers with the Ruritanian helmets and long rifles and their phlegmatic allies, specially if the latter happened to be Cockney. The poilus lavished all manner of good things on the Tommies, coffee, food, and wine, and departed with warm handshakes all round. There were aggravating complications all the same. Reserve ammunition, rations, even trench stores, all had to be replaced, range cards had to be remade and fresh direction signs put up. Officers were rather shocked to find the defences poorly developed in depth. The French assured them, however, that on this particular sector, which lay astride the swamps on either side of the River Oise, there could be no danger of attack.

These Londoners belonged to the 58th Division, which was one of three in France composed of battalions of this enormous territorial regiment whose history as such lasted only from 1908 to 1937. They had fought at Passchendaele with the Fifth Army and had now rejoined it in its new sector on the right of the British line—and this was ominous, for wherever the Fifth Army went battle always seemed to rage at its fiercest. None the less there could be no denying that the enemy was more remote, the scene infinitely less harrowing. The 58th's frontage was the last of a twenty-six mile stretch taken over from the French and, at ten miles, it was much the longest held by any division of the British Expeditionary Force.

The relief was complete by January 30th, 1918, bringing to belated fruition a decision taken the previous September at a conference attended by the Prime Ministers of Britain and France with their military staffs. Field-Marshal Sir Douglas Haig had not been present, being fully occupied with the Third Battle of Ypres, and when he received the resultant instruction a week later he wrote in his diary: "A great bombshell arrived today". He appealed to General Pétain, the French Commander-in-Chief, with whom he was to arrange details, explaining that he (Haig) could do more to help the French by continuing the offensive, thus absorbing German reserves, than by taking over

3

part of their line. Pétain could not agree. He had no enthusiasm for offensive action, except on a very limited scale, and indeed had aggravated Haig by the poor support he had given him for his Ypres offensive. He had nursed the morale of the French Army back to health, largely with the implied promise of no rash action, and an important part of the remedy was the provision of four leave periods a year for the poilu (whereas the Tommy had a fortnight every fifteen months) and this greatly increased the strain of holding a long frontage. Haig was outnumbered by three to one, for Pétain had the support not only of his Government but of the British one too, the Prime Minister, David Lloyd George, being willing enough to support a measure that would compel Haig to go on the defensive. There could be no escape. Having used the Battle of Cambrai and the sudden need to despatch five of his divisions to Italy as causes of delay, Haig went to see Pétain on December 17th and agreed to extend his front to the Oise by the date achieved.

It was aggravating for Haig to serve a political leader in Lloyd George with whom he had nothing in common save a burning determination to win the war. The men were complete opposites. Haig's strength lay in his steadfast calm, his weakness in his painful difficulty in stating his views verbally. Lloyd George's strength lay in his explosive powers of verbal exposition, his weakness in his very brilliance, because it contained too much mercury to inspire the loyalty of simple subordinates. Haig, the dour Scot, was conservative by upbringing and outlook and had old-fashioned ideas about a gentleman's code of conduct. Lloyd George, the volatile Welshman, had made his name by preaching radicalism and by taunting the gentry. Outwardly there was none of the apparent antipathy between them that there was between Lloyd George and his C.I.G.S., General Sir William Robertson. Yet their writings reveal a mutual loathing. Haig could seldom mention Lloyd George in his diary except in terms of scathing contempt. Lloyd George, although writing after Haig's death and before the publication of his diaries, poured such scorn on Haig in his Memoirs, and in such a childishly tendentious manner, that he appears to have been bitterly jealous of him.

"I should think shifty and unreliable," was Haig's diary

verdict on Lloyd George, when the latter paid his first visit, as Minister of Munitions, to General Headquarters in January, 1916. When Lloyd George made his next visit to France he had become War Minister and the Battle of the Somme had been raging for two and a half months. A photograph shows Haig and Marshal Joffre both trying to convince Lloyd George, who is oozing scepticism, that the cavalry are about to break through. That, at least, is Lloyd George's version of the conversation. The cavalry could not even attempt to break through, and from now onwards Lloyd George's foremost aim, as he saw it, was to protect the manhood of the nation against the lethal optimism of their renowned Commander-in-Chief. He even went to see General Foch to ask his opinion of British generalship. Foch in due course reported this to Haig. "I would not have believed that a British Minister could have been so ungentlemanly," Haig informed his diary.

No sooner had Lloyd George become Prime Minister in December 1916, than he made an attempt to make Haig subordinate to an Allied Supreme Commander. The idea was sound enough, but it was put over in a clumsy and underhand manner and when the great offensive by the intended Supremo, General Nivelle, ended by plunging the French Army into mutiny, Haig and Robertson could claim to be fully justified in their successful resistance to the expansion of his authority. His position weakened, Lloyd George found himself unable to prevent Haig's Ypres offensive from developing into a long-drawn, indecisive affair of mud, blood and agony. Haig kept it going because his Chief of Intelligence, Brigadier-General John Charteris, constantly told him that the Germans were on the verge of collapse. It was therefore a shock to find them react so vigorously in late November after being shattered by the great tank attack towards Cambrai, launched on the expiry of the Ypres offensive. No sooner had the church bells in England rung their victory peel than news seeped through that the Germans had regained the ground lost, putting one general to flight in his pyjamas. Gloom and indignation replaced jubilance.

Haig's fortunes were at their lowest ebb, yet his enemy in Downing Street could still do no more than wage a war of attrition against him, chipping away to reduce his power. He made one attempt at direct assault, asking the War Minister, Lord Derby, to dismiss both Haig and Robertson. Derby stood up for them and made it clear that if they went he would go himself. Lloyd George yielded and agreed merely to the dismissal of certain members of Haig's staff. One of them was Charteris and the other the Chief of General Staff, Sir Launcelot Kiggell, who was in poor health, and Haig consented to their removal only after prolonged pressure by Derby and Robertson.

Such was the personal loss suffered by Haig for the terrible things endured by his soldiers in their attacks from Ypres between July 31st and November 12th, 1917. Their casualties are officially estimated at 244,897. In terms of morale the loss cannot be measured so simply, nor can it be on the German side, although probably their losses were if anything the greater, both physically and morally. The opinion of two famous writers with first-hand knowledge of the subject is of interest. In *The Story of the 29th Division* Sir Philip Gibbs writes "For the first time the British Army lost its optimism". John Buchan, who served as a staff officer, goes further in his *A History of the Great War*: "Men felt that they were being sacrificed blindly . . . For a moment there was a real ebb of confidence in British leadership." Lloyd George, needless to say, goes further still. Of Haig's army as a whole in that sombre winter of 1917–18, he reports, "It was tired and without confidence in the wisdom of the leadership which was responsible for the stupid and squalid strategy of the last two months of Passchendaele, and for the egregious muddle which threw away the great opportunities of Cambrai".

On the other hand the report of the censor, covering the worst months, October and November, and submitted to the War Cabinet in December, was, "The morale of the Army is sound." It noted, however, a striking difference in the letters from men of the Second Army, which had borne the brunt of the recent fighting, and in those from others. In the Second Army, "the favourable and unfavourable letters were almost evenly balanced"—which is pretty amazing bearing in mind the conditions—". . . In other armies the favourable extracts greatly exceed the adverse." There were, of course, many men in these other armies who had played their part in this Third Battle of Ypres, and if anything is established by the censor's report, which was the nearest thing available to a gallup poll, it must surely be that loss of optimism was local and temporary. What is beyond doubt is that the British had withstood the strain of continual offensives, spread over a period of seventeen months, rather better than their allies. The store of courage, from which such massive withdrawals had been made, was not empty yet.

Various causes for this state of affairs emerge from discussion with those who were there. One is the quality of leadership at a lower level. The war had acted as a ruthless sorting house, and there were few in command of brigades, battalions, and, to a lesser extent, companies who did not owe their position to the prowess they had shown in battle. It was not in the least unusual for the commanding officer of an infantry battalion to be under thirty years old; men over thirty-five were no longer eligible for appointment. Some positively radiated bravery and, by understanding of their men, could inspire rather than intimidate; others were of the canny, fatherly, battlewise variety, real rocks of comfort when tempest raged. Binding together the leaders and the led was a high concept of a soldier's duties, which had been inherited from the reign of Queen Victoria and transformed to glowing pride by the example set by the Regular Army in 1914. The desire to emulate these heroes still burned bright in many breasts that would never have been enclosed by uniform in the normal run of events; army discipline was readily accepted, and in the realms of administration and regimental tradition a regular sergeant-major could exert great influence on a new battalion, even if he had to do so on his own. The foundations were firm. And as a longstop, keeping him sane when all was madness around him and giving him that extra ounce of stamina, the British soldier had a fund of humour to fall back on, from whichever part of the islands he came, and the joke he appreciated most was one against himself. He was at advantage here over his enemy.

One further factor that can easily be overlooked is that throughout their offensives the British had been steadily advancing. The Battle of the Somme had compelled the Germans to fall back twenty miles. That of Arras had opened brilliantly with an advance that at least made this important town inhabitable, and even from the oft deplored Passchendaele battles an advance of five miles had been made in places and two ridges gained, by which life in the salient was made very much more tolerable. Troops were now resting where once they could not have stood up, and this made them conscious of achievement, however hard it had been won.

It is curious that such mutterings as were voiced never seem to have been directed at the summit. This presumably was because most misfortunes could be attributed, as by Siegfried Sassoon in his famous poem, to some specific plan of attack, to the cheery general who made it, and the "incompetent swine" on his staff. General Gough and the staff of his Fifth Army headquarters were the most frequent absorbers of such shafts, though no doubt many were thrown on by injured subordinate staffs. Haig appears to have been quite immune. Major Sir William Orpen, who as an official war artist travelled around more than most, wrote: "Never once, in all the time I was in France, did I hear a 'Tommy' say a word against 'Aig." The same is true of the former officers and men questioned by the author during the writing of this book. The most common explanation of failures is: "It was all Lloyd George's fault."

The faith engendered by Haig is a phenomenon of the Great War ignored by his critics. Physically, no field commander can ever have lived further from his troops or been worse equipped for impressing his personality on them. It was beyond him to make an inspiring speech and he heartily despised what would now be called publicity techniques. There was no flamboyance about him whatever. If he inspected troops he did so for his own information and would offer no ingratiating gesture in return, nor was he in the habit of issuing rousing messages of the "Together-you-and-I" variety either through press or staff channels. The majority of the men he commanded never set eyes upon him. Yet those who did come under his steady, rock-like gaze felt the stronger for it. By some strange feat of telepathy and certainly without conscious effort, this stern, uncommunicative, and quite extraordinary man managed to transmit his own boundless faith in victory from his chateau at Montreuil to the vast sprawling network of mud-holes, hovels and burrows that housed his million fighting men.

This perhaps was because Haig's faith was so completely genuine, so free from doubt, that it gave him a majestic serenity that radiated all the stronger from its very lack of artificial aid. It was based partly on a deep-rooted religious belief, which in turn was backed by undoubting conviction in the "justice of our cause" and the consequent availability of divine guidance, provided it was duly applied for, and partly on a temporal belief, no less deep-rooted, in his own professional ability. These together made him impervious to such assaults on his self-confidence as the pressure to dismiss members of his staff. They also account for the absence from his prolific writing in his diary of any note of self-reproach or doubt about any decision. And they explain not only his faith in the final victory, but his certainty that such a victory could be won only in the West, by maintaining the pressure, and with Britain bearing the brunt, and that a large contribution towards that final victory had, in that bleak winter of 1917, already been made by the Somme and Passchendaele offensives. "Insane egotism" were the words used by Lloyd George to describe such faith, but the writings of Ludendorff show that it was not entirely misplaced.

It is significant that Haig commanded the devoted loyalty of his immediate subordinates, and this must greatly have aided the proliferation of confidence throughout the far flung reaches of the B.E.F. Examination shows that his army commanders were not the callous fools it has become popular to regard them. The senior of them was Sir Herbert Plumer, who at sixty (in 1917) was four years older than Haig. He had been commissioned into the 65th Foot in the days before it became the 1st Battalion, The York and Lancaster Regiment, and his first battles had been against the Dervishes, at El Teb and Tamai, before the murder of General Gordon. Plumer was of a type that the modern Army (according to officer recruitment advertisements) eagerly claims to be extinct : he had a plump face, a plump tummy, a bristly moustache, florid complexion and usually a peppery expression. Yet he was a very able, meticulously thorough commander, as was proved by his classic siege operation, the capture of Messines ridge, and he always took pains to ensure that everything possible was done on the men's behalf. The troops sensed this to a remarkable degree—hence the nickname 'Daddy'—and with that paragon, Sir Charles Harington, at their head his staff worshipped him. He had (according to Colonel Repington) been "heart and soul" for the Passchendaele offensive and with his step-by-step methods had retrieved the earlier misfortunes inflicted on the Fifth Army. Having taken over the Second Army from Sir Horace Smith-Dorrien at the end of April 1915, he had been responsible for the Ypres Salient for two and a half years. It had turned his hair snow white.

Since November 9th, 1917, Plumer had been temporarily in Italy, commanding the five British divisions sent to prop a tottering front. General Sir Henry Rawlinson (all the army commanders held the rank of full-general) had therefore taken over the Second Army's front with his Fourth Army head-quarters. He, too, had all the characteristics of a type that appears to be out of favour with the Army of today, being a tall, polo playing, hereditary baronet with a penchant for the military stance, thumbs hooked beneath the buttons of the breast pockets, weight carried on one elegantly field-booted leg, with the knee of the other bent and its foot aslant. Sir Oswald Birley painted him thus, and the face portrayed looks down from a height, with chin receding slightly beneath a military moustache, and seems about to open up with sublime confidence, "Gentlemen, allow me to explain my plans". This was the man who launched the Somme offensive, bringing greater grief to Britain in one day than in any other throughout her history, and the picture fulfils conventional expectation of the sort of man responsible. Yet in 1918 he became the key figure in some of the greatest victories gained by British arms, and it is worth making closer examination of his career.

'Rawly' was nearly fifty-four at the close of 1917, that is almost three years younger than Haig, and whereas Plumer regarded the coinage of nicknames as deplorable familiarity, Rawlinson was delighted to have his bandied around. His father, who had gained the baronetcy, was a distinguished man of learning, President of the Royal Asiatic Society and Royal Geographical Society and Fellow of the Royal Society. From him Rawlinson inherited a good brain, and also acquired great ambition and very considerable charm, and if the former demolished the gains of the latter as far as his general popularity was concerned, the two pulled together most harmoniously towards advancement. He joined the 60th Rifles from Sandhurst and soon became A.D.C. in India to the famous General Roberts, of whom he became a devoted friend. Some years later, having transferred to the Coldstream Guards, he took leave in Cairo at the time of the Nile expedition and to the envy of his colleagues he won a place on General Kitchener's staff, also becoming his devoted friend. His first big battle was the Atbara, and he gained close acquaintance of the carnage caused, being responsible for the disposal of 2,850 enemy corpses and as many animal ones. "I was thankful to get away to our hot quarters without being sick," he wrote in his diary, copious chronicler that he was. Five months later he was at Omdurman. As the Dervish hordes swarmed into view, he was sent to tell the commander of the Egyptian cavalry screen to withdraw to the right flank. This officer was Captain Douglas Haig. "I noticed that his confident bearing seemed to have inspired his fellaheen," Rawlinson wrote that night.

During the South African War, Brevet Lieutenant-Colonel Rawlinson was besieged at Ladysmith with Sir George White, served on the staffs both of Roberts and Kitchener, and ended the war in command of a column of 2,400 mounted men.

In 1904, now brigadier-general, he became commandant of the Staff College, and he was subsequently able to put theory into practice as commander first of the 2nd Infantry Brigade and then of the 3rd Division, taking time off for a world tour with Kitchener in between. Many unfashionable topics exercised his active mind, most of all co-operation between all arms, a thing of no interest to most members of the British Army in those days of proud parochialism. On manoeuvres he won a reputation for craft. "Rawly is a fox," his opponents were warned.

Soon after the start of the Great War he was given command of IV Corps of the B.E.F. He nearly lost it. Sir John French was the only general he encountered (so it appears) whom he did not please. In an attack on Menin, before First Ypres, he was censured for his caution, which in fact saved one of his divisions from annihilation, and he incurred the Commander-in-Chief's serious displeasure when his corps made the first big deliberate assault attempted by the British, at Neuve Chapelle in March 1915, and suffered the fate that was to become so common, costly stagnation after a bright beginning. Rawlinson made an unworthy attempt, later to be emulated by French himself, to lay the blame for failure on a subordinate commander. The latter proved the charge false and the axe was about to fall on Rawlinson's neck. Haig, as his Army Commander, saved him. He had been impressed, when a fellow corps commander, by his buoyant outlook under the stress of grim crisis; he thought him "a card" and regarded his "bright joviality a great asset". Now he resolutely resisted French's craving for a scapegoat. "It was very good of him," wrote Rawlinson, when Haig told him of his reprieve, "and I am certain that I have a strong ally in his strong character and personality."

Haig appears never to have fully trusted Rawlinson and it is interesting that he should have inspired such loyal devotion. Its immediate effect is to be seen in a letter written by Rawlinson to the Adjutant-General—he was also in regular communication with the King, through his secretary, Clive Wigram—in which he says of the failure of this Neuve Chapelle attack, "I find it was as much my fault as anyone's". This spirit of self-criticism was to persist and stand him in good stead.

The Fourth Army was formed on February 5th, 1916, and Rawlinson was appointed to its command from the start, having previously held temporary command of the First. He obtained many faithfuls from his old IV Corps headquarters. At their head was an artilleryman, Archibald Mongomery, who was promoted major-general to be Chief of General Staff. A fine looking man, he had genius for staff work and made as sound a consultant for his chief as Harington for Plumer; he was full of self-assurance and forceful in the expression of his views. (In later years he was to add Massingberd to his surname, rise to the post of C.I.G.S., and sadly disappoint military realists.)

Sir Edward Spears, who made many visits in his capacity as liaison officer with the French, was much struck by the efficiency and helpful outlook of Headquarters Fourth Army. He was also an admirer of Rawlinson, as witness his book, *Prelude to Victory*. Having mentioned some frustration as typifying the trying occasions when "his humour, kindliness, tact, and responsive comprehension of the difficulties of others were never at fault" he says later, "What I admired most in him was the uncomplaining fortitude with which he took hard knocks. There were moments when I knew he had been badly and even unjustly treated, but he never, even by implication, complained."

Certainly there were some hard knocks by the Somme. Crude though the opening was, it would inevitably have been less disastrous if the attack had gone in at dawn, as Rawlinson wanted, instead of two hours later as requested by those acknowledged experts, the French. Rawlinson did not complain, but he absorbed the lesson about co-operating with his allies. A fortnight later he did attack at dawn and gained brilliant success, which would none the less have been greater but for the delay imposed by Haig. Rawlinson did not complain. Indeed he wrote of Haig when at long last the offensive ended, "He is a splendid man to serve." Of his soldiers he wrote to Lord Derby after three months of fighting, "They have fought with a bravery and determination one had never dared hope for." He fully accepted that the wearing-out battle had to precede the break-through—indeed, the theme running through his diary is that there could be no short cut to victory—and he also believed that there could be no substitute for the test of battle to rectify weaknesses, whether in his infantry, artillery or in that new and very raw arm (which he was the first to put into battle) the tanks. "During the battle of the Somme," he wrote, "we have learned many lessons, and are continuing daily to benefit by experience." Whether they could have been learned less painfully is a question to which there can be no conclusive answer, with theory and the fraudulent advantage of hindsight as our only guides.

Like Plumer, Rawlinson favoured painstaking methods, and it was probably for this reason that Haig chose the more dashing Gough for the leading rôle in the Third Battle of Ypres. The choice was proved unwise. Rawlinson, who admitted in his diary to being "very much disappointed", was assigned the task of launching an amphibious operation to outflank the Germans if their defences around Ypres collapsed. They did not, and Rawlinson was left champing until called in to take over the

Second Army's front on the departure of Plumer for Italy. He was therefore the freshest of Haig's army commanders.

On the right of the Fourth Army, holding the line from Armentières to Vimy Ridge, their proud possession since the previous April, was the First Army under a Scot, Sir Henry Horne. He was the odd man out among Haig's army commanders. Whereas the other four were divided evenly by origin between the Infantry and Cavalry, Horne came from the Royal Artillery, and whereas the others were all Old Etonians, Horne was a Harrovian. (Haig by contrast had been educated at Clifton.) He was also the least conspicuous of the five, being dour, highly professional, a zealot for detail, and quite without ostentation. He had started the war as brigadier-general commanding the 1st Corps artillery under Haig, of whom he was an exact contemporary. Soon promoted to the command of the 2nd Division, he had ordered his men to advance, with disastrous results, into their own stationary gas cloud at the Battle of Loos. Raised to the command of XV Corps for the Somme, he had served under Rawlinson and gained some notable successes by the skilled handling of his artillery, in particular the development of the creeping barrage. They won him promotion to the command of the First Army in September of that year, 1916.

The Third Army stood on the right of the First, holding on the left the gains it had made in front of Arras and on the right, some twenty miles distant, the remains of the thrust towards Cambrai achieved by the tanks in November. The Army Commander was the Honourable Sir Julian Byng. He was the fourth and comparatively impecunious son of the Earl of Strafford and had entered the Regular Army through the Militia, being commissioned into the 10th Royal Hussars in 1883. He was a happy young man, gay, friendly, and dashing, and so he remained. He gained great success in South Africa in command of the eccentric and far from regular South Africa Light Horse, and after that war he commanded his own regiment.

Byng's first command in France was of the 3rd Cavalry Division, to which he was appointed in September 1914. So successful was he that the following August he was rushed to Suvla to take command of IX Corps and salve what he could from an invasion on the rocks. He could devise no alternative to a withdrawal, and having carried it out with great success he was back in France by February 1916, taking command of XVII Corps, which he exchanged in May for the Canadian Corps. It was not easy for an English commander to win the confidence of the 'Colonials', especially if he were an aristocratic cavalryman. Byng succeeded magnificently. Indeed, according to Cyril Falls, he gained not only their confidence but their affection—"nowhere in the world at war was there a formation so large in which the links between the commander and the troops were so strong"—and he achieved this by the happy combination of an endearing personality and skilled generalship, which together sped the Canadians to their greatest triumph, the capture of Vimy Ridge in April 1917. The following June, on Allenby's departure for Palestine, Byng was raised to the command of the Third Army. Typically, he was keen to let the Tank Corps have a fling after they had turned in disgust from the mud around Ypres. Unfortunately, his enthusiasm caused him to attempt too much with too little and after the moon (not to mention Cambrai) had seemed within grasp he was left with a dangerous outward bulge in his line and a dent in his reputation.

Next and furthest on the right was the Fifth Army, spaced along a forty-two miles' frontage, twenty-six of which, as already stated, had just been taken over from the French. This of course was the army of Sir Hubert Gough. At forty-seven, he was far the youngest of Haig's army commanders. His regiment was the 16th Lancers, and on the outbreak of war he was in command of the 3rd Cavalry Brigade, which he took to France from the Curragh, gaining release from foolish involvement in the political battle for Northern Ireland. (Gough came from a family of land-owning Protestants from Southern Ireland.) It took him twenty-one months to rise from command of a brigade to that of an army, with the 2nd Cavalry Division, the 7th Infantry Division, and the 1st Corps (originally Haig's) his stepping stones. He achieved it by his fighting instinct. Small of build, with a long, lean face, he had the guts and tenacity of a terrier and had rare talent for inspiring his men, partly by his own indomitable presence, partly by his genuine sympathy for them and his admiration for their courage. There was gripping intensity about this man; for half an hour he grasped a certain commanding officer by the arm while he discussed with him points of basic infantry tactics before a battle.

Formed in May 1916, the Fifth Army was originally termed the Reserve Army. Its first task in battle could hardly have been more forlorn. In order to allow Rawlinson to concentrate on his more prosperous right wing, Gough was brought in to take over his two defeated left-hand corps on the day after the great Somme offensive began. It was a long time before he could reduce the fearful redoubts of Thiepval and Pozières, but Gough persevered and in November he gained marked success with a thrust leftwards beyond the Ancre. Presumably on the strength of this, he was entrusted with the leading assault rôle in the Third Battle of Ypres. He did not make a success of it. Indeed, men began to revile the Fifth Army and its commander so bitterly that Lord Derby, as War Minister, wrote to Haig imploring him to dismiss Gough. Haig knew Gough's qualities, as he had known those of his brother John, who had been Haig's Chief of Staff until shot dead by a stray bullet in February 1915. He refused to sacrifice his subordinate, although Derby wrote again a month or two later to say, "It has been borne upon me from all sides, civil and military, that he does not have the confidence of the troops he commands." However, Haig made him remove his Chief of Staff, Major-General Neil Malcolm, whose overbearing manner and failures as a staff officer clearly made a large contribution to the unpopularity of the Fifth Army. Thus both Haig and Gough faced the next battle with the ground made slippery beneath them by the enforced dismissal of trusted members of their staffs.

A much greater worry, incapable of solution by the simple process of replacement, was the shortage of men. This was an old complaint, which reached crisis proportions as 1917 drew to its weary close. A Cabinet Committee was convened to consider claims on the nation's manpower. The Army had to compete against sea and air power, industry, and agriculture, and finished last, despite the shrill, "reiterated warnings" of the Army Council. The latter asked for an immediate 250,000 men, of which 95,000 were required to bring the infantry battalions in France up to strength, and a further 350,000 to cover wastage over the next seven months. They were told that their estimate of wastage was excessive and that a total of only 100,000 men could be provided. What was not explained, but was subsequently admitted, was that the Government feared serious civil disturbances if there were drastic combing of labour to fill the ranks of Haig's army group. There was, however, an enormous Home Army, one and a half million strong, and it was admitted by the Army Council that it included 449,000 men—fit and over nineteen years of age—who could be made available for drafting overseas. It became a common charge made by soldiers that these men were deliberately kept at home by Lloyd George in order to deprive Haig. It does not bear close examination. The men were there in theory and their availability was agreed, but for each individual there was a reason, usually compassionate, against his immediate despatch. The Army Council were unwilling to squeeze too tight.

If the Committee's parsimony towards the Army was depressing, the recommendation that accompanied it was insulting, and in accepting it the Cabinet made a purely military decision over the heads of, and in the face of strong protest by, their military advisers : to keep divisions in being, their three infantry brigades were to be reduced from four to three battalions, as had already been done in the French and German armies. This solution to a problem that the Government had, in the eyes of the deprived B.E.F., themselves created ran directly contrary to the recommendations of Haig, who was loath to alter an organisation "which has stood the test and time of war". Its wisdom has subsequently been accepted, but at the time it created heat of feeling that fell little short of fury. Divisional and brigade commanders felt like men in half-made suits, and the trimming had been done, not by a master tailor, but by the insolent, interfering hand of a Welsh ignoramus.

Haig had in the course of three months been deprived of five divisions to the Italian front, compelled to extend his line by twenty-six miles, and now ordered to disband 141 battalions (that is three from each of his forty-seven British divisions; the Dominion ones and those in Italy were unimpaired). Lloyd George, who was bent on defence until the Americans were fully assembled and trained, which meant waiting until 1919, maintains with typical vigour in his Memoirs that Haig's forces were quite adequate for this task provided they were properly disposed; the War Cabinet, in other words, could not be blamed for failure to provide the tools. He had, in fact, increased the ratio of fire support available to the infantry, for one of the principles on which he acted was that there must be no reduction in the ancillary arms.

Thus the nine remaining battalions of an infantry division (plus one pioneer battalion) retained the forty-eight guns (divided into two brigades each of eighteen 18-pounders and six 4.5-inch howitzers) and the thirty-six mortars that formed the divisional artillery. The divisional machine-gun battalion, of the Machine Gun Corps, also kept their sixty-four Vickers guns, whose use in mass had been much developed as a feature of an overall fire plan. As for the battalions themselves, they retained their four-fold organisation, that is of four rifle companies, each of four platoons, each of four sections. The establishment of a battalion was exactly 1,000 officers and men, but any with 800 was considered strong and at 600 could still adequately perform its task. Similarly a subaltern was entitled to fifty-three men in his platoon but would be lucky to have thirty. He would also have one Lewis gun, the American design light-machine-gun prone to various stoppages, and might have two, for the scale was in process of increase. A division up to strength after the reduction would have 13,035 officers and men, 3,673 horses and mules, 768 carts and wagons, 314 bicycles, 44 motor bikes, 11 cars, 3 lorries, and 21 motor ambulances.

A German division, incidentally, was rather weaker, consisting of 11,643 officers and men, organised on the same lines, except that brigades were known as regiments. It was much stronger in machine-guns, having 144, but not in light-machine-guns, even before the doubling of the British quota. Its artillery numbered thirty-six guns, of slightly smaller calibre, as opposed to forty-eight, but since large increments from army sources were available to both sides this was of no great importance.

Decreed in January, the executions of the doomed British battalions lasted until the beginning of March. They caused sadness, specially among the many men who had spent all their service with the one battalion and felt genuine love for the old

8th, 12th, 19th, or whatever it was; they went to others of their own regiments, but it was not quite the same. They caused perplexity among the more rigid-minded of the commanders and staffs who had to reorganise their defensive lay-outs and relief routines on a triangular, as opposed to quadrilateral, basis. And they also caused greater upheaval among some divisions than others, because only battalions of the New Army divisions (of which there were twenty-four in France numbered from 9 upwards) were eligible for disbandment. This meant that these divisions had to lose more than an average of three battalions each to make room for the surplus from the Regular Army divisions (of which there were eight) and those of the Territorial Force (of which there were fourteen, numbered from 42 upwards). There was also the 63rd Royal Naval Division, which now consisted of one brigade of sailor reservists of battleships, who dressed for battle as soldiers, one of marines, and one of soldiers. Despite all the wear and tear and misery, the individual characteristics of these various elements had been preserved. Whether regular, 'terrier', or war service, each battalion was both conscious and proud of its status, and fiery ties of loyalty bound the divisions together, nowhere more strongly than in Kitchener's New Army. It was not pleasing for some of these latter to be turned into hybrids.

The rundown of the British Expeditionary Force was accompanied by a steady build-up on the other side of the line. The collapse of Russia had freed some seventy German divisions and the trains had long been bringing them westwards at the rate of ten a month, thereby enabling the Germans to gain the numerical lead on the Western Front for the first time since 1915 and to increase it to an eventual thirty divisions, assessed at 197 to an allied 164. It was obvious that the Germans would attempt an all-out blow in the hope of demolishing France and Britain before the enormous potential of America, so leisurely in its conversion to fighting strength, could be of serious avail. Haig was well aware of the menace, and equally he was aware of the risk the Germans would themselves be running. "If Germany attacks and fails she will be ruined," was the forecast of his Intelligence Branch. The problem was to make sure the attack did fail. There was not much time.

2

RIVAL PLANS

(February–March)

"Depth in the defensive organisation is of the first importance," Haig had told his army commanders early in December when he expounded his measures for meeting the "strong and sustained hostile offensive" that he anticipated. The Germans, of course, had had the most experience of the defensive during the last three years, and Haig based his plans on the teaching in the latest German manual, copies of which had been captured soon after their issue in August 1917. Three zones, themselves developed in depth, were to be constructed, or in some cases merely renamed, for in many parts the system was already extensive and elaborate. The Outpost Zone was to drain the momentum of the attack; the Battle Zone was where it was to be halted; and the Rear Zone, some four to eight miles further back, was to be "prepared for defence as labour becomes available" but more often went by the name of Green Line, indicating that it had been selected for defence but was as yet undisturbed by shovel.

A month after Haig's conference, orders were issued changing the name of the Outpost to the Forward Zone, and a dilemma is discernible here which had also caused the Germans much brain and heart searching. The word outpost implied withdrawal, and there was a danger that it might begin before sufficient loss had been inflicted to break the cohesion of the attackers. The word was therefore altered and troops holding this zone instructed to "do all in their power to maintain their ground against every attack." The danger now was that good troops might be sacrificed holding ground of no vital tactical importance. In some parts of the front there was a distance of over two miles between the forward trenches and the start of the battle zone, which made mutual support virtually impossible. Depth here could give the advantage to the attackers, since the defences were vulnerable to assault in detail.

To hold his 126 miles of frontage Haig had fifty-nine infantry divisions, of which forty-seven were British, four Canadian, five Australian, one New Zealand, and two Portuguese. He also had three cavalry divisions. He appreciated that there were parts of his line that must at all costs be held and others where a withdrawal could be made without serious consequences. Of the former, Arras was pre-eminent. By breaking through here the Germans could split the B.E.F. and speed for the coast in two directions, and Haig therefore described the buttress of high ground protecting Arras, from Vimy Ridge southwards, as "the backbone and centre of our defensive system". He was also very loath to yield any ground on his left flank, especially around Ypres. This may partly have been due to pride in hard-won possession, but undoubtedly a stronger factor was an obsession about the security of the Channel ports, which had already done much to shape British strategy. There was little room for manoeuvre to counter enemy gains towards Dunkirk, Calais, or Boulogne, and consequently the B.E.F. stood like a man with all his weight on one leg, straining to keep open the door to his homestead. It was a case of sea power imposing rigidity instead of flexibility.

Just how sensitive Haig was to the vulnerability of his left is clearly shown by the allotment of his divisions. The Fourth Army, custodian of Ypres and nearest to the Channel (except for the Belgian Army, which held a twenty-mile sector adjacent to the coast), had eighteen divisions for a front of only twenty-three miles; the First had sixteen for thirty-three, stretching as far as Vimy; the Third had fifteen for twenty-eight, running from Arras; and the Fifth initially had only ten infantry divisions and three of cavalry (equal in fire power to little more than one infantry division) for far the longest frontage, forty-two miles. However, evidence obtained in January that General von Hutier had arrived opposite the Fifth Army, fresh from triumphs in Russia and with a newly-inserted army headquarters, procured a further four divisions for Gough, at the expense of the Fourth Army.

It had originally been supposed that the Fifth Army was safe because the Germans would not wish to attack over the ground they had devastated during their retreat to the Hindenburg Line a year earlier. This theory was now beginning to evaporate, but Haig could still give three reasons for parsimony towards Gough. The first was the paramount importance of holding his key bastions and the alarming scarcity of reserves for this purpose. The second was that there was a leeway of forty miles between the front line of the Fifth Army and the nearest point of strategic importance, the great railway centre of Amiens. The third was that General Pétain had promised to take Gough under his wing, with the necessary provision of reserves, should his army be in danger.

Haig had obtained this undertaking in exchange for his acceptance of the extra frontage when he visited Pétain on December 17th. Pétain was still left with 324 miles, but by greater elasticity of method, combined with the defensible nature of certain tracts, he had only sixty divisions in the line, including those in corps reserve. This left him with thirty-nine in army or G.H.Q. reserve, and indeed it had been with the expressed object of building up a central reserve that the French had asked the British to take on the extra commitment. Haig's reserves included divisions in corps reserve and numbered only fourteen. It was therefore reasonable enough that the French should provide support for the British right.

Haig had suddenly acquired great faith in Pétain. The previous October he had been fulminating against his failure to support the Ypres offensive as promised. "What a wretched lot the majority of the French are!" he told his diary. Yet on his visit to Pétain's headquarters on December 17th: "I was much struck with the different bearing of the present officers at G.Q.C. The present ones seem much more simple, more natural and practical than their predecessors, and are more frank in their dealings with the British. In fact, the relations between G.Q.C. and G.H.Q. are better than I have ever known them."

Optimism had for long been a feature of French generalship, and Haig does not at this stage seem to have appreciated that the French Army now had a pessimist as C.-in-C., or that pessimism was the prevailing mood, even though he (Haig) was well aware how acute the crisis had been the previous summer. Having done a marvellous repair job on morale, Pétain was determined not to subject it to overstrain. His aim was to guard the homeland until the Americans could arrive in sufficient strength to win the day, and in his parochial gloom he could see the need to concentrate his effort on defending the heart of the homeland, Paris. It was well known that the French Army was as strongly tied to Paris, both strategically and emotionally, as the B.E.F. to the Channel ports. A consequence of this, which escaped both Haig and Gough, was that despite his undertaking Pétain stationed only four divisions within thirty miles of the British right.

A plan had been devised, on the instigation of Lloyd George, for removing these hazards endemic in the policy of mutual reliance on which Haig, for all his experience, still put store. Following the Italian disaster at Caporetto, the Supreme War Council had been formed with its own permanent staff, the military representatives of France, Britain, Italy and the U.S.A., sitting at Versailles. At the third meeting of the full Council, which began on January 30th, these military representatives were formed into the Executive War Board, with the power to raise and control a central reserve. General Foch, who until then was Chief of Staff to the French Government, was elected president. The Board met and sent out demands for thirty divisions to be made available as their central reserve, thirteen French, ten British, seven Italian. (Only five American divisions had as yet arrived in France and, with strict instructions that they should not stray from his command, General Pershing, their Commander-in-Chief, gave a firm negative to covetous enquiries.)

Haig took a sceptical view of the general reserve and thought it absurd that the control of troops should be entrusted to a committee. He did not let it worry him. He merely made reply, when at length the War Board's requirement was formally conveyed to him, that he had "already disposed of all the troops under my command" and that the only division he could earmark was one expected back from Italy. Pétain made an offer of eight divisions, but withdrew it when he learned of Haig's reply. Thus the War Board had no meaning as far as the Commanders-in-Chief were concerned.

It meant a great deal to General Robertson, Britain's Chief of the Imperial General Staff. He described the scheme as "unworkable and dangerous" and objected in particular to the Board's independence from his authority. Lloyd George, its chief architect, offered him the post of military representative, but he refused it with disdain and was relegated instead to Eastern Command, deposed at last by his master and tormentor. Thus Haig lost the services of a staunch ally, indeed his one loyal friend in government circles. He accepted it all with his usual composure and with scarcely a word of sympathy for him.

Plumer was offered the job of C.I.G.S. He turned it down with all the horror of the honest field commander for the meshes of the political net. It therefore went to General Sir Henry Wilson, the inveterate intriguer disliked by many of his contemporaries. He was Britain's representative on the War Board, and this post therefore became vacant. Haig agreed that Rawlinson should fill it, on the understanding (duly fulfilled) that Plumer should return from Italy and re-assume responsibility for the Ypres sector with his Second Army headquarters.

Rawlinson was in London when he was asked by Haig to take this appointment. Although there was great risk for an ambitious general in fishing in political waters, he accepted it without qualm. "It will be an immensely interesting and historic time," he informed his journal. Two days later, on his fifty-fifth birthday, he had breakfast at Buckingham Palace and, unlike the other two at the table, the Queen and Princess Mary, he was treated to some cream by the King, who was allowed some on doctor's orders. Next day, February 21st, Rawlinson returned to France and "spent a sad day in saying good-bye to my dear old Fourth Army". However, he took Montgomery and several other members of his staff with him to Versailles. The move marked an advance in his relationship with Haig. Whereas previously it had been "Dear F.M." now it was "Dear D.H.".

Although he was loyal to his subordinates, Haig was in the habit of making scathing comments, in letters to his wife, about people who were loyal to him. He wrote that Lord Derby, "like the feather pillow, bears the marks of the last person who has sat on him," and a month previously Derby had stoutly resisted pressure from Lloyd George for Haig's removal. Robertson he despised, most unfairly, for yielding to "the bidding of his political masters", and now that Rawlinson had taken Wilson's place at Versailles the two were together chastised under the comment, "they are both humbugs, and it is difficult to decide exactly what is at the bottom of the mind of each of them". Rawlinson was no doubt bracketed with Wilson because he was one of his few close friends. Haig had, in fact, gained an ally at Versailles, whatever the machinations that might be processed around Whitehall. "I am myself opposed to the General Reserve," Rawlinson recorded, "as I do not think it will serve any useful purpose, and I am quite satisfied to allow the two Commanders-in-Chief to fight their own battles in unison." And so they nominally prepared to do.

For the Germans, planning was a less elaborate business. It was not a question of reaching agreement between the politicians and generals of two, three, or sometimes four countries, but of awaiting decision from a single mind. "His Majesty commands" began the orders to the generals, and His Majesty commanded as he was bidden, not by his Chancellor or Cabinet, nor by the Chief of the General Staff of the Field Army, but by his First Quartermaster-General, General Erich Ludendorff. "I alone had to decide," he wrote in his War Memoirs; "of that I remained conscious throughout."

This, of course, did not mean that he did not need advisers, and as if under the guidance of some oracle of doom he chose Mons on November 11th, 1917, as the rendezvous for a conference with the chiefs of staff of his army groups, their aristocratic commanders being left to fulfil their customary functions of decorating their headquarters. About the only definite decision at this stage was that the British should be the target; with them gone the rest would follow. Two rival plans emerged. One, named Saint George, was to smash through around Armentières, envelop the Ypres Salient, and with the British pinned against the coast, roll up the remainder of their line southwards. The other, Saint Michael, was to launch an enormous left hook by first overrunning the right wing of the British line and then wheeling north-westwards to envelop Arras, while the German left stood fast on the Somme to repulse counter-attack by the French. It was an essential feature of this plan that the French should be deterred by a diversion from bringing swift aid to their allies, but there was no intention to break through to Amiens; protection, not exploitation, was the rôle assigned the left. One further solution, which was put forward by a Lieutenant-Colonel Wetzell and would probably have hurt the British most, was that George and Michael should be combined, Michael coming first with the object of softening resistance to George.

George had the disadvantage that the axis of advance along the Lys valley was considered unsuitable for traffic until April, and Ludendorff therefore opted for Michael, keeping George in reserve as a second string but with no definite plans for its execution. He issued his orders on March 10th. The assault was to be made at 9.40 a.m. on March 21st on an enormous frontage, over fifty miles wide, stretching from the Oise on the Germans' left to Croisilles (ten miles south of Arras) on their right. To strengthen his own hold over events, Ludendorff divided the task between two army groups. The Crown Prince Rupprecht's had the main task, employing General von Below's Seventeenth Army, newly arrived from Italy, on the right nearest Arras and General von der Marwitz's Second Army on the left. The furthest objective assigned these two was Bapaume, and they were then "to push forward in the direction of Arras-Albert . . . and upset the balance of the British front on the [German] Sixth Army front". The Crown Prince Wilhelm of Germany's Group of Armies had the protective rôle on the left and was to "seize the passages over the Somme", using the redoubtable von Hutier's Eighteenth Army.

The orders were loose, with no detailed tabling of objectives or timings. This was in accordance with the new doctrine. Initiative was its essence and infiltration its means, the two being afforded maximum scope by the vast expanse of the blow. "There must be no rigid adherence to plans made beforehand", ran an instruction embodying the one: "The strongest form of attack, envelopment", summarised the other. The teaching of

26

the old maestro, Clausewitz, with its insistence on concentrating all against the enemy's citadel, was spurned.

Sixty-three divisions were selected for the assault, withdrawn for special training, and provided with men and equipment which set them apart as shock troops. There was further discriminatory selection at battalion level. The best, in some cases complete battalions, were chosen as 'storm troops' and divided into mobile teams, armed with light machine-guns, mortars, and flame-throwers, each with the task of penetrating the enemy lines where the resistance was weakest, regardless of the position on the flanks. Behind them were to come 'battle units', which included artillery, charged with the task of mopping up the strongpoints by-passed by the storm troops. "The Army pined for the offensive", Ludendorff informs us. This does not appear entirely consistent with his admission that "skulkers were already numerous", but there can be no doubt that after the long, sullen years of defence there were plenty of soldiers eager enough to grab this last great chance of victory for the Fatherland.

If the tactics were to be fluid, the assembly plans were meticulously regulated and industriously supervised. Great pains were taken gradually to feed in row upon row of guns and heaps of ammunition without detection from ground or air; by careful staff work the move forward of the assault divisions, from their training in the back areas, was delayed until four nights before the start; ingenuity in many forms sowed an enduring conviction among the French that the main blow would fall on them; and faith in instrumental precision, which was not shared by all the German gunners, eliminated nearly all ranging on targets.

None the less British Intelligence was not without its clues and the more they accumulated the stronger grew the feeling in the British Fifth Army that the day of destiny was at hand. The presence of von Hutier, craftily deduced from an obscure obituary tribute written by him, had, as we have seen, gained Gough extra divisions. He had had to put them in the line. There were now eleven holding his forty-two miles' front, dwindling in density from the left; all had fought in the Third Battle of Ypres and some at Cambrai as well. He had three in reserve, of which two could not be moved without the consent of G.H.Q. and were fifteen and thirty miles from the front line. What depth there was had to be provided by the divisions themselves, and they did this by distributing their battalions in the rough ratio of three, four, and two between the forward, battle, and rear zones, forming a studded belt between four and seven miles wide, with plenty of gaps between the studs. This was different from the familiar system of continuous trench lines and had the disadvantage that it was hard to conceal the strongpoints and redoubts, specially from air observation. Some felt they were making bull's-eyes of themselves for the enemy as they made deeper excavations and put up more wire.

Gough also had three cavalry divisions, each capable of providing a mobile reserve of some 3,000 rifles, and three battalions of tanks, each with thirty-six Mark IVs. The latter were held back for counter-attack, a task for which the needs of speed and concentration were in serious conflict; the monsters moved at 3 m.p.h. and were incommunicado when so doing. There were 360 guns additional to the divisional artillery, of calibres ranging from 60-pounders to 12-inch howitzers.

There were twelve squadrons of aircraft allotted to the Fifth Army and placed directly under Gough's command. The great majority were single-seaters, used either for reconnaissance or fighting. The Allies had recovered from the mauling they had received the previous spring and had slight numerical superiority and rough parity in performance. Spotting was still the most useful task performed by the air arm, although much effort and thought also went into night bombing, at both tactical and strategic level, and into close support work for the troops. The Germans had grown tiresomely, though not very lethally, active at night, and this made the British army and corps headquarters more warlike in appearance and brought a welcome reduction in the visits paid them by M.P.s and suchlike.

Two anxieties in particular agitated Gough's mind. One was his growing doubts about the invulnerability of his right sector, which on February 1st he had reported as "not likely to be the scene of a serious hostile attack". An unusually dry spell of weather and the reputation of von Hutier had caused him to express a very different opinion to his corps commanders shortly after making this report. An extra division had been inserted on this flank by the marshes of the Oise, but the frontages held were still very wide.

The other problem concerned the water obstacle behind his main positions. The combined river and canal of the Somme ran from south to north at a distance of about fifteen miles from the front line, and running into it, from the south-east, was the Crozat Canal, which tapered nearer the front line. (Incidentally, at Peronne the Somme wheels westwards and was therefore of very different significance from this point in tactical terms. To distinguish between the two stretches it is proposed to call the south–north one the Somme Canal and the east–west one the Somme River.) There was an obvious temptation to make this the main line of defence, to which a planned withdrawal would be made, especially as the Third Army on the left could with advantage make a conforming withdrawal. The issue was discussed in a G.H.Q. memorandum, but the project was over-ruled because of the difficulty of carrying out the withdrawal and the importance of maintaining lateral communication through Peronne, which was on the enemy's side of the Somme. It was added, somewhat contradictorily, that "the possibilities of having to execute a withdrawal should receive careful consideration".

Shortly after this instruction, on February 9th, another arrived for Gough : "The Field-Marshal Commanding-in-Chief considers that in the event of a serious attack being made on your Army on a wide front, your policy should be to secure and protect at all costs the important centre of Peronne and the River Somme to the south of that place, while strong counter-attacks should be made both from the direction of Peronne and from the south, possibly assisted by the French Third Army." He was then told that the forward and battle zones should be defended as laid down—which meant to the last—but that "the provisions regarding the reinforcement of the Battle Zone and its re-establishment by counter-attack require some modification".

Poor Gough! It was not explained how he was to hold the line of the Somme if he was going to fight hard in the battle zone, nor who was to make the strong counter-attacks from Peronne, nor how the French Third Army was to be persuaded to assist. He could, if he wished, have taken this instruction as an invitation to withdraw to the Somme after offering only token resistance in the battle zone, but it came more naturally to him to inspire his men with the determination to fight it out in the positions they held. This he did vigorously, making many spirited addresses, and the men set with a will to making their battle positions impregnable. As for the emergency positions on the Somme, these were added to the already imposing list of tasks assigned the labour force of British, Indians, Chinese, and Italians, whose number with the Fifth Army had at Gough's urging been doubled in the course of six weeks to a total of 48,154. They arrived too late to achieve very much.

The fighting troops were in need of field training, for large gaps had been torn in the battalions during the autumn and filled for the most part by fledglings who had been able to learn little more than the rudiments of trench life from the veterans, some of whom wore three or four wound stripes, in rare cases more. They also needed rest—when did they not? They could have neither. There was far more work to be done—digging, wiring, sandbagging, the marking of dug-outs, pill boxes, and tracks—than could be managed by the pioneers and sappers on their own. The defences developed, impressively in places. But many communication trenches sunk no deeper than eighteen inches, and in the rear zone the turf often remained green and uncut, save for some spitlocking to define the line of an intended trench.

Whatever the feelings roused against Gough at the time of his Ypres offensive, there is ample evidence that confidence ran high in the Fifth Army as the day of battle drew near. The surroundings helped, being remarkably salubrious by normal front-line standards. There was a touch of spring in the air, the weather had been dry, bringing wonderful freedom from mud, and the enemy were both inactive and ineffective, falling easy victims to raiding parties. This was because the crack divisions had all been withdrawn to prepare for the coming assault. It had been impressed on the British soldiers that, when and where it came, the attack would be tremendous, but the plans for meeting it had been explained in detail and those who had seen what machine-guns could do could not but feel sorry for any

German who had to cross the wide open slopes that abounded all along the Army line.

The III Corps was on the right, with the 58th, 18th, and 14th Divisions in the line from the right. Only here was there any shortage of experience at the top. Lieutenant-General Sir Richard Butler, the corps commander, had until January been Deputy Chief of Staff at G.H.Q. Haig had wanted to make him Chief of Staff on the removal of Kiggell, but had been told that "he was not liked by any of the 'Authorities' at home" and had again yielded to pressure. Now he was in charge of eighteen miles of the front with no previous experience of command other than of the 2nd Lancashire Fusiliers from September to November 1914 and of the 3rd Infantry Brigade from then until his elevation on to Haig's staff the following February. But his inclination had always been towards command, and it was because he had more pugnacity than tact, combined with a tendency to take refuge behind a fearsome frown, that he was "not liked by the Authorities".

On Butler's left was Sir Ivor Maxse's XVIII Corps, with the 36th, 30th, and 61st Divisions in the line. Originally a Royal Fusilier, Maxse had transferred to the Coldstream Guards as a captain and had commanded the 1st Guards Brigade in the retreat from Mons. In October 1914 he had raised one of the New Army divisions, the 18th—which plays a notable part in our story—had trained it diligently and commanded it on the Somme with such success that in January 1917 he had been given his corps. He had served under Gough, who was nearly eight years his junior, in the Ypres offensive. Dapper, meticulous, bursting with energy, and for ever expounding ideas for "killing more Huns", Maxse was a great man for detail. He had a system for knowing the names of junior officers and a system for frustrating every trick the Hun might devise. Even so, Haig noted of this corps in his diary, having visited them on March 7th: "I thought that they were taking it too much for granted that enemy would do what they had planned that he should do."

Next on the left stood Sir Herbert Watts's XIX Corps, with the 24th and 66th Divisions in the line, the latter under the command of Gough's discharged C.G.S., Neil Malcolm. Watts,

who was rising sixty, had retired as a brigadier-general just
before the war, having belonged to the Prince of Wales's Own
West Yorkshire Regiment. He had served under Gough as a
brigadier in the 7th Division and followed him in command of
it in September 1915. Promotion to the command of his corps
had come in February 1917. Gough much admired his elderly
subordinate and describes him in his book as "a spare, active
man, quiet and very modest in demeanor, but one of the most
courageous and experienced of our commanders".

On the left of the Fifth Army line, was Sir Walter Congreve's
VII Corps, with the 16th, 21st and 9th Divisions committed.
Congreve had won the V.C. at Colenso in a vain attempt to save
Sir Redvers Buller's guns. Nearly eight years older than Gough,
he had started the war in command of the 18th Infantry Brigade
and during 1915 had graduated through the command of the
6th Division to that of the XIII Corps. Renowned as a front-
line general, "absolutely indefatigible in getting to see for himself", he was the only successful corps commander at the start
of the Somme offensive. A few weeks later he lost his son Billy,
who was serving in his old regiment, the Rifle Brigade, and in
his own corps. A gay, shining spirit, the young Congreve had
already won the D.S.O., M.C. and Legion d'Honneur, and for
the feat cut short by death he posthumously joined his father as
a V.C. The following June Congreve lost a hand, chopped off
by an army doctor to complete the work started by a German
shell. He was sent protesting on sick leave and did not reappear
in France until January 1918, to be given VII Corps. He
admitted privately that he was not in the best of health. Asthma
added to the toll taken on this gaunt and gallant man.

Despite their industry, the Germans could not conceal all
trace of their preparations. Air photographs revealed telling
changes in the shapes of trees and buildings, the gunners found
it increasingly easy to start explosions in hollows and copses
where ammunition might be dumped, and sentries even spotted
officers issuing orders with maps spread out and fingers pointed.
Raids produced prisoners, and the prisoners, being men of mere
'trench' divisions, talked. Gough, having studied the methods
of von Hutier, had already told his commanders that they should
expect a night bombardment of six to eight hours, followed by a

dawn assault. On the morning of March 19th he was able, with further aid from prisoners, to pin-point the chosen dawn : March 21st. He asked for permission to move his two G.H.Q. divisions nearer the front. It was refused.

The refusal came from Haig's new Chief of General Staff, Lieutenant-General the Honourable Sir Herbert Lawrence. He was a former cavalryman and had retired well before the war because Haig had been appointed over his head to the command of his regiment, the 17th Lancers. Smooth of manner, he obviously thought Gough needed calming down and gave him a quiet lecture over the telephone on the principles of war, avoiding detailed analysis of the issue in question. Haig had rebutted all the past criticism of his young army commander, but there is evidence here of its corrosive influence : Lawrence spoke to Gough as his superior and senior, as he had been to the measure of some ten years during their regimental days but was no longer. Gough lacked the confidence to demand to speak personally to his Commander-in-Chief and, as he relates in his book, never discovered whether or not his request was referred to him. All that there was left for him to do was to grit his teeth and send out the curt message (on the afternoon of Wednesday, March 20th) : "Prepare for attack."

A weird feeling of unreality came over the men in the dug-outs and redoubts, in farm buildings and villages that seemed unbelievably well preserved for their distance from the line, and in huts and shelters nestled against some hillside seldom scarred by shell. Beyond the hill men were preparing to come at them, grappling with that agony of suspense which had so often wracked the British when it had been their turn. Or were they? Was it a false alarm?

There had been rain, the first for eight weeks, and it had freshened up the countryside, implanting a mocking sense of uplift. Major W. E. Grey, who wrote the history of the 2nd/2nd London Regiment, described the scene as follows : "The evening of the 20th of March was strangely still and peaceful; few of war's usual discordant sounds disturbed the last quiet hours of the departing day. The whole countryside was instinct with the sweetness and vigour of approaching spring; woodland scents filled the keen, crisp air; a gentle breeze played among the yet leafless branches of the trees; and away from the line, only the Very lights, waxing and waning noiselessly above the tree-tops, served to dispel the illusion, bred of the enshrouding darkness, that peace had returned to this beautiful land. Yet over all there was a presage of impending disaster."

As night set in there were sudden eruptions at various points along the line. They ended in two instances with the return of British raiding parties, bright-eyed, panting, and hustling along prisoners. The latter begged earnestly to be evacuated rearwards with all speed; one obliged with the information that the bombardment was to begin at 4.40. Some British guns fired concentrations of gas on the likely approaches. The shelling then subsided to intermittent.

3

BLIGHTERS EVERYWHERE

(March 21)

The Germans had massed 6,473 guns, of which over 2,500 were heavy or super-heavy, and at 4.40 on this Thursday morning, March 21st, they duly opened up in unison along the fifty-four-mile stretch chosen for the assault, while others co-operated on the flanks to conceal its limits. There had never been a bombardment on a scale such as this, and it seems most unlikely that there has been one since. The black, murky sky was lit with wobbling light from end to end as with belches of flame the shells were sent screeching on their journey to land with orange flash and deafening crash, followed by the noisy fall of earth or masonry and the startled cry perhaps of a man pierced by a jagged piece of steel. So thick did the shells fall that the ground rocked with the crazy monotony of a cake walk, and interspersed with the vibrant crunch of high explosive came the hollow plop of gas shell. Old shell cases were struck as the gas alarm, but their clangs were as hard to hear above the shindy as the crack of the British guns firing their response. The darker the night, they say, the stronger the fear. This was a very dark night.

The initial 'stonk' fell most heavily on the battle zone, while the troops in the forward positions were deluged by mortar bombs. It became painfully apparent from the start that by careful observation from ground and air the Germans had been able to pin-point most of the British positions and that their gunners could match the accuracy of the observers. Groping in their gas masks, often clinging on to each other for direction, the infantry in some places had to creep through the crashing shells for two or three hundred yards, for only in the forward zone did the men sleep by their posts and despite the warning so clearly given others further back did not leave their cellars and dug-outs for their battle stations until the codeword 'Bustle' arrived. The gunners also had a bad time of it, receiving most of the gas and some fiendishly accurate crumps from the famed 5.9-inch howitzers, and even batteries that had anticipated events and moved to alternative positions before the bombardment had

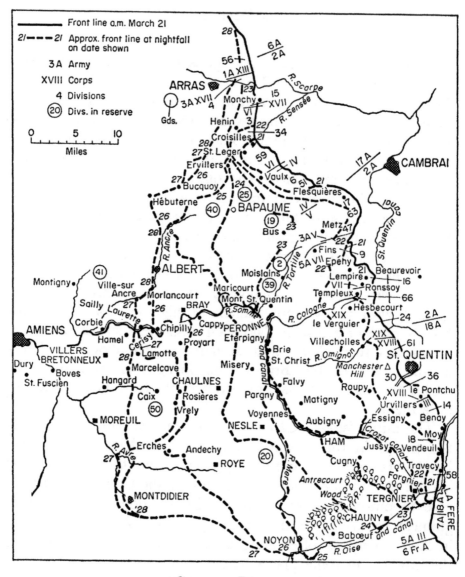

German Progress

their losses. There was some ghastly horse slaughter, both among the gun teams and infantry transport parks, and a sad toll was also taken of those who had to venture forth to bring in the wounded or repair telephone lines. Care had been taken to bury the latter deep, but equal care had been taken by the Germans to detect their filled-in entrenchments on air photographs and to place selected heavy guns in exact alignment.

All such refinements were the work of Colonel Bruckmüller, who although still officially on von Hutier's staff was the guiding brain behind the whole fire plan and was recognised by Ludendorff as such. He had sound instinct for creating hell. Pauses on targets were of the exact length required to get the evacuation of wounded under way when the next crash came down, crossroads were pounded by the heavies always at the most awkward moments, and a clever mixing of gases kept the troops in and out of their masks with tears streaming down their eyes. Yet despite all the horror and the fury the shells as usual missed many more men and weapons than they hit, and the nerves of men were not jangled as harshly as by the prolonged bombardments that had formerly been the vogue.

The great day so long awaited by the Germans scarcely dawned at all. The rising of the sun merely transformed the pitch blackness of night into a shroud of chill white mist, stagnant in the valleys and rather more wispy on higher ground, but at no point penetrable by the eye beyond a distance of forty yards or so. The attacks developed spasmodically, from 7 a.m. onwards, and by 9.40, the hour commanded by His Imperial Majesty, the mighty tide of grey was in full spate from the Oise in the south to the Sensée in the north. There was one gap, where blister gas had been released and was now causing much torment. It covered the salient around Flesquières, the strongly defended remnant of Byng's gains towards Cambrai, which the Germans planned to lop off intact by severing its shoulders. Only large scale raids were made here on this opening morning, the repulse of which cheered the defenders.

Thus the German assault fell on two distinct sectors. Von Hutier's Eighteenth Army (of the German Crown Prince's Group) and von der Marwitz's Second Army (of Prince Rupprecht's Group) together engaged Gough's Fifth Army, putting nineteen divisions against eleven, with a further twenty-one in second- or third-line reserve against only three available to Gough. North of the Flesquières salient, von Below's Seventeenth Army fell on the two centre corps of Byng's Third Army, putting ten divisions against five, with eight against two as immediate reserves. As for the Kaiser, he was accommodated with his son, Crown Prince Willie, in an observation post on the front of the Eighteenth Army, and from there he watched his men streaming past into the fog.

Conditions were favourable for Ludendorff's infiltration tactics, especially at this moment when enthusiasm was at its height. He himself complained that the fog "retarded our movements and prevented our superior training and leadership from reaping its full reward . . . but a few thought it an advantage". That few would include all who had personal experience of the havoc a single machine-gun could inflict across the type of ground, with its long sweeping curves, that the Germans had to cross in so many places. The stormtroopers were practically immune from such peril as they darted forward in their manifold groups, some with bayonets fixed, some with rifles slung and stick grenades in hand, and all with machine-gunners in close attendance. Unseen from front or flanks, they arrived at many a post to find its occupants sprawled around in mangled, moaning distortion, for terrible destruction had been wrought on those portions of the forward zone that lay on the forward slope under direct observation from German-held hills. But from some posts came the fierce smack of bullets and the crump of grenade fired from discharger cup, and here the stormtroopers were laid moaning as they grappled with tangles of wire. Their comrades went on, leaving these strongholds for the battle units behind them and making short rushes through the mist to probe the next defended locality and find a way round its flanks. In the manner of any other incoming tide, they were drawn towards the low ground and spread deepest along the valleys that conveniently coincided with their required direction of advance.

The Germans knew they fought shoulder to shoulder, vying with each other for glory across a gigantic front. The British knew no more about the battle than their interpretation of the noises around them and of the forms that suddenly loomed out of the fog. It was a soldiers' battle on a scale far beyond the imagination of the heroes of Albuhera and Inkerman. All told, 127 battalions met the onslaught in the forward and battle zones, and they fought their own individual, disjointed battles, sometimes as complete battalions, more often as isolated companies, platoons, or even sections. It dawned gradually on the forward garrisons that they were cut off : their telephone lines had long been cut, the Very lights they fired soared fatuously through the fog without response, and nothing more was seen of the runners —it was a bad day to be a runner—who set off for headquarters with messages asking for counter-attacks, for artillery fire, for instructions. Men fought on, dying unseen, their bravery unknown. For some, recognition would come when prisoners returned with their stories at the end of the war—as in the case of Lance-Corporal J. W. Sayer, of the 8th Queen's in 24 Division, who was posthumously awarded the Victoria Cross for the persistent and indomitable vigour with which he defended his post, undaunted by wounds from which he was to die. Inevitably, other Sayers were devoured without trace, word, or recognition.

Few commanders knew more about the battle than what they could assess from the ominous noises of firing steadily creeping nearer. Odd tit-bits of information came in, from a repaired telephone cable, a runner, or some wide-eyed and gasping person who claimed to be the sole survivor of a post. Anxious eyes peered into the fog, straining to distinguish the shape of helmet on top of each emerging form, as fingers quivered round triggers. There would be a hiss of "Boche!" followed sometimes by fire, sometimes by the timely correction, "No—it's one of our fellows."

Only the airmen could see beyond the fog, and they sent many calls to the gunners asking for fire on the swarms of Germans moving forward across hills into the fog belt. This could be a very effective means of co-operation, but the gunners had been thrown into disarray, either by the bombardment itself or by their haste to move to alternative positions, and were too pre-occupied with more pressing problems to get their wireless sets to the aircraft tuned in. With the infantry line and light signal were their only means of communication, and neither was of much avail. It was the start of a long nightmare of obfuscation which was to strain relationships all round, between infantry, gunners, headquarters and neighbouring units. However, light came as the morning advanced, gradually dispersing the fog from north to south, and as prodigious targets were revealed to them the guns let fly.

The density of the attack roughly corresponded to that of the defence. The 58th London and the 18th Eastern, the right pair of Butler's III Corps, held the longest frontages of Gough's divisions, and although von Hutier, living up to his reputation, defied the former French veto on the possibility of attacking across the Oise swamps, he did not employ quite the strength he used elsewhere. South of the Oise, the one brigade of the 58th were unmolested. Further northwards, beyond the bend in the river bed, the fog was at its thickest, affording ample protection for the Germans as they threw floats or planks across the canal, river and adjacent dykes, but they had a hot reception from the widely dispersed positions in the forward zone. The 2nd/2nd London (Royal Fusiliers) held out until almost noon, when they fell back on the battle zone, bayoneting Germans who loomed out of the fog and leaving behind them one company trapped in Travecy. A furious battle was meanwhile developing for Fargnier, a suburb of the little industrial town of Tergnier, divided from it by the Crozat Canal. The Londoners lost it, but regained it after dark that evening and in this fighting they captured men from twenty-seven German battalions.

On the front of the 18th, a Kitchener division unadulterated by the purge, there was such resistance in the forward zone that the battle zone was in danger only from the flanks. The 7th Buffs were the right forward battalion, holding redoubts near the banks of the Oise, chief of which was the old fort behind Vendeuil. Lieutenant-Colonel A. L. Ransome (of the Dorset Regiment) their veteran commanding officer aged thirty-four, was not much impressed by the spirit of the attackers; one officer prisoner kept telling his captors how much he liked them. The redoubts were soon surrounded but most held out all day. There were two 18-pounder guns close behind Vendeuil ahead of battalion headquarters, placed there as much for moral as for fire support, and they were able to do much execution when the fog began to lift. One of them was eventually overrun but no sooner had its detachment been marched off as prisoners than the other gun opened from 200 yards and blasted the Germans to smithereens; the horses then came up and galloped it away. Ransome, who had watched all this, was still happily ensconced in his headquarters, the only one still open in the entire forward zone, when at midnight a patrol reached him with orders to withdraw. He sent his adjutant to brigade headquarters on a bicycle in order to obtain confirmation before complying, but he had to leave most of his men behind in their surrounded redoubts.

On the left of the Buffs, the 7th Queens' Own Royal West Kent were around Moy, almost three miles from Vendeuil. Having had two of his companies overrun, with his adjutant dead and the German dead lying thick around him, their commanding officer, Lieutenant-Colonel J. D. Crosthwaite (from the London Regiment), sent his last runner off at about 12.30 p.m. with the message : "Boche all round within 50 yards except rear. Can only see 40 yards, so it is difficult to kill the blighters." An hour and a half later Crosthwaite was hit and knocked unconscious and by about 4.30 the remnant of his battalion had fallen into the blighters' hands. The 8th Royal Berkshire meanwhile were resisting attack on a farm about a mile to the left of the Royal West Kents. It began in mass at 10.30 a.m. and by gradual accumulation won through at 6 p.m. A number of the Royal Berkshires then fought their way through to the battle zone.

The frontage held by these four batalions, the 2nd/2nd London and the three of 18 Division, measured eight miles, and at least four divisions were employed against them. They very adequately carried out their task of breaking the cohesion of the attack but broke themselves in the process, fighting on in posts which they had orders to defend to the last and hopefully awaiting counter-attacks which never came. They received no help from the troops in the battle zone, who merely blinked into the fog or themselves grappled with the enemy. This was the pattern all along the line.

The left wing of III Corps had meanwhile been shattered. Here the 14th Light Division held as their battle zone an important plateau from which two spurs ran gently down towards the enemy lines. With no water obstacle to impede assembly the Germans massed tremendous strength and quickly swamped the forward zone. Battalions of famous Rifle and Light Infantry regiments were swallowed at a gulp while their brigade commanders fretted in their gas masks without knowledge of their fate. By one o'clock the Germans were in the villages of Benay and Essigny, key bastions of the battle zone. Various groups still held out behind them, notably the 9th King's Royal Rifle Corps at Urvillers, but they could do no more than cause nuisance. A breach had been made from which not only the battle zone of the 18th Division could be turned but the right flank of XVIII Corps too.

Butler, at Corps Headquarters, had alarming news of the extent of the penetration from air reports that reached him as early as 10.40. Except for one brigade of the 18th Division, his only reserves were scratch ones, and men were soon being bundled out of billets and lecture huts to start the interminable process of plugging gaps. The 5th Cavalry Brigade were among the first into action. Beginning a long separation from their horses, men of the Royal Scots Greys, 12th Lancers and 20th Hussars dismounted at the foot of the plateau and marched to the aid of the reserve battalions of the 14th Division grimly clinging to the edge of the battle zone. Other cavalrymen, with details from the Corps Reinforcement Camp and Corps School, hurried to guard the bridges over the Crozat Canal.

On the XVIII Corps front Maxse's carefully laid plans were soon creaking beneath the stress of fog and mass. He had a deep forward zone, over three miles in places, and it was intended that the troops in the most forward positions should fall back on to the Line of Redoubts, from which no further withdrawal could be contemplated, far less anticipated. These redoubts were wired for all-round defence and were rather more than a thousand yards apart. Most were constructed to accommodate a complete battalion, but in the event few of the outpost companies were able to extricate themselves from the hordes that swept all round them and it was estimated that only one man out of four managed to achieve his intended withdrawal. As for the redoubts themselves, inevitably they were surrounded and the guns close behind them overrun, and it had to be the last fight for their occupants.

With three divisions to oppose fourteen (of which five were in second line, three in third) Maxse was the most heavily beset of Gough's corps commanders, and it could be argued that he had no alternative to making a sacrificial offering of the eight battalions in his forward zone. It is certain that they caused great destruction before themselves being liquidated. One company of the 12th Royal Irish Rifles (since renamed Royal Ulster Rifles), of the 36th Ulster Division, not only had Germans lying thick all round them when at last their very forward position at Le Pontchu quarry was overwhelmed at 4 p.m., but as the survivors were marched back towards St. Quentin they were able to see at close quarters the terrible carnage they had made of a transport column caught in their sights by the lifting of the mist. The 15th Rifles and the 3rd Royal Inniskilling Fusiliers held out until 6 p.m., although for long pounded, surrounded and assailed both with shot and flame. There was no sign of hesitance here on the part of the Germans; one made a charge all on his own after the rest of his company had been caught in the open and demolished. On the left of the Ulstermen, separated from them by the St. Quentin Canal, redoubts were held by the 2nd Wiltshire, 16th Manchester and 2nd/8th Worcestershire, of the 30th Division, and by the 2nd/4th Oxfordshire and Buckinghamshire Light Infantry and 5th Gordon Highlanders, of the 61st South Midland Division. All forced the enemy to pay dearly for possession, but could delay his progress no longer than the late afternoon.

The stand of the 16th Manchester is perhaps the most famous of these, and there is a certain symbolism about it that makes it a fitting epitome of this terrible day. It was made on a small hill—Manchester Hill—standing in the very centre of the Fifth Army line and shaped like the hump of a camel whose head would be facing St. Quentin, that catacomb of German activity, two miles distant, of which little was visible from the British lines except the great towering, towerless slab of stone that was its cathedral.

Obviously this was a position that the Germans needed to

capture with all speed. Lieutenant-Colonel W. Elstob, commanding the Manchesters, was not concerned about merely delaying them. "There is only one degree of resistance", he instructed his men, "and that is to the last round and to the last man." There was something about 'Big Ben', as Elstob was known, which inspired acceptance of such words, not as melodramatic exhortation, but as a simple definition of task, to which he would himself give effect. He glowed with that radiance of spirit which gives the words 'lost generation' their peculiar illumination.

Even by 8.30 a.m. the two forward companies on Manchester Hill were completely surrounded, and soon afterwards the scream of a bayoneted sentry announced the entry of the Germans into the headquarter redoubt. Elstob drove them out, using in turn revolver, bombs, rifle and bayonet. He rallied his men, cheered them, and formed cooks, clerks and signallers into resolute fighting teams. The Germans made another breach. Again Elstob repulsed them almost single-handed and at once organised the construction of a fresh stop. He was wounded. He fought on. He was hurled flat by a shell burst. He got up, laughingly dusted himself, and fought on. Ammunition ran out. He dashed across the open and returned with a box full. As the fog lifted, the Germans could be seen in droves all round Manchester Hill, dead, dying, and very much alive. Miraculously, the line to brigade headquarters was still intact. Elstob's cheerful voice had been heard on it at regular intervals, always reiterating the claim that the Manchester Regiment would hold Manchester Hill to the last. At 3.30 p.m. he said that there were very few of them left; he had himself been wounded again. It was his last message. The Germans had now brought up their field guns to a range of some sixty yards. Their shelling and incessant, strangulating machine-gun fire blared forth until 4.30, and then there was silence. The hill was taken and Elstob was dead. He had been shot through the head after answering a demand for his surrender with, "Never!" It seems almost superfluous to add that he was awarded the V.C.

It was said of Elstob by a historian of the Manchester Regiment, "His was one of those fine natures which combined in a remarkable degree tenderness and strength, innate dignity

and humility, generosity and restraint. Men instinctively trusted
him." There is steadfast serenity in the eyes that gaze from a
picture opposite these words, making the description as credible
as the deed is incredible.

Elstob was not a soldier by profession, but a schoolmaster
who had graduated through Manchester University. He joined
the 16th Manchester as a private when it was formed as a
result of Kitchener's appeal, and he served with no other. He
fought with it, and was twice wounded, on the Somme as a
company commander, winning the Military Cross, and although
still in his twenties he commanded it in the Third Battle of
Ypres, winning the Distinguished Service Order. "If I die," he
wrote to a friend in this fateful month of March 1918, "do not
grieve for me, for it is with the Sixteenth that I would gladly
lay down my life." Here surely lies a clue to many deeds of
valour enacted on this forlorn and ferocious Thursday. King,
country, division, regiment—all acted as magnets of loyalty,
but nothing stirred the hearts of the soldiers, specially those
who had answered Kitchener's call, as did the bonds of comrade-
ship within the family forged into intimate unity by experience
shared and tribulation endured, the battalion.

It is mark of the ubiquity of the weaving, ardent Germans
that long before the fall of Manchester Hill and while the
Wiltshires were still holding out in their redoubt on the right
a strong attack had been made on Roupy, which was midway
between these two redoubts and two miles in rear. It had been
repulsed by the 2nd Green Howards, and the battle zone here
and on the front of the 61st Division was still intact. But in the
late afternoon the attack was resumed on Roupy, under the
cover of skilfully handled guns, and an ugly gash made in the
Green Howards' line.

On the front of Watts's XIX Corps the six battalions in the
forward zone were soon overwhelmed and there was dangerous
penetration along the valleys flanking the corps' battle zone
before the fog lifted soon after 11 a.m. In the Omignon valley
a scratch force of gunners, 9th East Surrey, and 12th Sherwood
Foresters, all of the 24th Division, halted the Germans in front
of Villecholles at the rear end of the battle zone, while on the
higher ground to their left the 3rd Rifle Brigade, 8th Queen's,

and 8th Royal West Kent put up a very stubborn defence on either side of Le Verguier. Swift and deadly tribulation was wrought on those Germans revealed swarming about this valley when the fog lifted, but with fine offensive instinct fresh waves plunged forwards to release themselves from the trap. By nightfall they had all but surrounded Le Verguier and on the opposite (southern) slopes had dented the left flank of 61 Division (XVIII Corps), despite the efforts of the 8th Argyll and Sutherland Highlanders and the 2nd/4th Royal Berkshire, whose colonel, Lieutenant-Colonel J. H. S. Dimmer, V.C., was killed on his charger as he led up two companies for a counter-attack.

In the Cologne valley, along the left flank of XIX Corps, the 6th Lancashire Fusiliers and 5th Border Regiment, of the 66th East Lancashire Division, were gradually beaten back during a furious battle for Templeux le Guerard, a plain but prettily-sited village and an important link in the battle zone defences. It fell just after dark, for the second and final time, thanks largely to some well placed mortar bombs which split the worn out bodies of some and the jangled nerves of others. Watts had already thrown in his last infantry reserve, the 9th Royal Sussex of 24 Division, and he had to call on the 1st Cavalry Division to provide stops along his two flanking valleys, where the enemy pressure was at its strongest.

On the front of Congreve's VII Corps, the 16th Southern Irish Division on the right held a slight salient with the forward zone across the spurs of a ridge. It was overrun with such rapidity that the Germans were in among the 7th/8th Royal Inniskilling Fusiliers, holding the important village of Ronssoy in the battle zone, before the latter realised that the attack had begun. The Germans had won the village by noon, having forced the Inniskillings into submission, and with the fog lifting earlier here than further south had observation up two valleys running into the rear zone of the 16th Division. A counter-attack by two battalions was ordered and then cancelled, but the cancellation did not reach one of the two, the 6th Connaught Rangers, who thus became typical victims of the dilemma facing commanders as to whether to employ their meagre reserves on plugging gaps or retrieving losses.

The Connaughts had the comfort of Absolution, given them

by their priest, Father McShane, who went round the whole battalion before they moved forward for their attack. They needed it. They passed half-dead horses sprawled in a vain attempt to pull out some guns. They entered a shallow trench under heavy shell fire and found it full of the dead and dying. They were told two tanks would be attacking with them, but never saw them; probably they were knocked out by artillery fire. Two companies moved boldly forward across the open and reached a sunken road, from which every attempt to move was shattered by withering fire. A third followed in supposed co-operation with some troops on their right who turned out to be Germans and shot them down. In the course of a few minutes the flower of Connaught had been trampled into the ground and left to sigh, die, and groan like so many of their enemies who had been caught on those wide open slopes without coverage by the mist.

On the far side of Ronssoy, the 2nd Royal Irish made a brave stand around Lempire, until breaking out in the afternoon and reaching a revised line of defences three officers and fifteen soldiers strong. Fortunately for Congreve, he alone had an infantry division—the 39th—nearby in reserve and was able to form a ring round the remaining infantrymen, pioneers, sappers and ungunned gunners of the 16th Irish battling to stay the flood rolling down the slopes from Ronssoy.

Elsewhere on the front of this corps the situation was less perilous. North-west of Ronssoy and connected to it by a ridge were the extensive ruins of Epéhy, and these the 21st Division retained, thanks to some stalwart work by a brigade of the Leicestershire Regiment and on their left by the 12th/13th Northumberland Fusiliers and the 1st and 2nd Lincolnshire, the latter forming a rare partnership for regular battalions. North of Epéhy the enemy made a narrow breach across the ridge, but were caught by well-planned fire on the slopes beyond and paid the price infiltration invited but seldom received. The 21st Division, together with the 24th, were singled out by Haig for special mention in his despatch, the 16th for scornful mention in his diary.

On the left of the 21st stood the most senior of the Kitchener divisions, the 9th Scottish, composed now of a Lowland brigade, a Highland brigade and a South African brigade. Their front overlapped that of the German attack, and although they had their scares, they preserved their battle zone and their losses, on this day, were easily the lightest of the eleven divisions holding the Fifth Army line.

On the Third Army's front, beyond the six-mile salient reserved for subsequent treatment, the Germans swept through the forward zone quite as easily as on the Fifth's. It lay across gentle spurs and valleys running from the open, rather higher ground of the battle and rear zones. There had been heavy fighting here during the preceding year and there were many trench systems, some new, some decrepit, and some too exposed to offer much protection.

Five divisions held the line chosen for attack by eighteen of von Below's Seventeenth Army. Initially it fell hardest on the right-hand three, and swift penetration was made into the battle zone of the 51st Highland and the 6th Divisions, forming IV Corps, and on the 59th Division, of VI Corps, on their left. By frantic endeavour the Highlanders and the regular battalions of the 6th were able to improvise a line along the rear of their battle zone, which the Germans tried vainly to storm, their vigour waning as the afternoon advanced. Since around 10.30 they had been without protection from the mist and had had more to endure than their colleagues around St. Quentin, with heavier weight of artillery against them and thirty-seven squadrons of the Royal Flying Corps plaguing them with bombs and bullets. Furthermore, the British had reserves at hand, and from around midday these two divisions of IV Corps had the support of the 19th Division, in the form both of guns and men.

For the 59th Division the situation became desperate. The two forward brigades, composed of the Staffordshire Regiments and the Sherwood Foresters, went down almost in toto fighting fiercely for two villages, and two reserve battalions, sent up from four miles back, ran headlong into the enemy and were swamped. There was a race for a ridge at the left rear end of the battle zone between the Germans and a hotpotch of 'details' —drivers, grooms, clerks, batmen—which the latter won, thanks to some effective work by gunners, machine-gunners, and airmen in delaying the advance. Major-General C. L. Nicholson, commanding the 34th Division on the left of the 59th, was meanwhile skilfully redeploying his troops to meet the threat to his right flank, where he held the villages of Croisilles and St. Leger in the valley of the River Sensée. The Germans duly made a tremendous effort to turn this flank, but the 34th stood firm, the 16th Royal Scots at Croisilles and a brigade of Northumberland Fusiliers around St. Leger particularly distinguishing themselves. Waves of Germans, split into their battle groups, were then seen advancing against the left flank of this division. They too were brought eventually to a crumpled halt, with the aid of the 3rd Division on the 34th's left and the hastily summoned 40th Division.

It was here, five miles from Arras, that the Germans most wanted success, here alone that they were decisively thwarted. Luck for once was on the side of the British. The 34th held the ground of greatest importance, namely a gentle ridge, topped by Henin Hill and shaped as an outer shield for Arras, the capture of which was an essential prelude to the cherished project of rolling up the British line. The defenders were in rather greater density than on the Fifth Army front, the 34th holding a frontage of $2\frac{3}{4}$ miles as opposed, for example, to the $3\frac{1}{4}$ held by the 24th. They had reserves closer behind them and they had the incentive of holding ground which was of obvious importance to the whole B.E.F. Their luck lay in the fact that the attack did not gain full momentum until the mist had lifted. Commanders could thus follow and anticipate the course of the battle.

Gough and his subordinates, on the other hand, had to compete with a situation as obscure as their instructions were indefinite. Without knowing very often which of their battalions still existed, commanders could do no more than chafe at their headquarters and wrestle with hypothetical problems concerning the employment of their few reserves. Gough soon disposed of his. He had by previous agreement allotted the 39th Division to Congreve, the 1st Cavalry to Watts, and the 2nd Cavalry to Butler. As soon as the scope of the attack was realised he gave Maxse the 20th Division, on its release from G.H.Q. strings, and Butler the 3rd Cavalry, and he ordered the 50th Northumbrian, also released by G.H.Q., up from the back area to come under Watts. The first part of the journey was made by rail and around noon the battalions marched to the station with their drums and fifes at their head. Having been lifted twenty miles, they were on the march again, all through the night. One more division was promised Gough by G.H.Q., but two days were needed for its delivery.

However, there were the French, and the French Sixth Army, adjacent to the British Fifth, promptly ordered a division across the Oise to Gough's aid. Even more was expected of the French Third Army, which had been relieved in the line by the British Fifth and was meant to be in reserve to support it. The arrival of its commander, General Humbert, at Gough's headquarters at Nesle was therefore welcome. He appears to have been a sardonic fellow. At the time of the relief he had expressed the opinion that the Germans could deliver *"un vilain coup"* from St. Quentin, and now that the blow had fallen he answered Gough's eager greeting with the words, *"Mais, je n'ai que mon fanion,"* meaning that the penant on his car was all he commanded. It was the first sombre dawning of Pétain's selfishness. Plumer meanwhile was telling Haig, with a comforting hand on his shoulder, that he could take any divisions he wanted from the Second Army to replace lacerated ones and that he (Plumer) would still hold on to the Passchendale ridge.

4

IN RETREAT

(March 21–23)

Gough visited all his corps commanders during the afternoon of the 21st. They were not the men to despair. Indeed, they were more vulnerable to optimism than gloom, and with a strain of robust self-confidence seeping down to lower levels of command rather too rosy a picture may have been painted. Butler was the only one whom Gough found at all anxious. It was agreed that he should withdraw his troops behind the Crozat Canal and that Maxse should bring most of his right-hand division, the 36th, back in order to comply. The only other adjustments agreed were local ones to keep the dented flanks of the various corps in touch. Their commanders were happy to cling on to what remained of their battle zones, even though their frontages were elongated by bulges and there were fewer troops left to hold them, about one quarter having been lost. Gough, to his credit, stressed the importance of keeping the divisions intact. He told his corps commanders, and sent out a written instruction in confirmation, that they should withdraw if strongly attacked and fight a delaying action "in complete co-operation with each other" rather than incur further losses by standing fast. Having thus authorised the withdrawal to start and having already disposed of his reserves, there was little he could do from now onwards to sway the course of events.

That evening Gough rang up Lawrence, Haig's Chief of Staff. He emphasised the weight of the onslaught against him and expressed (in his own words) "very considerable anxiety for the next and following days." The response rankled so deeply that he recorded it at length in his book, *The Fifth Army*. Lawrence refused to be impressed; after their severe losses, he

51

maintained, the Germans would need to rest and recuperate and "would be busy clearing the battlefield." Gough tried un-availingly to shake him out of this maddeningly complacent view. No one seemed interested in his plight. While the Chief of Staff contributed the 'There-there-now' of a nanny to a child, the only communication from the Commander-in-Chief was a parental message of congratulation on the fight Gough's men had made. Both, in fact, had their eyes on a more northerly portion of the line and were not convinced that the main assault had yet been delivered. However, orders were issued at 11.15 p.m. for the despatch of a second division from the Second to the Fifth Army, indicating that Gough was not quite the neglected orphan he felt.

Night brought some respite for the men of his battered divisions, so long beset by their swarming, skilled, agile, enter-prising, and in most parts determined enemies. The Germans had expended a huge store of energy and now they flopped down where they fought, paying no heed to an order that the attack would continue "even during the night". The British wearily cleaned their weapons and made what adjustments they could to meet the renewal of the onslaught. The various with-drawals ordered were carried out without interference, being announced on the right flank by the blowing-up of bridges. There were some other impromptu and splendidly welcome with-drawals by men who had been submerged without trace beneath the tide. Three companies of the K.R.R.C. and Scottish Rifles, who had laid low at Benay, broke through complete to swell the meagre ranks of the 14th Division, and many other smaller parties or lone individuals crept past the corpses around them, plotted course by a moon that shone until 1 a.m. and groped hopefully for gaps between drowsy German sentries during the pitch darkness that followed. Some made successful ventures in the opposite direction, notably some field gunners and infantry-men of the 30th Division who succeeded in hauling in ten abandoned guns, bringing a prisoner with them. But local counter-attacks here and there aroused more vigorous response.

There was no sleep for the denizens of the many headquarters whose moves had been ordered before darkness fell. There were cars and lorries to be loaded, cables to be taken up and relaid, office and mess accoutrements to be dismantled and removed from well encrusted dens, stacks of papers to be thrust in incinerators. Headquarters Fifth Army moved back as far as Villers Bretonneux, only ten miles east of Amiens, and all its corps headquarters came back west of the Somme Canal. Divisional headquarters were also moved rearwards, although with rather less elaboration, being more accustomed to the process, and further forward still matches were put to files and code books that the battalion orderly-room sergeant could not carry in his pack. Theoretically, it was wise to pull back the big headquarters at this early stage, and thanks to the exertions of the signallers and the anticipatory arrangements that had providently been made, a telephone service was maintained, much to the benefit of cohesion over the next few days. Morally, the moves were harmful. The staffs had embarked on a habit, the habit of leading the retreat, and were to draw much mockery for their alacrity at "going out of the line".

Aided again by fog and by hard-won knowledge of the British defences, the Germans swarmed into the attack again as dawn broke on the 22nd, under arrangements made on a divisional basis. The pressure was heaviest where the gains were already the greatest, and the four corps of Gough's army were consequently tugged back from the right like men with arms outstretched. With the extreme left virtually static, grasps gave way under the strain and there was much anxious groping.

Butler's corps were momentarily safe behind the Crozat Canal, but their withdrawal left Maxse's right flank hideously exposed and a heavy price had to be paid for his proud reluctance to give up more ground during the night. Despite a great fight by the 1st Inniskillings on this exposed flank, Maxse felt compelled to order a general withdrawal shortly before one o'clock and because no proper defences had been dug on his reserve, or green, line he ordered his three divisions right back to the Somme Canal, covered by the newly arrived 20th Division from an intermediate position. He has been censured by Sir James Edmonds, the official historian, for withdrawing too fast and too far, thus endangering Watts's corps on his left, but from the supremely vivid account written by the adjutant of the 2nd

Green Howards, Captain Herbert Read, it appears that the orders came too late.

The Green Howards, who were in 30 Division, were at Roupy, a key village on the St. Quentin–Ham road in the centre of the corps battle zone. A wedge, it will be remembered, had been driven into the battalion redoubt the previous evening. The attack was renewed at 7 in the morning but could make little progress, except round the flanks. A stronger attack came in at midday, with the mist still thinly persisting, and some platoon keeps were overrun in the face of desperate fire from the Green Howards. Nagging, unrelenting pressure was maintained while a yet stronger attack was prepared. By the time it came in Read had been raised to the command of his battalion, and a company of the King's with them, by a British shell that wounded his colonel. A message arrived from brigade headquarters as the Germans tightened their clutch round the flanks. Reinforcements or withdrawal? Read wondered, tearing the envelope open. Neither : he was to hold on to the last.

An hour later, at about 5 o'clock, with the enemy still pressing on "with a determined, insidious energy, reckless of cost", he suddenly decided to order a withdrawal to the reserve line before it was too late. Having sent a runner off with the necessary message, he agonisingly watched the result from his command post in rear. The Germans had gradually been bombing their way round the rim of the redoubt. "And now we only held it as lips might touch the rim of a saucer. I could see the heads of my men, very dense and in a little space. And on either side, incredibly active, gathered the grey helmets of the Boches. It was like a long bowstring along the horizon, and our diminished forces the arrow to be shot into the void. A great many hostile machine-guns had now been brought up, and the plain was sprayed with hissing bullets. They impinged and spluttered about the little pit in which I crouched.

"I waited anxiously for B. to take the open. I saw men crawl out of the trenches and lie flat on the parados, still firing at the enemy. Then, after a little while, the arrow was launched. I saw a piteous band of men rise from the ground, and run rapidly towards me. A great shout went up from the Germans: a cry of mingled triumph and horror. '*Halt*

Eenglisch!' they cried, and for a moment were too amazed to fire; as though aghast at the folly of men who could plunge into such a storm of death. But the first silent gasp of horror expended, then broke the crackling storm. I don't remember in the whole war an intenser taste of hell. My men came along spreading rapidly to a line of some two hundred yards length, but bunched here and there. On the left, by the main road, the enemy rushed out to cut them off. Bayonets clashed there. Along the line men were falling swiftly as bullets hit them. Each second they fell, now one crumpling up, now two or three at once. I saw men stop to pick up their wounded mates, and as they carried them along, themselves get hit and fall with their inert burdens. Now they were near me, so I rushed out of my pit and ran with them to the line of trenches some three hundred yards behind.

"It seemed to take a long time to race across those few hundred yards. My heart beat nervously, and I felt infinitely weary. The bullets hissed about me, and I thought : then this is the moment of death. But I had no emotions. I remembered having read how in battle men are hit, and never feel the hurt till later, and I wondered if I had yet been hit. Then I reached the line. I stood petrified, enormously aghast. *The trench had not been dug, and no reinforcements occupied it.* It was as we had passed it on the morning of the 21st, the sods dug off the surface, leaving an immaculately patterned 'mock' trench."

This empty mockery of a trench, in fact, lay in the battle zone. There could be no holding it and, covered now by some machine-guns, the Green Howards withdrew to Fluquières, on the edge of the green line, where they found a trench but were encircled by Very lights fired by the Germans to denote their positions to hovering aircraft which quickly brought artillery fire down on the anguished men. Back Read led them, until he came to another trench, and here, just as darkness was falling and with the enemy still tirelessly afflicting them, a despatch rider arrived with orders for a withdrawal beyond the Somme Canal through Ham. Having limped through this little market town, recently so cosy and now deserted, except by looters, the survivors of the stand at Roupy tumbled down on the floor of a school in a village two miles further on. Rations arrived for them in the morning. They consisted of tinned bully beef, biscuits and cold water.

Further to the left, the 61st Division had a longer march, of about twelve miles, back to the Somme. Disengagement presented no great problem, since the enemy had been well repulsed in the morning, but against his infiltration tactics withdrawal was a perilous manoeuvre in daylight, and the Scottish and West Midland battalions of this division became sadly depleted as they trudged back to the Somme. Night brought no relaxation, for fresh German divisions had entered the battle. The 20th Division—a Light division, like the 14th— drew some of the sting from their fiendishly persistent attacks, but both they and the 61st had to face some desperate crises before they reached the Somme in the early hours of the 23rd. The 2nd/6th Royal Warwickshire, for instance, having been marooned without orders by the wounding of their brigade commander and the capture of the brigade major, were down to eighty officers and men when they plodded across the bridge at Voyennes at 6 a.m.

General Watts, of XIX Corps, ordered the retirement of his two forward divisions at 12.45 p.m. Despite the early fog, great destruction had been wrought on the Germans, especially by the men of the 24th Division with dismounted Dragoon Guards-men and Hussars of the 1st Cavalry sprinkled among them. Indeed, only Le Verguier had been lost, and that after a noble stand by the 8th Queen's. But up the Cologne valley on the left flank of the 66th Division the grey swarms were harder to check. A brave infantry charge by the 19th Hussars cleared them from a wood, despite the breakdown of the tanks support-ing them, but withdrawal there had to be, and again it proved more costly than defence.

On the corps green line the 50th Division—tough, stocky men from the Tyneside mining towns—were burrowing away to improve the scanty defences after their march forward from railhead. They had a vivid insight into what lay ahead as the battle-stained, wide-eyed groups of men, many of them limping and bandaged, stumped back through their positions, too pre-occupied with their own plight and experience to give more than an occasional nod of greeting. Only one quarter of the fighting men—all Lancastrians—of the 66th remained. The 24th had suffered less heavily, and indeed many men of their battalions, most of which came from counties around London, were bewildered at being made to withdraw when they had been felling Germans with such effect. Momentary exhilaration, as so often in war, had plunged dizzily to gloom. There were few yet who realised that the complete army was in full retreat, and for the 24th there was still a long way to go. Having halted that evening five miles east of the Somme, they were ordered at 3.30 next morning to take up position to cover the right flank, belatedly realised to be exposed. Limbers reached them with ammunition, having galloped through enemy patrols en route.

Among those left behind on this front were a company of the former corps reserve battalion, the 9th Royal Sussex. They had been thrown in on the 21st to stem the onrush up the Cologne valley and found themselves surrounded next morning. The company commander, Captain H. A. Saxon, wrote: "Even to me who knew them well and expected much of them, the spirit which the men showed to the end was a revelation. For twenty-four hours they had seen the enemy advancing until they were lost to view in the rear, and no unit except our own seemed to offer any resistance or even to stay. They were surrounded and gave up expectation of any relief—the mist gave a feeling of blind helplessness. They were shelled by their own artillery, and even for the wounded, for some six hours there was no way out, and yet they never for a moment considered there was any other job for them but to stay and fight until the ever-increasing numbers round them should find the courage to overwhelm them. To the end they held themselves better than the enemy, and to the end they jeered and dared him to come on."

Congreve's VII Corps were in the most delicate situation of all. His Irishmen of the 16th Division were already in a desperate plight, and although they and the 39th Division repulsed five mass attacks on this Friday morning they were forced to yield further ground. The Leicestershire brigade, of 21 Division, exacted a heavy price for entry into Epéhy but themselves suffered heavily when at last squeezed out of it and compelled to make a downhill withdrawal. And now the 9th

Scottish Division were in mortal danger, with their right flank wide open. Thanks partly to some guns of the 21st, which were fought to the last, the 9th fought their way back without great loss, except to a sacrificial company of the 9th Royal Scots and two batteries of guns, to link up after dark with the remnant of the other three divisions on the green line. But now a deliberate withdrawal by 50 Division, not notified to Congreve until 4 a.m. because of the bombing of Watts's corps head-quarters, opened an inviting gap on the right, and there was another gap on the left, because the 9th Division had come back much more precipitately than the right division of the Third Army. An enterprising German colonel seized his chance here, grabbing the village of Fins, astride an important supply route for the Third Army. Like many another commander on either side, he defied the expectations of his gunners and had to endure shelling from his own side.

There had been a voluntary retraction of the line by the closely placed divisions of V Corps, Third Army, holding the Flesquières salient. The mustard gas had done its beastly work effectively, and many men had been evacuated while others who stayed at duty were racked by vomiting and could speak only by whisper. But a massed attack on the left haunch, clumsily carried out by von der Marwitz's Second Army, crumpled hopelessly before the weapons of the 17th Northern Division. On the right only desultory attacks were made, and the only cause for alarm, until the nocturnal penetration to Fins, was the suspicious lack of determination shown. The salient had, in fact, grown bigger, because the enforced withdrawals on the flanks were larger than the voluntary one inside it. V Corps were in no mood to be stampeded.

Further leftwards along the Third Army line, sheer persistence won the Germans gains after they had suffered terrible losses, in inflicting which the British ran short of ammunition. A breach through the 6th Division in the late afternoon was repaired by a counter-attack by twenty-five tanks of the 2nd Tank Battalion, which would have been as inexpensive as successful if the tanks had not been picked off by artillery while loitering on their objective awaiting the arrival of infantry : a familiar weakness. On their left the 40th Division were eventually driven out of

Mory, beyond the green line, and, more serious, the 34th lost Henin Hill despite great slaughter of their Bavarian assailants. The trenches on the hilltop disintegrated under artillery fire well directed by German aircraft. But the British stood firm on the other side of the hill.

Compared to Hutier's spectacular advance, the progress here was a great disappointment to Ludendorff, but being nearer their vitals it made the British writhe and enforced a withdrawal which Sir Charles Fergusson, the corps commander concerned, accepted with anguish and his troops of the 15th Scottish Division carried out with grudging perplexity, having played a a proud part in the capture of the ground they had to yield. The long, squiggly, wide-topped ridge known as Monchy Hill protected Arras from the east and provided observation deep into the German lines, but the capture of Henin Hill exposed it to attack from the south and meant that more men would be required to hold it than Byng could spare. He therefore ordered the abandonment of the eastern part of the ridge, which included the village of Monchy and its magnificent view across the Douai plain. No risk could be taken here. "I expect a big attack to develop towards Arras," Haig wrote in his diary that night.

While Byng admirably anticipated events with his left hand, his right was beginning to grope. Gough came to his head-quarters at Albert this evening, Friday the 22nd, much worried about the gap that was opening between the two armies, even though news of the fall of Fins had not yet arrived. Byng ordered V Corps to make a further, limited withdrawal. Haig was quick to see that something more drastic was required, and soon after midnight written orders arrived from G.H.Q. enforcing belated awareness on Headquarters Third Army that their right wing was in considerable peril. Byng was directed to conform with the withdrawal of the Fifth Army and "be prepared in case of necessity" to fall back on the River Tortille, which was in alignment with the Somme Canal and well behind the green line of V Corps. The divisions of this corps were at once told to prepare for this radical withdrawal, but orders for its execution did not reach them until after daylight, and by now the Germans were coming near to winning the race for the gap.

They had already, at midday on Friday, March 22nd, provided chastening evidence of their dash and initiative, for at this hour they made their first breach across the water obstacle which was intended to be the Fifth Army's longstop line. It happened on the extreme right, near the junction of the Oise with the Crozat Canal, on which III Corps had fallen back in the night. The mist had cleared by now. Under cover of it the Germans had brought their mortars and machine-guns into position and with them all blazing in unison the stormtroopers dashed across the collapsed but not demolished remnant of the road bridge into the once busy little town of Tergnier. An hour later they made another crossing over the deep, 20-ft. wide canal a mile further north by using similar tactics over another ruined bridge. One and a half battalions of the London Regiment— virtually all the infantry left of 58 Division, except for five battalions still south of the Oise—strove bravely to stave them off, reinforced by sappers, machine-gunners, cavalrymen, students from the signal school, and an entrenching battalion. Not until after dark did the Germans gain full possession of Tergnier and consolidate their little bridgehead which so menaced the new line to which the bulk of the Fifth Army were still retreating.

Tergnier was not the only place to fall with the coming of darkness over the III Corps front. At Vendeuil, four miles east of the Crozat Canal, two parties of the 7th Buffs still held their forward-zone positions thirty-six hours after the attack began, one of them an odd assortment of company strength in the fort, the other a platoon detachment further south and nearer the Oise. At Travecy, a mile to their right, A Company of the 2nd/2nd London similarly held out. Since long before dawn on the Friday it had been obvious to the occupants of these posts that they were cut off and abandoned without hope of relief. Yet when the mist lifted they had turned their Lewis guns on the transport columns that made such splendid targets for them on the road to Tergnier. The Germans attacked again and again and did not gain entry until exhaustion, hunger, lack of ammunition, and the sorry plight of their ever-mounting rows of wounded led to the more or less simultaneous capitulation of these three forlorn posts around 8 p.m. on this Friday night.

Elsewhere hope still burned bright. At Jussy, five miles to

the north of Tergnier, men of the sadly depleted 14th Division beat back attacks across the canal deep into the night and at 1 a.m. some 5th Lancers and oddments of the 7th K.R.R.C. smartly flattened a lodgement gained under a heavy bombardment. Further south there was a railway bridge, the destruction of which had been entrusted without fulfilment to the French authorities. The Germans crossed it at dusk, but were beaten back by the 6th Northamptonshire of the still pliant 18th Division. Surrounded on the far bank, 2nd Lieutenant A. C. Herring of this battalion put up a desperate resistance with a handful of men, thwarting further attempts to cross here for eleven hours. Herring, who was an accountant recently transferred from the Army Service Corps, survived, to be rewarded with a congratulatory handshake from the Kaiser at St. Quentin and (much later of course) the V.C. from his King.

Meanwhile Frenchmen of the 125th Division had been arriving, bringing cheer to various details of the 58th Division preparing a reserve line west of Tergnier. Their Sixth Army commander had ordered them to counter-attack, and at dawn on the 23rd two battalions set off for Tergnier and two others for a wooded hill to the left. There was a marked air of nonchalance about these men as they marched off into the mist, attended by staff officers on chargers that had filled the railway trucks earmarked for ammunition, leaving nothing more available than the thirty-five rounds carried by each man. They were soon in trouble. Despite losing their way, the right assault force reached the fringe of Tergnier but was there stopped by a hail of bullets, and the left one met even fiercer fire, their commander going down at an early stage.

Two companies of the 7th Queen's were allotted for the protection of the left flank of the French. Their commanding officer, Lieutenant-Colonel C. Bushell, who had accompanied his 1st Battalion to Mons in 1914, was another of those extraordinary men who could will themselves, despite all that had been endured, to display no trace of fear whatever. He galvanised the men, both English and French, who lay withered by sickening machine-gun fire. A bullet gashed his head as he strode among them. He treated it like a gnat bite. The shells began to fall, presaging a counter-attack. With blood streaming down his face, Bushell regrouped his mixed force to meet it, spreading courage about him across many acres. The Germans were held. Bushell had his wound dressed and returned to bring further inspiration as the situation worsened, until at last he fainted and was carried from the battlefield. Soon afterwards the French broke, having run out of ammunition. The Queen's made a cool and skilled retirement, conscious of the example set by their commanding officer, as indeed were the whole of the 18th Division. It was a well-won V.C.

The Germans had by now erupted in spate across the Crozat Canal. Morning fog and numbers combined to swamp the defences around Jussy, aided by agile use of the bridges that lay smashed in the water but could still be used. Proper foot and vehicle bridges were constructed with remarkable speed during this Saturday morning and fresh German infantry came up by lorry. The 18th Division inflicted some heavy casualties on them as they debouched, the 11th Royal Fusiliers catching a marching column complete with band at its head. But from Jussy the Germans soon turned the left flank of Butler's weary assortments and their French colleagues and drove them into a forest, in which control was a nightmare. The 18th Division fought a desperate battle at Rouez Wood, $2\frac{1}{2}$ miles west of Tergnier. Colonel Ransome of the 7th Buffs—a connoisseur in such matters— thought the volume of machine-gun fire mounted by the Germans was the densest he ever heard. The men stuck it out. The French arrived and counter-attacked with startling gallantry. But again they had not the ammunition to sustain their effort, and back they came, spreading alarm and confusion where previously the exhausted British had stood defiant and firm. But the Germans missed their chance. Some sort of order was re-established, and with the merciful fall of darkness the British and French plodded further back.

Maxse's XVIII Corps had found the canal line, beyond the flow of Crozat into Somme, no easier to hold. The four divisions of this corps had been marching all through the night, having had precious little sleep on the previous two, and the rearguards on the left, west of Ham, were still crossing the river when the defenders of Ham—a brigade of the King's Regiment in 30 Division—were attacked from the rear at 6 a.m., the fog, as usual, lying thick. The town stands in the watercourse, flanked on the north by the river and on the south by the canal. The Germans had wormed their way round it, and the bridges over the canal had to be blown with many Kingsmen trapped inside the town, where they held out for another two hours or so. But the Germans were over the collapsed bridges long before Ham had fallen and they also forced the passage of an undamaged railway bridge further east. Pushing on southwards they routed a company of Inniskillings at a hamlet a mile from the river, but turned tail when the Irishmen returned cheering wildly with the brigade major, Captain J. G. Bruce, mounted at their head. However, only two hundred men, from six different units, could be scraped together for a corps counter-attack, and by the time they had toiled in from a reserve position four miles away the Germans were far too firmly ensconced in front of Ham to be troubled by their aching exertions or by the four aircraft that provided their only fire support.

On the right Light Infantry remnants of the 14th Division and Ulstermen of the 36th yielded slowly and with grim, numb courage to the mounting pressure on their right flank applied by the ever growing number of Germans come across the river from Jussy. In the late afternoon the assault was resumed from the direction of Ham, and by darkness Maxse's men lay forlornly along a jagged, unstable line across the plain about three miles beyond the canal, with their tormentors still coming at them during the night. On the left of the corps line the 20th Division still held the banks of the canal, having comfortably repulsed various attacks made in the afternoon uncloaked by fog.

It will be remembered that Watts's XIX Corps still had two divisions in some peril east of the canal as dawn broke on this Saturday morning. They were successfully withdrawn. Having had a hard and costly fight on their first contact with the Germans on the Friday evening, the 50th Division shook them off by disengaging without detection during the night—a manoeuvre that begged more frequent use—and had an easy passage back to the Somme Canal. The 24th had difficulty only in getting their rearguards across at Falvy. The 3rd Rifle Brigade made a text-book step-by-step withdrawal after being nastily caught in enfilade, but some of the 9th East Surrey nearby found their bridge blown and the canal unfordable and the non-swimmers were obliged to make a forlorn last stand, while the 8th Hussars and a squadron of the 19th had to leave behind their horses, plunging and writhing under machine-gun fire, after an attempt to swim had foundered in the boggy approach. Five tanks also had to be abandoned, not because of the premature firing of a bridge, but because the one they chose, although the main one on the Roman road from Amiens to St. Quentin, was too narrow.

After dark the Germans made two crossings in this sector, but the 8th Division, the first of two sent to Gough from the Second Army, had taken over and promptly drove them back; it was a regular division, composed of battalions that had been in Mediterranean stations on the outbreak of war. One breach had been made into the village of Parny, and the Germans were ejected with a hundred killed and twenty captured by forty-five headquarter men of the 1st Worcestershire, led by the acting commanding officer, Major F. C. Roberts, who won the V.C. for the exploit. The 8th held a frontage of some eight miles along the canal and its curtain of poplars and rushes, and they needed to be on their mettle, for eight German divisions had been identified opposite them.

For Congreve's VII Corps the 23rd dawned and continued sombre. A weak brigade had been despatched by V Corps of the Third Army during the night to maintain touch between the two armies, but had failed to do so, and there was also a vacuum on Congreve's right, caused by the withdrawal of the 50th Division rather sooner than advice of it reached him. This latter event took place at 4.40 a.m. (on the Saturday) and Congreve thereupon issued orders for a withdrawal of two to three miles to positions covering Peronne. The morning fog, still persisting, enabled the survivors of the 16th Irish Division, of which the pioneer battalion (11th Hampshires) and the 17th Entrenching Battalion formed half, to sneak back unseen on the right, and also the stronger 39th Division alongside them, thanks to a well struck blow by the 17th K.R.R.C. as the Germans made their customary dawn attack. The orders took longer to reach the other two divisions and did little more than confirm what the Germans had already done. A weak composite brigade of the

21st gave way, making extrication very hazardous for the Yorkshiremen of the other brigade, who had to abandon well-held trenches and rush away uphill in view of the enemy, but with less disastrous results than were to be expected. The far-flung 9th Division retired beyond the Tortille four to six miles north of Peronne, the rearguards of the 6th King's Own Scottish Borderers and the 8th Black Watch escaping destruction by a combination of skill, guts and luck.

Peronne, of course, was the "important centre" by the bend of the Somme that Gough had been instructed to "protect at all costs". It was not a large town. None the less a host of refugees streamed away out of the town across the bridge over the Somme, making a heartbreaking and militarily exasperating procession with their handcarts and cumbersome oxcarts, their grannies, kids and pigs. In some houses meals lay unfinished on tables, providing a few fortunate British soldiers with their first brief taste of cooked food since the battle started. The military police herded the procession along, keeping with difficulty a passage clear for the jumbled columns of military vehicles, horse drawn and motor mixed, and finally for the guns. There were military refugees, too, and among them, emotions numbed by fatigue, were nursing sisters hobbling along with belongings to carry and wounded to assist. Black clouds of smoke, from burning stores, provided the appropriate air of devastation. The only mercy was that the German air force had an off day.

North-east of Peronne there is higher ground from which two ridges run towards the town, and it was here that the defence had to be made. But there were no troops for the task other than those who had been fighting, suffering and with-drawing. The trouble about withdrawing is that once begun it is liable to become a habit, and the habit had begun to take hold. It was easy enough for the Germans to find gaps in the ex-tenuated and hastily occupied British line, and rather than make them pay for their daring the first concern of the troops out-flanked was to avoid being cut off, for however weary the British were the determination still ran high to fight and live for another day. There were thus further withdrawals all through the after-noon, some roughly co-ordinated by senior commanders or staff riding their chargers across the slopes—for there was no means of communication below divisional headquarters other than by personal delivery—some spontaneous. The 39th Division held the village of Mont St. Quentin, on the toe of the more northerly ridge, until 4 p.m., and as the infantry withdrew, their gunners remained firing over open sights and then pulled all but one gun out as the shells burst in among them, hitting men and horses. Soon the bridges were blown and heavy German boots tramped the cobbles of Peronne.

Already the 21st and 9th Divisions had fallen back from the Tortille, which was little more than a brook, into the hills beyond, where all around there was nothing but ruts and ruination, left by the fighting of eighteen months ago. In attempting to keep touch with the Third Army, the 9th had become perilously far spread and at nightfall Brigadier-General H. H. Tudor, commanding the division, decided to concentrate his brigades, leaving a gap of unknown width on his left, which it was by rights the responsibility of the Third Army to fill.

But the Third Army were in trouble, too, at any rate on their right. The rearguard of V Corps, holding a reduced salient round Metz-en-Couture, were scheduled to withdraw at 1 p.m. on this Saturday, but the Germans began to work their way round their right flank four hours earlier. They did not exploit the situation with the dash that had won them Fins and in the 47th London Division encountered a force with the guns, machine-guns, visibility and men to take a heavy toll. The divisions of V Corps fell back on their green line without great loss. But no sooner were they there than the Germans again appeared behind their right flank. There was further withdrawal, some confusion, and further widening of the gap between the two armies. The Germans attacked again soon after dark and captured a village deep in the vitals named Bus (as if to empha-sise how V Corps had missed it), just as Byng, apprised of the plight of the Fifth Army by another visit from Gough, issued orders for a junction to be made three miles south of Bus, and as Major-General Sir George Gorringe, the commander of the 47th, sent officers into the night to find his brigades and listened in exasperation to mocking noises on the telephone.

For the sickened (by mustard gas) and worn-out men of the 47th, the 63rd Royal Naval, and the 17th Northern Divisions it must have seemed that the end of the world had come. To the south the sky was ablaze with the bonfires made of abandoned stores, ammunition dumps were being blown up around them, and by various means the enemy advertised his presence every-where, sometimes singing drunkenly as he lurched into the attack, celebrating the capture of stocks of whisky. Yet somehow communications were re-established, discipline held, and by some complicated, devious and splendidly endured marches combined with calm resistance elsewhere, the line was reknit and at 8.30 in the morning tenuous junction was made with the bedraggled 9th Division of Gough's Army.

Further leftwards along the Third Army line there were moments of crisis as von Below's Seventeenth Army smashed at IV Corps and its hinge with the bulging V. Divisions had been intermixed as reserves came up to strengthen the line. The 10th Royal Warwickshire and 8th Gloucestershire of the 19th, for instance, won distinction fighting alongside Highlanders of the 51st who had withstood the offensive from its start; five battalions of the 19th and 41st Divisions went down fighting through being caught with both flanks turned in a position inaccessible by runner; and on their left men of these two divisions and the 25th, holding a reverse slope position, piled massive heaps of grey upon their wire as six violent attempts were made on their trenches. Nearer Arras the Germans had great difficulty, according to their histories, in gaining positions which they imagined to be held by "brave defenders, unshaken and not disheartened" but had, in fact, already been evacuated by the 15th Scottish in order to shorten the line. The all-important left still held firm.

But for Gough the one flank was in as sorry a plight as the other. It was early on this Saturday afternoon, as the Germans were swarming over the canal line at Ham and Jussy, as the refugees were streaming even through Villers Bretonneux, and as rumours waxed wild, that he received his one and only visit —and a brief one at that—from his Commander-in-Chief. Haig's calm was undisturbed. He had not allowed the battle to interrupt his diary writing, and the result indicates that he had a some-what airy notion of what was going on. "All reports show that our men are in great spirits," he began his entry (after reporting

67

on the weather) on the Friday night. Later he accorded the drama of underlining to the words : "At 8 p.m. Gough tele-phoned, 'Parties of all arms of the enemy are through our Reserve line.' I concurred on his falling back and defending the line of the Somme and to hold the Peronne Bridgehead in accor-dance with his orders."

One can be sure that Gough, too, was calm and each attests to the other's cheerfulness. Gough no doubt took some pleasure in telling Haig that identifications had been obtained of forty-five enemy divisions facing him, but he would have liked to have discussed the situation in greater detail, specially on the question of liaison with the Third Army. That neglected feeling still rankled, as is illustrated by the hurt tone of his description of the occasion in his book : "Haig was calm and cheerful, but all he said to me was : 'Well, Hubert, one can't fight without men'—a fact which I could well appreciate."

It does not seem that Haig himself fully appreciated the fact or grasped even then the plight of the Fifth Army. In his diary this night he recorded his surprise on visiting Gough "to learn that his troops are *now behind* the Somme and R. Tortille", and Gough himself was in for a surprise when an order from G.H.Q. reached him, issued at 5.30 p.m. : "Fifth Army must hold the Somme at all costs. There must be no withdrawal from this line. . . . Third and Fifth Armies must keep in close touch in order to secure their junction and must mutually assist each other in maintaining Peronne as a pivot." The line of the Somme had already been levered open, as Haig must have known, and Peronne had fallen just before the signing of the order.

5

THE FLOW STEMMED

(March 23–28)

It was on this Saturday, March 23rd, that Ludendorff changed his plan. Orders were issued at 9.30 a.m. and amplified at a Chiefs-of-Staff conference in the afternoon. Instead of co-operating in a gigantic turning movement against the British, with the left standing firm to prevent interference, the three armies were now to sprout forth in divergent directions like the leaves of a *fleur-de-lys*. Von Hutier's triumphant Eighteenth Army, so far from standing on the defensive, was to press south-westwards and carry the offensive to the French. Von der Marwitz's Second was to advance on Amiens along both banks of the Somme, forming the blade for the newly conceived concept of cutting the French and British apart. Von Below's Seventeenth, notwithstanding its disappointing progress, was assigned the most ambitious task of all. Reinforced only by three fresh division, it was to attack vigorously through Arras towards St. Pol (twenty miles further west) and was to co-operate with other armies further north "in order to drive the British into the sea".

Two principles of war, long taught to every cadet at Sand-hurst, were violated here—Maintenance of Object and Con-centration of Force—and the fact that so renowned and highly professional a soldier as Ludendorff lapsed into such elementary error throws revealing light on the distortions, expectations, and seductive spectre of opportunity confronting a commander at the moment of decision. His War Memories, not surprisingly, make no mention of any change of plan, far less illuminate his motives. Two impulses were probably at work. One was his obsession with the doctrine of infiltration, as a result of which he could not bear to halt troops in full flow and tended to regard strategy as the slave of tactics. "I forbid myself to use the word *strategy*," he even told Prince Rupprecht. "We chop a hole. The rest follows." Opportunism had become the creed of this stern, stodgy, and so Prussian general.

The other impulse was the elation of the moment, the thrill of brilliant achievement after the grim years in defence and the hectic months of preparation, breeding what has been aptly described as "the shout-hurrah mood of August 1914". Either way, stark facts were ignored. The hole had not been chopped; the British had fallen back but not disintegrated, and they stood ominously firm where most it mattered. Yet the new orders presupposed their total defeat. Wanting victory too dearly, the Germans—even the great Ludendorff—frolicked with its image.

Even so, they were near to victory, and if their effort might in the long run be dissipated over too wide a frontage beneath the new wave of optimism, no slackening of it was yet apparent to the poor, gasping, dog-tired troops on whom it fell. Meanwhile a case of pessimism on the Allied side had a surprising and far-reaching outcome. Pétain had come to see Haig at his advanced headquarters at Dury in the afternoon of this eventful Saturday, the 23rd. Although worried that an attack was about to fall on his front, he told Haig that he was bringing eleven divisions to the Amiens sector, which was nine less than Haig had asked for. Six of these had come into action in relief of the right wing of Gough's army by the Sunday afternoon, but being short of guns and ammunition they showed greater inclination to retain alignment than to repel the enemy. The retreat was if anything accelerated in this sector, and it is clear that the French generals, including Humbert, who at last had something more than his *'fanion'* to command, laid the blame on the lamentable state of the Fifth Army.

At 11 p.m. on this Sunday night Pétain returned to Dury and, having previously had Haig rather worried, he now astounded him. "Pétain struck me as very much upset, almost unbalanced and most anxious," Haig reported in his usual long entry in his diary. Having stressed the likelihood of an attack on his own sector, Pétain handed Haig a copy of an order he had sent to his army group commanders that day. Its dynamic was compressed under the heading (translated) Intention:

"Before everything to keep the French Armies together as one solid whole; in particular not to allow the G.A.R." (the nearest group to the British) "to be cut off from the rest of our forces. Secondly, if it is possible, to maintain liaison with the British forces." Pétain admitted that if the Germans pressed their advance further he would be forced to abandon the British right flank in order to carry out his orders to *"cover Paris at all costs"* (underlined and given inverted commas by Haig in his diary). It was tantamount to admitting that the war was lost.

While his enemy and his ally strayed from their prearranged courses, led on by illusions respectively of victory and defeat, Haig remained determined to stick to his. He had been husbanding the reserves stoically provided by the First and Second Armies and had six divisions available either to prop up the Third Army or combat a fresh offensive elsewhere. But his whole position would collapse without the aid to his right flank promised by Pétain to meet this very eventuality. He himself was resolved to retain contact with the French (according to his diary) "even at the cost of drawing back the North flank on the sea coast". If Pétain shrank from his commitment, Haig swiftly decided, an overall commander must be appointed with the power to hold him to it, and at 3 a.m. on the Monday morning—that is on Haig's return to Montreuil from Dury accompanied by his Chief of Staff, Lawrence—a telegram was despatched to the C.I.G.S., Sir Henry Wilson, asking that this should be brought about.

Wilson, remarkably, was at Montreuil by 11 a.m. After one false start and much motoring and telephoning, he arranged for the great men of France to come to Doullens, but not until the Tuesday, March 26th. He spent the Monday night with his friend Rawlinson and one suspects that he may have asked him how he would fancy being entrusted with the defences of Amiens, for it was Wilson's intention that he should have this vital task in place of Gough. It is certain that Rawlinson, who had already decided that the Executive Board "never was a workable proposition", was eager enough for the chance. He knew the area well and was fully aware of the threat. "It is a race for Amiens," he wrote that very night, "between the troops we and the French can bring up against those which the Boche can push forward. He means to divide us, if he possibly can."

Meanwhile the retreat continued. Gough's men had clung to most of their positions still adjoining the Somme Canal during the Sunday, but on either side of them the line was wrenched back alarmingly, specially on the left where Congreve's VII Corps had already fallen back from the Tortille and at 8.30 a.m. on this Sunday had regained contact with Byng's Third Army.

The contact was short lived. Almost at once the Germans came on again, under cover of mist, and the diminished brigades of the 9th and 21st Divisions fired a few rounds, heaved their heavy legs out of the meagre holes they had made for themselves, and continued the rearward trudge for survival, some dropping beneath the savage bark of shrapnel. But one brigade stayed, the strongest of 9 Division, the South African Brigade. Unlike the others, they had received orders the previous evening that their position was to be held at all costs. The order was obeyed. From 9 a.m. to 4.30 p.m. the South Africans fought and fell, pounded by ever increasing weight of artillery and assailed under cover of blazing grass, until, reduced to a hundred, they were at last overwhelmed, with the brigade commander, Brigadier-General F. S. Dawson, emerging from the fallen crew of a machine-gun, whose duties he had taken over. The cost was total, but the gain considerable and with Gough's second newly arrived division, the 35th, and the 1st Cavalry Division coming to their aid, together with the motley, hastily formed battalions of Hunt's Force, VII Corps retired to a fresh line with some semblance of order.

For the right wing of the Third Army the agony of the Sunday surpassed even that of the Saturday. Desperate contortions had been made all through the night to evade the enemy clutch. They began again at 5 a.m. when a heavy attack came in. As bright sunlight dispersed the mist, groups of bedraggled soldiers were to be seen everywhere winding intricate courses with pitifully laboured gait across the ghastly, churned up, corroded wastes which before the Battle of the Somme had been villages and countryside. Only the roads had received any repair work. Here and there a stand was made against attackers showing signs of wear themselves, and then a flank would be turned and the British would struggle to their feet again. Sometimes friend and foe marched on parallel courses in full view of each other, and often the British were obliged to make a detour to circumvent infiltrators. Yet some order was maintained, usually by generals riding horses that floundered among the ruts and shell holes, and a thin thread of cohesion was kept in being, though it depended as a rule solely on the instinct of the officers in command of groups that might represent brigades or battalions but could be mistaken for companies or platoons. Other groups, with no responsible officer in charge, thought only of getting away.

Supply was a matter of luck. Either the troops passed a dump or they did not, and there were some who lasted the whole day without food and, worse, without water. Many tanks had to be abandoned for lack of petrol, and their crews extracted their Lewis guns and joined infantry parties. A tortoise could have kept up on the march—one brigade took two hours to cover a mile and a half—and if there were halts it was a despairing task trying to get the men to their feet again.

At 3.45 Byng ordered a general retirement to a line that conceded Bapaume to the enemy. The divisions from the salient —the 17th, 63rd, 47th and their original reserve, the 2nd—had the furthest to travel and darkness was falling as they staggered in to occupy some defensive relics of the Somme battle. Many had been kept going in the belief that they were falling back through fresh troops, and now they had not only to prepare and man their own defences but in many cases had to make further moves during the night because much sorting was needed to get the divisions deployed according to plan.

Fresh troops, however, now sustained VII Corps, which during the night had been transferred from the Fifth to the Third Army, with the inter-army boundary now conforming with the east–west line of the Somme. The fresh troops were the 35th Division, the original Bantam Division but no longer so named to avoid reinforcement by weaklings in place of the stocky, brawny men who formed the original material. Holding almost the whole of the corps front, these men gave the Germans a violent jolt when they attacked in strength early on the Monday morning. Prompt counter-attacks paid a good dividend when

73

ground was lost, and in one on Maricourt Wood, Lieutenant-Colonel W. H. Anderson of the 12th Highland Light Infantry routed the enemy at the head of a mixed force which included cooks, clerks and batmen from brigade headquarters. He drove the Germans from a timber yard, where they had massed their machine-guns, but the V.C. he won was posthumous, for he was killed as he rushed in at the head of his men.

For the divisions of V Corps Monday brought further anguish after a night of little rest. They fought back with marvellous spirit when the Germans resumed the attack, but gaps appeared in their hastily manned line and once again they had to drag themselves out of their trenches and run the gauntlet of shrapnel and machine-gun bullet. Thinking them beaten, the Germans came on intrepidly. They were sent flopping by a hail of shells and bullets. Even so, these maddeningly persistent troops of Marwitz's Second Army kept gnawing away at their utterly exhausted enemies and made further gains. Immediately to the north von Below made a massive assault on the jumbled divisions of IV Corps, leading with a blow against the already battered 19th Division delivered by "a battering ram of six divisions". Fearful toll was taken of the German masses assembled with such industry and committed so crudely, but inevitably ground had to be yielded and such was the congestion on the roads behind the British lines that ammunition replenishment drove officers to near frenzy. It was as well that the Royal Flying Corps chose this day for an all-out effort.

With an ugly gap appearing between his V and IV Corps, Byng decided on a further withdrawal, to be carried out that night to the line of the Ancre, running through his old headquarters, Albert. It was achieved with some alarms and at the cost of more agony. The survivors from the furthermost positions—a few hundred Londoners of the 47th, rather more sailors, marines, and North Countrymen of the 63rd and 17th—had withdrawn twenty miles westwards in the course of three days and nights, covering probably twice that distance through the diversions forced on them and fighting all the way, never so hard as during the final stage. Now at last some could sleep lying down, out of reach to the German infantry, and oblivious to the bombs and shells dropped around them. The 12th Division had arrived to take over the Albert sector, and there were new divisions too, the 42nd and 62nd, in position to bring respite to the desperately hard fought men of IV Corps.

On the front of Gough's Fifth Army the trend that had set in on the first day of the battle remained constant: the right wing kept subsiding, pulling the remainder back. The process was in fact speeded by the arrival of the French. They had assumed responsibility for III Corps' sector on the Saturday and during the Sunday their strength rose to six infantry divisions and one of cavalry, providing Humbert with a real Third Army. But the men arrived and went into battle faster than their beloved 75 mm. field guns, and although British artillery was available to support them there were grave problems of communication and from the start they displayed an alarming reluctance to stand and fight. Read, of the Green Howards, describes the cheer that the sight of the French in their sky-blue helmets brought the British, but soon: "I saw the French retiring on the right, about 1,000 yards away. They were not running, but did not seem to be performing any methodical withdrawal." On the plain between the canal and the heights of Antracourt such a scene was watched by many bewildered British officers.

While the troops of III Corps fell back through the French V Corps during the Saturday night, the right wing of Maxse's XVIII Corps became increasingly jangled. Near Cugny the 2nd Royal Irish Rifles and a few Kingsmen were stranded in the open. They had been fighting all night and by 2 p.m. on the Sunday their ammunition was almost spent. 150 were left to meet the last assault. "Many," wrote a survivor, "had only their bayonets left. Rather than wait for the end, they jumped from the entrenchments and met it gallantly. It was an unforgettable sight." Only fifty remained on their feet to be marched off as prisoners when the Germans finally entered the corpse-strewn defences.

Nearby, and only an hour later, cavalry intervened to help and hearten the wilting Ulstermen in their agony of exposure to the pernicious, maiming fire that was ever growing in volume round their right flank, where the French were meant to be. The charge was made with 150 sabres of Major-General A. E. W.

Harman's detachment. Cleverly approaching unseen up a re-entrant, a troop of the 3rd Dragoon Guards drove a party of Germans into a wood and pursued them through it dismounted. One of the 10th Hussars then swept round the wood and swung round to catch a line of infantry in enfilade, slashing and scattering them. A troop of the Royals followed to round up prisoners, returning with ninety-four and a claim that a hundred more were lying dead with sabre gashes. Seventy of the cavalry-men had been sent crashing by machine-gun fire from a flank; some were brought in by Ulstermen who returned cheering to regain lost positions, their aches momentarily forgotten. But the Germans recovered their demeanour and initiative, and soon the 36th were in retreat again. They struggled back that night to take refuge behind the French.

The left wing of Maxse's corps also fell back, but Watts's far-strung men in XIX Corps clung to the line of the Somme Canal all through this Sunday, except on their extreme right, where the rearward movement further right had begun to exert its fatal leverage.

During the night (March 24th–25th) Gough was deprived of three parts of his command. VII Corps, as has been related, was transferred to the Third Army, leaving a portion south of the Somme River to come under Watts. XVIII Corps, like III Corps, was made subordinate to the French Third Army, which had the task of relieving it, and Gough himself, with only XIX Corps under his direct command, was removed from the operational command of Haig to that of General Fayolle, the commander of the G.A.R., or Reserve Army Group. An exasperating day for Gough followed. He received no orders from Fayolle and was not to know (perhaps it was as well) of the order issued by Pétain on the need "before everything to keep the French Armies together as a solid whole." But he could sense its effect acutely enough, which was to tear the Allies apart.

The French V Corps on the right began withdrawing even before the Germans opened their attack on this Monday morn-ing. No serious attempt was made to hold the commanding ridge that stretches north-eastwards from Noyon, and it was left to Brigadier-General L. W. de V. Sadleir-Jackson, a dashing, dressy cavalryman, and some three hundred men—the fighting strength of the 11th Royal Fusiliers and 7th Bedfordshire—of his 54th Brigade (18th Division) to show what could be done, and incidentally to demonstrate that the morale of the defenders was standing the strain better than that of the attackers. The Fusiliers and Bedfords had already had plenty of fighting during the day, for the French still relied on the British to take their share, and after extricating themselves from a situation of great hazard were on their way back to the Oise at about 5 p.m. when there was a clatter of hooves and Sadleir-Jackson galloped up with his brigade major. There were some French guns behind them, with nothing to protect them from the enemy in the village of Baboeuf. The men were turned about and led straight into the attack, forming the equivalent of two large companies. They were sore and exhausted and must have wanted to weep, but the sheer audacity of the venture provided inspiration and they rushed the village with fantastic spirit, catching the Germans off guard. Soon they had rounded up 270 prisoners and plunged their bayonets into many more, with ten machine-guns as spoils, at remarkably small loss to themselves.

These battalions held on to Baboeuf until 2 a.m., when they withdrew southwards across the Oise, where practically the whole of the French V Corps, and Butler's too, had now taken refuge. Gough was annoyed with Butler for allowing his corps to be sucked southwards with the French. There was little chance of their early return to the Fifth Army. The Germans this night entered Noyon, one of Hutier's key objectives and a communication centre of great importance between the British and the French. The French were already overstraining, with their own troop movements, all routes further south.

Maxse, whose XVIII Corps was now the junior partner to Robillot's II Cavalry Corps, resisted the magnet from Paris. The day began with a typical frustration which did nothing to strengthen the partnership. Arrangements had been made for a combined counter-attack by a newly arrived French division and one from XIX Corps on the breach across the Somme Canal at the junction of the two corps. The French did not even assemble for the attack; Germans penetrated the line unopposed because they were thought to be Frenchmen; and the British 24th Division came under heavy enfilade fire from where the French were meant to be in attempting their part of the counter-attack. *"Mais, ce n'était qu'un projet,"* Robillot explained on Maxse's protest, shrugging off the fact that written orders for the attack had been issued. The French division, which had not ventured within a mile of the intended start-line, went backwards instead of forwards. Gaps on the right precipitated a general withdrawal and the route chosen was through Roye, away from XIX Corps.

Maxse's men were bound to comply, suffering further losses in the process, but instead of following the French through Roye and south-westwards, the limping, jumbled remnants of his four divisions were shepherded to the north-west of this link town between Noyon and Amiens, which until that evening had contained Maxse's headquarters. Here, after toiling through a moonlit night, they at least reduced the gap that imperilled XIX Corps, to a matter of some two miles. Meanwhile the French had retained the XVIII Corps artillery. A verbal bombardment, opened by Maxse and supported by Gough, produced its release, but not until next day.

With enemy shells whistling in from over their right shoulders, drawing mistaken complaints against their own gunners, it was impossible for Watts's XIX Corps to hold on to their thin line along the canal, which was already twisted back at its end. None the less they put up a tremendous fight, highlighted by the stand of the 2nd Middlesex (of 8 Division) at Brie, where their motto 'Die Hard' was steadfastly obeyed, and at Eterpigny, where Captain A. M. Toye won the V.C., and of the 1st Sherwood Foresters at St. Christ, from which they withdrew, when ordered that evening, through a village appropriately named Misery, and although the Germans barred their way to it, the Foresters carved themselves a passage, carrying their wounded with them. By dawn next morning the corps were entrenched in what two years back had been the front line of the Germans, five miles west of the Somme Canal. The 24th Division were on the right, and on their right was a void.

The 9th East Surrey held the right of the line. Like other battalions of this division, they had endured the retreat well and were at a strength of some three hundred, despite being heavily engaged the previous evening. The enemy attacked at about 8 a.m. on this Tuesday morning, swarming round the exposed right flank. Orders to withdraw were received, but it was found impossible to carry them out and the acting commanding officer, Major A. C. Clark, decided to fight it out. His men did so as long as their ammunition lasted. Out of the three hundred, only two officers and fifty-five men were in a state to surrender when the Germans rose from among their dead comrades and stormed the last trench.

As the Surreys paid with their lives for the divergence of French from British, the men at the top began to assemble at Doullens. This was not a town of great distinction or beauty, but it was conveniently placed and had a new and imposing town hall, with iron railings around it and an elaborate bell spire on top. Placed within twenty miles of Albert, which the night before had been entered by the Germans, Doullens had taken a sudden, alarming plunge into the war. Major-General Sir John Monash, whose 3rd Australian Division were due to detrain at the town that very day, described his arrival as follows: "I tumbled into a scene of indescribable confusion. The population were preparing to evacuate the town en masse, and an exhausted and hungry soldiery was pouring into the town from the east and south-east, with excited tales that the German cavalry was on their heels." His first trainload of troops to arrive were at once deployed to provide a protective screen round the town.

The British generals came first, to be met by the Mayor and ushered into the smart town hall. Haig had summoned his army commanders, Plumer, Horne and Byng, for a preliminary conference. Ever neglected, Gough had not been invited; he was of course no longer under Haig's command operationally and was denied the opportunity to comment on the eccentricities of the French. Byng was quietly confident, which was as well, since the other two could offer only one more division between them. "Near the Somme," he reported, "the enemy is very tired and there is no real fighting taking place there. Friend and foe are, it seems, dead beat and seem to stagger up against each other."

At about midday the President of France, Raymond Poincaré, arrived with his Prime Minister, Georges Clemenceau, the shaggy, 78-year-old tiger, blunt as a peasant and quivering with belligerence behind his enormous white walrus moustache. Then

79

came the President of the War Board, General Foch, personifying the fighting cock of France, his small, erect, bandy-legged figure aquiver from the tips of his boots to the spikes of his moustache. Then Pétain, melancholy and so drooping with defeatism that not only did Haig write of his "terrible look" but Clemenceau took Poincaré on one side to express his dismay at finding their Commander-in-Chief *"agaçant à force de pessimisme"*. Last to arrive were the representatives of the British Government, Lord Milner, who had come to France a few days earlier at Lloyd George's request, and the C.I.G.S., Wilson, with the usual expression, half whimsical, half cynical, on his face. Rawlinson, who remained at Versailles, was represented by his Chief of Staff, Montgomery; probably Wilson had warned him that it would be tactful to stay away.

It was an affair strictly between French and British; there was no American, no Belgian, no Italian there. But a notable contribution had already been made by Pershing, the American Commander-in-Chief. At 10 p.m. the previous evening he had come to Pétain's headquarters (which were about to be moved nearer Paris) and offered to release his five large divisions, which had been so jealously preserved under American command, for use wherever required as long as the emergency lasted. Pershing, too, was struck by Pétain's "very worried expression", but his offer caused great joy when it reached the ears of Foch and Clemenceau.

Because no one shared Pétain's pessimism, which had brought about the conference, it was easy enough to reach agreement at Doullens. The first step was to dispel the illusion of pessimism conveyed by a recent memorandum from Haig in which he had stressed the importance of "covering the Channel ports". This done, Haig, who not surprisingly is reported to have looked somewhat haggard, gave a calm appraisal of the situation on his front. At mention of the Fifth Army, Pétain interrupted him with, "Alas, it no longer really exists, it is broken," an impression he had no doubt obtained from his own commanders with colourful illustration. Wilson, who abominated Pétain, contradicted him with some heat. None the less Wilson, when the conference ended, would persuade Haig that the commander of the Fifth Army should be replaced.

When it was his turn to speak, Pétain claimed to be doing all he could to defend Amiens and he had, in fact, ordered up more divisions than the eleven he had previously promised Haig. Foch intervened with some fighting talk about not yielding an inch. This gave Haig the chance to say he would be glad to follow any advice Foch might give, and it led eventually to a proposal from Clemenceau that Foch should co-ordinate the operations in front of Amiens. This did not go far enough for Haig, who proposed instead that "Foch should co-ordinate the action of all the allied armies on the Western Front." All readily agreed, and thus the Allies at last had an acting Generalissimo, although he was not as yet designated as such. "Douglas Haig is ten years younger tonight," wrote Wilson that evening. A year ago he had stubbornly resisted subordination to a French general. But circumstances had changed, the most compelling of which was the capsizing of his "special arrangement" with the French Commander-in-Chief, and Foch had more to commend him than Nivelle.

However momentous the occasion, lunch was a thing not to be overlooked, and Haig records that after the conference he "lunched from the lunch box at Doullens." Ignoring rumours of the approach of the enemy, Foch went to the Hôtel des Quatre Fils d'Aymon and it was here that Clemenceau unkindly said to him, "Well, you've got the job you so much wanted." "A fine gift," Foch retorted; "you give me a lost battle and tell me to win it."

Yet little more was needed than an injection of his own restless resolve, which had already made its impact on all who attended the conference. Gough was chosen as its next recipient, but unfortunately the dose was clumsily administered. Foch made his headquarters, which had been moved to Dury, three miles south of Amiens, his first call on leaving Doullens, and presumably accepting Pétain's version of the state of the Fifth Army, sought to remedy the situation by insulting poor Gough. He shrieked rhetorical questions at him—why he did not fight as he had in 1914, why did his men retire, what were his orders to them?—and even chided him for being at his headquarters instead of in the firing line, when in fact he had been told to be there to meet Foch! Gough was stupefied, knowing nothing about the Doullens conference or the slanderous things said about him, and while he was trying to explain the true situation in his best French, the excited little Generalissimo departed, expostulating that there must be no more retreat, not another inch. Gough knew that his troops were putting up a far better fight than the French. "I have never forgotten Foch, nor ever forgiven him," he wrote in old age, for a book published in 1954.

Next to receive a pep talk was the commander of the French First Army, General Debeney, formerly Chief of Staff to Pétain and a true Pétainist at heart, melancholy and very conscious of the need to nurse the morale of his men. His troops were due to come in on the left of Humbert's Third Army and protect Montdidier. Foch told him to bring them into action with all speed and hasten the relief of Maxse's XVIII Corps. Fayolle's Army Group headquarters and even Pétain at G.Q.C. were similarly galvanised, and from the latter orders emanated that evening changing Fayolle's task from mere avoidance of being separated from the rest of the French armies to the protection of Amiens at all costs, with an emphatic ban on further withdrawal. Extra divisions for this purpose were being churned through the groaning transportation machine at the rate of two a day.

On the other side of the Somme the immediate effect of the Doullens conference was to add to the reigning confusion. Despite his confident pronouncement, Byng had overnight issued orders that called for the need to stand firm but none the less envisaged further retirement if "the tactical situation imperatively demands it" and gave one more rearward line to be occupied in that event. It was, of course, as much an invitation as an order, and Congreve, whose VII Corps was slanted forward ahead of the Ancre on the right of the army line, issued orders that seemed to presuppose that the tactical situation would demand further retirement. It duly began, but was cancelled by an instruction emanating from Army headquarters at 3.40 p.m. as a direct result of the Doullens conference : "there must be no withdrawal". Not until 6.30 did it reach the forward battalions and by now most of them were behind the Ancre. There were brave counter-marches, counter counter-orders, exasperation, exhaustion and much riding about by officers, and in the end the corps line formed a spreadeagled V, with its left wing holding the line of the Ancre and its right on a ridge east of the river, resting against the Somme, and with the much worn 9th Division intermixed with the fresher 35th and the 1st Cavalry.

Elsewhere on the Third Army front the Germans were held. Riding out in the morning, staff officers found harrowing gaps in the line, following the withdrawal the previous night. The largest was between V and IV Corps, where the line of the Ancre had been lost and the Germans had entered Hébuterne. But its exits were blocked effectively by troops of the 19th and 51st Divisions, who had done so much to earn respite, while behind them Ford tractors pulled out farm machinery, to be mistaken for German armoured cars and radiate waves of panic which were quick to reach Doullens. That evening the weary defenders saw a wonderful sight. Fresh troops strode in with sprightly gait, the New Zealand Division counter-attacking from the south, the 4th Australian Brigade from the north. Hébuterne was recaptured. Meanwhile Germans trying to debouch from the ruins of Albert on to the high ground beyond ran into the fire of the newly arrived 12th Division and were accorded shattering repulse.

The Third Army was static once more. The instruction issued that day from Doullens was now observed: there was no further withdrawal, none at least of any account. On the right the line was a little further back than the old front line before the Battle of the Somme, when the British held Albert, and having laboured across the devastated zone the Germans had the depressing experience on the 27th of encountering fresh Australian troops—the 3rd and 4th Divisions—in process of relieving Congreve's battered assortments on either side of the Ancre. Monash, commanding the 3rd, had after endless exasperations located Congreve at midnight, having belatedly been placed under his command. He was in a chateau at Montigny, the corridors of which were full of hastily dumped staff baggage. The only light was a candle, by which Congreve calmly and briefly gave his orders. "The enemy is now pushing westwards and if not stopped tomorrow will certainly secure all the heights overlooking Amiens." The Australians were brought from

Doullens in London buses and began the march forward to the relief an hour after dawn. The enemy was stopped.

North of Albert the line zigzagged across spurs that descended from the defensible Artois plateau and were criss-crossed with old trench lines, some of German origin, some of British, and although most of the troops here, such as the 62nd, 42nd, 31st, and Guards Divisions, had been fighting hard for some four days, repeated efforts by the Germans on this Wednesday the 27th could gain only one local success.

On the left the Third Army line still lay along the rolling ups and downs east and south-east of Arras. On the extreme left the 4th Division, standing astride the Scarpe, held the only part of the army line as yet unblemished. The 15th Scottish were on Monchy ridge on their right and had easily withstood such attempts as had been made against their revised line of defences. The 3rd Division, below them on the right, had been harder pressed and were now on the rear of their original battle zone. Alone of the Third Army, these three left-hand divisions had been in the line since the battle started. They had worked like ants on their defences and could see for themselves that their trial was near at hand.

It came on Thursday the 28th. Abandoning his theories about attacking at the weakest point, Ludendorff reverted to the Clausewitz doctrine and ordered the direct attack on Arras, which bore the code name Mars and had originally been intended to hasten, not set in motion, the rolling up of the British line. The sector chosen was one of eight miles wide due east of Arras, bisected by the Scarpe, and it was held by the three divisions just mentioned together with the 56th London Division, of Horne's First Army, on their left. These worthy representatives of the Regular (3rd and 4th), Territorial (56th), and New Army (15th) divisions were attacked by nine fresh divisions, with two more in support, of von Below's somewhat discredited but still (at the top) supremely confident Seventeenth Army.

All the heavy artillery had been assembled and opening at 3 a.m. the crash was as loud as that of the 21st. The British guns were the first target, being treated both to high explosive and mustard gas, and then after an hour's pounding of the forward positions by the guns, a long line of aircraft zoomed in at about 5.15 and machine-gunned the trenches as waves of stormtroopers grappled with the wire and swarmed through the gaps they could cut. They were churned mercilessly by shells, mortar bombs and machine-gun bullets. Fresh attempts were made and some ground gained. The 3rd and 15th fell back on systems they had prepared in rear, and scratch reserves were mustered behind them, as had so often been done a few miles to the south. North of the Scarpe the attackers had greater weight of numbers, and although some suffered awful slaughter from resort to mass tactics, others made penetration up a swampy valley dividing the 4th and 56th Divisions and perilously turned the flanks of their inner brigades. But always, always Germans were falling, brought down by well sited, red hot machine-guns or by field guns tirelessly manned. Around 5 p.m. the attacks petered out and, amazingly, no more came in. The great Mars onslaught had failed totally.

The British had shown what they could do when unhampered by fog, even though most telephone lines had been cut by the bombardment. But they had other advantages, denied specially to Gough's Fifth Army at their initial moment of trial. The front lines was held only by outposts, with the result that few troops were swamped by the initial onrush or left to fight it out unsupported. Thanks to nearly a year's occupation, the defences were extensive, providing ample depth, and the dug-outs were deep, affording good protection. Furthermore, the bombardment was less accurate than the one on the 21st, and being warned of its coming, a number of British batteries moved position during the night. As for the German infantry, they were not in such overwhelming numbers, and although their tactical prowess was impressive in places, it seems unlikely that the ardour shown was quite as high as that displayed by the troops to whom the honour was accorded of opening the offensive. Indeed, despite the miles of ground they had lost, it was the British who were making gains in the matter of confidence.

It was the same along the whole of the Third Army front. All through this day and all along the line the Germans came on, lacking the support of many heavy guns, except at Arras, but attacking hastily improvised defences. Some, attempting mass tactics, were turned into ghastly moaning heaps, others sank sourly to the ground and stayed there, and though twenty divisions were thrown into the battle (not counting the ones in the Mars attack) every attempt was called off during the after-noon, "partly by order of the commanders, partly by the attitude of the troops themselves". (Colonel W. Foerster). It was here, on the desolate slopes of Artois, that Ludendorff's abused project of rolling up the British line begged fulfilment. It had ended in the sort of day that, if experienced by British troops, would have brought their commanders eternal execration.

In the meantime von der Marwitz's Second Army and von Hutier's Eighteenth were bringing their new task alarmingly near fulfilment, the former driving straight at Amiens along the south bank of the Somme River, the latter plunging tirelessly on and throwing into confusion every plan made for the French reinforcements well before they clambered out of their '40 hommes/8 chevaux' trucks at an ever-receding railhead. As has been mentioned, the right flank of Watt's XIX Corps was turned early on the 26th, with the East Surreys trapped, after a night retirement from the Somme Canal. The possibility had been foreseen and Watts had, at 11.30 that night, issued tentative orders for a further retirement, but such were the difficulties of communication that they did not reach brigade commanders until 9 in the morning, and by then the corps line had not only been turned on the right but dangerously pierced near the left. Retirement therefore was turned into a hectic and painful business of extrication, to which congestion and divergence caused by the bends of the Somme added further complication. However, a new line through Rosières, some ten miles west of the Somme Canal and nearly twenty miles east of Amiens, was successfully occupied and the enemy, with little artillery yet in support, were held. Watts now had six divisions, most of whose brigades had been turned into composite battalions. Of these the 16th (transferred from VII Corps because they were south of the Somme) and his original 66th and 24th had come all the way, with one brief respite afforded by the stand on the Somme Canal; the 39th (also from VII Corps) and 50th had joined the battle in the reserve line after long marches forward; and the 8th had joined on the canal.

North of the Somme Congreve's VII Corps had spent most of the 26th retreating, with less cause than Watts's corps, and the latter consequently discovered that his left flank was still exposed next day. But on his right Maxse had made contact after a day of many adventures by his four haggard and meagre divisions, of which those experienced by the 36th Ulster provide a good sample of the retreat. After a fifteen-mile march, carried out in a numb trance without regulation halts because of the near impossibility of getting men on their feet again, the Ulstermen flopped down in the houses of some villages six miles west of Roye around 1 a.m. on the 26th. A number had broken boots and bleeding feet. At 8 a.m. an order arrived for a line to be occupied three miles nearer Roye and the men were bustled out of their billets and led off in their composite groups in the direction they had come from. Now the Germans could be seen in the distance, having brushed past the French rearguards, and as they limped towards them, some men passed a dignified old peasant just starting his morning's raking. An officer told him the Germans were coming. *"Eh bien, monsieur, il faut partir alors"*, he replied with striking dignity and returned homewards to collect his wife and chattels and join the long, sad procession of fugitives.

The Ulstermen took up position, some in old trenches near Andechy, which they reached just ahead of the Germans, others in improvised positions short of their intended ones, and there they remained all day, holding the right of the corps line with flank against the Avre, beyond which French posts were visible, while the other divisions struggled through to link up with XIX Corps on the left. They had no artillery, yet not until after dark were the Germans able to make penetration through the Ulster Division's positions, when they entered the village of Erches after submitting it to heavy bombardment. This was the first breach in an Allied line that for an hour or two had been continuous and stable from the Somme to the Oise. The Germans, sensing they had found the weak link, brought up more men and guns during the night and stormed onwards next morning (the 27th). But their enthusiasm was waning, as is illustrated by the following account of a haphazard counter-attack delivered and described by an officer of the Machine

Gun Corps, Captain Densmore Walker. The Gilmour mentioned was an elderly rifleman transferred to an entrenching battalion, a hero in action, a blot on any barrack square.

"Things were looking as black as conceivable. I suppose it would be about 7.30 a.m. when the attack came. We heard shouting straight behind us and saw about a dozen men a mile away, coming towards us in a line. One waved a white flag and they all shouted. Some said they were English, and we were relieved; some said they looked like French; and I said that any way we would fire on them—which we did. They were perfectly good Huns! They took cover when we opened, and then, when we were really interested in them, the real attack came from Erches. He swarmed on to the road and came down the trench. This looked like the finish of it. There was a general movement backwards, but Evans prevented the machine-gunners from dismounting the one machine-gun with the 107th Brigade, and got it into action on the top of the trench. This changed the aspect of things, as the Huns checked. We all got out of our trench (most people with the idea of clearing over the open, I fancy), and there we stood for quite a while, our people firing towards Erches, and the Huns hesitating. Seeing this latter tendency, Gilmour and I moved slowly towards Erches, trying to urge the troops to attack, but they were too undecided. . . . Then we saw a Hun in the trench just below us. I fired my revolver at him and he ran back. So we chased him. That settled matters! The Huns turned tail and our men followed."

Walker and his hotpotch of tired and hungry men chased these Huns back into Erches and took up position on the village's edge, but they were soon all but surrounded and obliged to fall back towards the north-west. The 36th Division had been cut in two and the Germans streamed through towards Montdidier, which was seven miles to the south-west, and at the same time (around noon) they cut a gap in the French line some seven miles to the south and swept two corps into retreat in divergent directions, Robillot's hingeing on its right to face north instead of east, the newly arrived VI Corps, which had been between Robillot's and Maxse's corps, retreating to the south-west with both flanks exposed, while the remnants of two battalions of the Royal Irish Fusiliers remained behind cut off on the Avre, where they went down fighting. The gate into Montdidier was flung wide open, and the French VI Corps, which was the spearhead of Debeney's First Army, made no attempt to defend it but continued its retreat to the high ground beyond, presumably in order to allow time for fresh troops to come up on either flank. The Germans entered the town at 8.30 p.m. (Wednesday 27th). It was grim news, coming rather more than twenty-four hours after Foch had issued his first order as Generalissimo: no more retreat.

On the Fifth Army front greater heed was paid to this order, but with dire results. Here Watts's XIX Corps held a nine-mile front through Rosières with all six divisions in the line. On their right they were at last in touch with XVIII Corps, who were in the fretful process of being relieved by the French, but their left, resting on the Somme, was six miles ahead of the right of the Third Army on the opposite bank: a not unpredictable consequence of making a river a boundary line. Behind the corps, Carey's Force had since the Tuesday been working on the old Amiens defence line, constructed originally by the French as a longstop line. It formed an arc, eight miles long, fourteen miles in front of Amiens and three of Villers Bretonneux. To improve and man this line Brigadier-General G. G. S. Carey, who had arrived as a divisional commander designate, had 2,900 men under command, of whom the great majority belonged to specialist companies of the Royal Engineers. There were 500 Americans among them, of two railway companies, and there were also some Canadian motorised machine-gunners and, a useful increment, the staff of the Fifth Army Musketry School. It was a larger version of the many scratch bands that had been fighting alongside the front-line infantry since the battle started, and it had the advantage, which none of them enjoyed, of more than a day's freedom from the attentions of the enemy and an opportunity to get organised and entrenched.

The attack on XIX Corps opened all along their line around 7.30 a.m. (Wednesday 27th), that is about fifteen hours after its hectic occupation. It was made by eleven German divisions, of which six were comparatively fresh. Their first success was the capture of Proyart, a village at the head of a valley running from the Somme, held by the left-hand division, the 16th Irish,

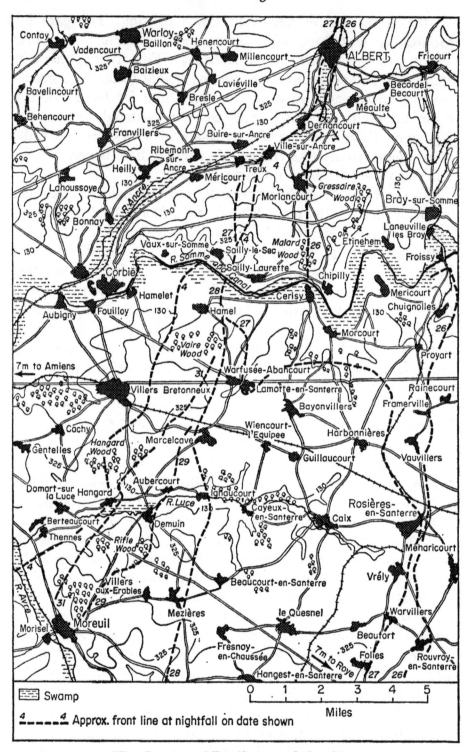

The Battles of Rosières and the Arre

whose positions were deluged by machine-gun and artillery fire from the northern bank of the river. Proyart fell at 10 a.m. and, debouching from it, the Germans inflicted great tribulation on the 16th and 39th Divisions until they were driven back towards the village at 4 p.m., past a blazing sugar factory, by two battalions of the 8th Division—the 2nd Devonshire and 22nd Durham Light Infantry (pioneers)—and a mixed sapper-infantry group of the 50th, all of whom had come five miles in the face of mounting torment by shell and machine-gun bullet. But the enemy still held Proyart and could command the river bank.

Rearward adjustments had to be made to meet this threat, and these in turn caused further unauthorised withdrawals nearer the centre, and indeed one of the problems, after so much retreating, was to impress the change of policy on minds dulled by fatigue. As the war diary of the 50th Division explained: "The troops were dazed . . . There was no sign of panic, and any attempts to withdraw were quite orderly, and the men obeyed willingly when ordered to return to their position, but they appeared to have lost the sense of reasoning and it was difficult to make them understand". None the less, some amazingly spirited counter-attacks were launched. Brigadier-General H. C. Jackson, who had just been placed in command of the 50th Division, led one himself, blowing a hunting horn, and the mere sight of him and his snarling men put the Germans to flight; headquarter men went into the attack alongside their infantry in another staunchly sustained effort by the 8th Division; and a captain of the Manchesters, in the 66th Division, kept twenty men going by singing 'Onward Christian soldiers', and the Germans, to his joy and amazement, threw up their hands in surrender on his approach. In will-power the British were gaining the ascendancy, and although some ground had to be yielded to the debilitating, ever insidious, but no longer so determined pressure by these ubiquitous Germans, the withered battalions and heterogeneous groups of Watts's divisions seemed well able to hold their own against frontal attack.

But on the exposed left flank the situation turned from serious to alarming. Forced into retreat from Proyart, harrowed by shells whistling in among them from over the river, and with three battalions cut off behind them the Irishmen of the 16th met heavy fire ahead as they withdrew down the river bank. The Germans were in possession of Cerisy, a village on the Somme's south bank four miles west of Proyart. They had crossed at about noon, throwing planks over the gaps in a ruined bridge while shells pounded the positions held by some eighty Irish sappers, who had fought stoutly but soon been overwhelmed. This discovery precipitated the retreat from Proyart. After stopping stragglers and collecting less disordered groups of men, a brigade major led a counter-attack. It reached a position from which to stop the Germans advancing out of the village, but soon receded beneath a ferocious weight of machinegun fire. The Germans had fed four battalions over the river and by 7 p.m. they had advanced three miles up a valley and with hardly any fighting entered Lamotte, a village on the corps axis, the main Amiens–St. Quentin road, four miles east of Villers Bretonneux, where Headquarters XIX Corps were, and five miles west of most of their troops. The corps line was twisted into the shape of an S lying on its side.

It was the worst crisis Watts had had to face since the 21st, and, sadly and ironically, it had been caused by the unnecessary withdrawal ordered the previous day by his neighbour Congreve, whose corps had earlier been endangered by the hasty withdrawal made by Watts. Watts's divisions were either too disorganised or too far stretched to organise any counter-attack. Carey's Force were at hand, and indeed they held a village that touched Lamotte on the Amiens side, Warfusée-Abancourt, across the dip of the valley. But a counter-attack at night was regarded as too ambitious a baptism of fire for these specialist sappers. Gough therefore ordered Maxse to send over the 61st Division, who had just been relieved, to come under Watts's command and attack with aid from the 1st Cavalry Division, who had very briskly come trotting across from Congreve's corps when news of the crisis arrived. Lorries were sent to collect the much emaciated 61st, but it soon became apparent that there could be no prospect of their launching the attack before dawn, if not much later.

It was an awful night for Gough. On returning from a visit

to corps and divisional commanders at 5 that afternoon he found Haig's Military Secretary, a Major-General Ruggles-Brise, waiting to see him. "He told me as nicely as he could", Gough relates, "that the Chief thought I must be very tired, so he had decided to put in Rawlinson and his staff of Fourth Army to take command. I was very surprised, and I suppose I was very hurt, but beyond saying 'All right', I only asked when Rawlinson would be coming to take over".

The final problem facing him was whether to defy the orders given him with such bewildering frenzy by the Generalissimo and allow Watts to withdraw his poor divisions (as he wanted to) from the clutch enveloping them or to run the risk of their being trapped and destroyed. At first he said no, they must stand fast, but when a combined plea was received from the commanders of the 8th, 50th, and 66th Divisions, coupled with the news that the Germans had interposed themselves between the headquarters of the 39th Division and its three rump-brigades, he referred the decision to Foch himself. The latter was awoken at 3 a.m.—rudely, Gough must surely have hoped —and consented to a withdrawal. The news reached the divisional commanders at 4 a.m., but their command systems were not fluid enough to get the withdrawal under way before daylight, although they must have decided on their plans.

Meanwhile the three battalions of the Irish Division that had been cut off beyond Proyart were taking their own measures to procure salvation. They belonged to the Royal Dublin Fusiliers, the Royal Munster Fusiliers, and the South Irish Horse, and they averaged two hundred men apiece. After beating back spasmodic attacks they withdrew together at about 8 p.m. They decided that their best chance of escape lay in crossing the river, and having been blocked one way, they crept westwards along the towpath until they came to the Chipilly bridge, across which the Germans had made their penetration to Lamotte. The bridge being guarded, plans were made to rush it. The officer who led answered a challenge with the German password, and as the sentry fired, unfooled, a mass of yelling Irishmen careered over him and down on to the bridge, the girder of which had been snapped at the far end, with the result that there was a sheer ascent up the boulder on to the bank. There was a fevered pile-up at the bottom. "The more that arrived the tighter the crush. Gradually a few men were hoisted up, then more : the enemy was smashed or swept aside, running away screaming from the hideous turmoil." (To quote Colonel H. S. Jarvis in McCance's *History of the Royal Munster Fusiliers*.) The survivors then toiled through a bog, wiped out a German patrol complete and crossed back over the river and canal at the Sailly Laurette lock gate. A mile or so further on they were met by a challenge, and it was marvellous to hear, being made by an Englishman of Carey's Force.

Thursday the 28th, that day of triumphant repulse by the Third Army, was the day of the Fifth Army's greatest agony. At 8.30 a.m. the German guns opened a bombardment all along the line from the Somme to the Avre, complementing that on the Third Army positions as far as Arras. On the XIX Corps front it fell among staff officers urgently explaining plans of withdrawal to battalion commanders—some were wounded and their orders never arrived—and on the XVIII Corps front it struck men of the 20th and 30th Divisions and a remnant of the desperately hard-fought 36th, all of whom had spent the night enduring an exasperation that could be termed a speciality of the region, waiting in vain for relief by the French. The French in fact, of Mesple's Groupement, had taken up position two miles in rear, having decided to regard the British line as an outpost one. This information reached Maxse's men later in the day, coupled with the invitation to withdraw into reserve. It was accepted—and so too was the opportunity to inflict further loss on the shrivelled groups as they hobbled back across the open. Further to the south, however, the inspiration of Foch was at last seen to bear fruit. As the Germans sought to enlarge the bulge they had formed round Montdidier, their left flank came under sudden attack by the men of Humbert's Third Army, and for the first time since the offensive opened they were forced to yield a slither of their gains. It was only a slither, but it poured anxiety into the breast of Ludendorff when so much stood to be gained by daring all.

To revert to Watts's corps, the rich plain of Santerre afforded little cover at this time of year for the withdrawal of the five divisions placed in such peril by the German thrust to Lamotte.

Many sagging men in these divisions, with their set, gaunt faces, their parted lips, and their pink, strained and vacant eyes, had fired a hundred or more rounds from their rifles on most of the last seven days, and when the Germans swarmed forward again that morning they sent them spinning and crumpling as so often before. But once begun, the withdrawal degenerated into a scramble, largely because some were off before others received orders. Units spilled into each other and became mere crowds, the men stumping along with heads bent and rifles slung, intent only on getting away, and all the time machine-guns chattered from gaps on the flanks, found so unerringly by the persistent Hun, black shellbursts carved holes in the throngs, and iron-cross biplanes swooped down almost to ground level, roaring and belching bullets but making more men duck than collapse. Brigadier-generals courageously rode around restoring order and confidence. One was captured while extricating the rear-guard of the 39th Division, and another disturbed the men of an entrenching battalion at their dinner and sent them off on a counter-attack that put to flight some hitherto audacious Germans and released the remains of the 50th Division from the jaws of a trap.

Meanwhile at noon—almost eighteen hours after its occupation—two rump-brigades of the 61st Division began their long-projected attack on Lamotte, with the 1st Cavalry aiding them from the flanks. A long advance across the open had to be made, under cover from thirty-four guns, and not surprisingly the attack ended in agonised failure, 200 yards short of the objective. Soon afterwards Carey's Force won their spurs by repulsing an attack on Hamel, by the banks of the Somme, but on their right flank they crumpled beneath a furious bombardment on Marcel-cave and a serious breach in their line was made. Watts, who had moved his headquarters across the Avre to St. Fuscien, south of Amiens and only two miles east of Army headquarters at Drury, called out his last reserve, his headquarter signal company, all except one operator left on the telephone exchange. They were not needed. The 61st Division—that Territorial mixture of the South-west Midlands and Scotland—manfully disentangled themselves from perilous exposure on the open fields between Marcelcave and Lamotte and helped Carey's men patch up a revised line of defences.

Fortunately for the divisions making the retreat from the Rosières line, the Germans did not pester them unduly once out of sight of the positions they had left, and by a superhuman feat of organisation the throngs were sorted out and formed into a co-ordinated line two to three miles in rear. But Mesple's Frenchmen had also been withdrawing, and once again the right flank of the 24th Division, still on the right of XIX Corps, rested on a void. This division swung back to an old line of trenches, hingeing on the 8th, but it was not enough; their flank was still exposed. A further withdrawal was sanctioned, as the shells began to thicken among the trenches occupied by the 24th and 8th. It began soon after 4.30. Fine, squally rain beat down on the men as they staggered to their feet again and slunk off while the Lewis guns of the rearguards did their erratic best to provide covering fire. The rain may have added to their sense of desolation, if they were not past all feeling, but it helped them get away by blinding the Germans. And now at last respite was not far off. The French had not only relieved XVIII Corps but had extended their line, so that it overlapped that of XIX Corps. Orders reached the 24th, 8th, and 50th Divisions that they were to fall back through the French and go into reserve. They had a five-mile plod across open country, with the shellfire slowly relenting its terrible hold, and then the faces of the poilus, so comforting beneath their comic helmets, were to be seen in the dusk over makeshift defences. But their toil was not over. Positions had first to be occupied, while the rain still poured, in immediate readiness to support the French, but with the arrival of more French troops, the British were moved back across the Avre, where in the early hours of Good Friday, March 29th, they flopped down in the buildings of various villages, no longer liable to receive immediate assault.

The 50th were the last to arrive, having remained until 6 p.m. in position around Caix, one of the villages from which they had set out so boldly a week earlier. The padre of the 4th Northumberland Fusiliers, the Reverend R. W. Callin, who himself had been marching along fast asleep holding on to the mess cart, described the passage of the battalion through Moreuil, which lies on the Avre, thus: "Men dropped asleep on doorsteps for three or four minutes at a time, walked a few yards further, slept on another doorstep, and so on. The writer knows two officers who slept four times in this fashion . . . It was not so much a question of muscles being tired—though they were *very* tired—as of the very bones being sore, and all reserve force being utterly used up".

What was left of the 36th and 30th Divisions had also found refuge in this haven beyond the Avre, but the remains of the 16th, the 61st, and the desperately weak 66th—three of the old originals—held the XIX Corps line, intermixed with Carey's Force. Close behind them were the 39th, who had made a fine counter-attack to extricate the 66th near Caix, and the 20th from the now non-operative XVIII Corps. Such was the army that Gough passed on to Rawlinson. In the course of eight days it had been reduced from fourteen strong and confident divisions to a jumble of intermixed units, most of whose men were even past feeling sorry for themselves. But its frontage had been reduced from forty-two miles to barely six—a fair equivalent to its reduction in fighting strength—and with its right resting on the little river Luce in alignment with the French and its left on the Somme now in line with Byng's Third Army, its flanks theoretically were at last secure. It is ironic that Gough had to go just as he had achieved real prospect of stability.

6

UNDER NEW COMMAND

(March 28–April 5)

Rawlinson formally assumed command at 4.30 on this Thursday afternoon, March 28th. There is no record of the take-over except for four foolscap sheets on which Gough described his fighting state in pencil. They make poignant reading. The word "perhaps" appears against the strength of each division and there are a number of alterations. The 8th, 50th and 30th were the strongest with "perhaps 2,000", the 66th weakest with 500. Maxse's divisions were graded "quite unreliable", "unreliable", or "rather unreliable", except for the 61st which received "all but tired out, perhaps 1,500" and there is a note about this division, "Men are very tired—General says are unfit to counter-attack (have been ordered to do so—all the same—9 a.m.)". This, of course, was the abortive attack on Lamotte made at midday. Gough's assessment of his total infantry strength was 21,650, of whom 8,000 were with the absent III Corps, and it was made before the costly fighting on the 28th.

In artillery the position was brighter. About half the 500 guns lost had been replaced and Gough handed over 783, of which 225 were medium or heavy. They could provide a much greater density of fire on the reduced frontage than was available on March 21st. Of tanks there is no word. Poor use was made of the three battalions in support and they seem to have disintegrated north of the Somme Canal.

On a covering sheet of foolscap Rawlinson wrote his comments, also in pencil: "The units were in a state of lamentable confusion and demoralisation and in full retreat before the advancing German Army. It was a difficult task to stay the

98

hostile advance and save Amiens, but by superhuman efforts we managed to do it".

This was obviously written later, although dated the 28th, and one can only hope that Rawlinson was in humbler mood when he arrived to take over command, accompanied by Archibald Montgomery. It seems certain that he was, for he was sympathetic by nature and had for long been a champion of scapegoats. Yet no doubt he appeared abominably spruce having stepped straight from the elegance of Versailles. Gough had served as instructor at the Staff College when Rawlinson was commandant, and at least he was handing over to a man he greatly respected. Rawlinson suggested that he should stay the night, but Gough had un understandable urge to leave with all speed and, having pledged his staff to the allegiance of the interloper, he departed "not at all sure where I was going to get a bed or dinner that night".

Wherever he obtained these essentials, he dined next night with Haig (who had earlier received the King) and learned that he and his staff of the Fifth Army were to prepare a defence system between Amiens and the sea: a wise enough task, as Gough could appreciate, but scarcely one for a full general. The idea was to preserve the Fifth as a reserve army, as which it had originally been formed.

There is some confusion as to the circumstances leading to Gough's relegation to this rôle. Wilson's diary entry for March 26th runs from the signing of the agreement at Doullens to, "Then I discussed removal of Gough, and told Haig he could have Rawly, and Rawly's old Fourth Army staff from Versailles, to replace Gough. Haig agreed to this". Haig in his diary refers to a conversation with Milner and Wilson at 5 p.m. that day, as he was going out riding after his return from Doullens. "I said that whatever the opinion at home might be, and no matter what Foch might have said, I considered that he [Gough] had dealt with a most difficult situation very well. He had never lost his head, was always cheery and fought hard". Yet Rawlinson, according to his journal, received a telephone call from Wilson that evening and was told "that Gough is to be sent home, and I am to reconstruct the remnants of the Fifth Army as the Fourth Army".

The conclusion must be that Haig agreed at Doullens that Rawlinson should relieve Gough, and indeed he must have been glad to have him back, re-invigorated by a comfortable break. Wilson, according to the Official History, was just as keen to remove him from Versailles because he did not want a strong man there. Presumably the conversation at 5 p.m., as Haig set out for his ride, referred to the dismissal, as opposed merely to the relief, of Gough. Haig had resisted this before, when the case against Gough was stronger, and he was obviously keen that posterity should know, through his diary, that he had not lost faith in the man whom he himself had rocketed to high command. None the less it was naive of him to suppose that he could remove a man from command at a moment of crisis without imputation of blame or that with the wolves howling for a scapegoat Gough would be allowed to remain nominally in command of an army.

Realisation came when Lloyd George attended a conference at Beauvais on April 3rd, at which the powers of Foch were further defined and widened and he was formally appointed Allied Commander-in-Chief. (He had an admirer in Lloyd George, who was much irritated by Haig, and conversely Haig had an admirer in Clemenceau, who was much irritated by Foch). After the conference Lloyd George, in private, launched an attack on poor Gough, wildly blaming him in particular for his failure to hold the Somme Canal and destroy all the bridges. Haig stood up for him, but Lloyd George said he must go, to which Haig retorted (according to his diary) that he "could not condemn an officer unheard, and that if L.G. wishes him suspended he must send me an order to that effect". The order came, accompanied by a letter from Lord Derby claiming that there was intense feeling in England against Gough and that the great concensus of opinion among the wounded in hospital was that he was unfitted to command. Gough was removed, and Haig, not for the first time, offered his resignation. It was refused.

Meanwhile Rawlinson had gathered his old faithfuls about him. Unlike Gough's, his had always been a happy headquarters, and there was the feeling of an old boys' reunion as its members reassembled to renew long associations with their chief; some, including Montgomery, had been with him at Versailles, others not. It was matched by a certain grizzled nonchalance displayed by the comrades in crisis at Watts's headquarters up the road. "They may well get us by lunch time and you by tea time," Watts had cheerily replied when Rawlinson first rang up to hear how things were going.

The first thing Rawlinson did on taking over was to write direct to Foch, pointing out that the situation was serious and that unless fresh troops were sent within the next two days he doubted whether he could hold his positions. He also sent a staff officer to Fayolle, whom he knew well, asking for the return of Butler's III Corps and the cavalry with them, a request made often enough by Gough but to no avail. It was different now. The 2nd and 3rd Cavalry Divisions, who had done much good work in a mounted infantry rôle, were directed back at once, and French buses, with rounded chicken-coop roofs, were marshalled for the collection of the infantry. The 9th Australian Brigade, four battalions strong, were meanwhile despatched to Rawlinson by Byng, and more French divisions were directed to join Debeney's First Army on his right.

Good Friday, the 29th, was the quietest day enjoyed by the Fifth Army (as it continued to be called until April 2nd) since the 21st, as also by the Third; neither von der Marwitz nor von Below could mount an attack. However, an old source of trouble persisted, for von Hutier had not paused. The French under Mesple, who had much enraged Gough with his indecision, gave way under attack, and the British 20th Light Division were brought back into the battle to make a brave counter-attack beyond the Luce and extend the XIX Corps boundary by almost three miles, while the worn-out divisions beyond the Avre were yanked out of their billets to occupy stop positions in rear.

Next day the attack was resumed in earnest, Hutier and Marwitz combining in a drive against Amiens from south-east and east. The first crisis for the British came as dawn was breaking with the depressing but so predictable news from the 20th Division that the French were gone from the high ground beside them, above Moreuil. Watts called out the newly arrived Canadian Cavalry Brigade, who were commanded by a former British War Minister, toppled by the Irish dispute, the

Rt. Hon. Jack Seeley. The Germans were in a large wood, known as Moreuil Wood. The Royal Canadian Dragoons charged the nearest corners mounted, while Lord Strathcona's Horse plunged dismounted into the interior of thick saplings, with one squadron also making a mounted charge and capturing some guns at heavy loss to themselves. There was prolonged and gruesome grappling with sabres and rifles. The 3rd Cavalry Brigade entered the battle in the afternoon, with the 4th Hussars and 16th Lancers dismounted, and after driving the enemy from the wood they were in turn driven back to a line midway through it. The 8th Division took over from them in the evening and extended the line as far as the outskirts of Moreuil, from which the French had by now been driven back across the Avre. The 50th were also brought toiling back into the battle, and in a long ding-dong fight they helped the 20th to retain a clutch on that very important high ground between Moreuil Wood and the Luce.

On the other side of the Luce breaking-point was almost reached. The left still held firm, with the American sappers of Carey's Force making a brave defence of Hamel in conjunction with the 1st Cavalry Division. But south of the main road the line became very wobbly, specially where the Germans had made their breach through Marcelcave. The 39th made some brave attempts at counter-attack but with little avail : the men had borne too much. The Australians were summoned, and ahead of them rode the 12th Lancers. They galloped forward by squadrons, each in line, nimbly dismounted and dashed into a wood to take possession just as its garrison were moving wearily out and the Germans almost as wearily moving in. Men who had been shuffling back cheered and turned round to fight again. Two battalions of Australians arrived and lengthened the barrier formed by the Lancers. Sudden realisation came to the despairing men of the Fifth Army that they were not forgotten after all.

The men of III Corps had now begun to arrive after a journey in their French buses made hazardous by the utter exhaustion of the drivers. The 18th Division came first. They had had four days out of the line and, although played out by normal standards, were fresh compared with the men to be relieved; with the aid of leave details and ex-battle surpluses battalions had been raised to an average strength of around three hundred. They came in on the right of the Australians during this Saturday night, bringing an end to the agony of elements of four divisions—the 66th, 61st, 39th and 50th—and for some of Carey's Force too. The situation none the less remained one of extreme fragility.

Only Hutier could inspire his men to earnest effort next day, Easter Sunday, March 31st. He pushed the anguished 8th and 20th Divisions further down the slopes between the Luce and Avre, the latter being forced back from a little wood named Rifle Wood in their memory. Here, with vantage point from which to view the grime rising from Amiens eleven miles away and to enfilade the British line beyond the Luce, even Hutier was forced to pause. The long advance had posed tormenting problems of reinforcement and supply, and the Royal Flying Corps had been greatly aggravating the torment—making their final effort as such, for on April 1st they became the Royal Air Force. Furthermore the German soldiers, wearying of the search for the green uplands beyond, were turning sour. The British did the attacking on April 1st. The 2nd Cavalry Division made an infantry assault under heavy bombardment and regained some of the ground lost south of the Luce. But the cost was heavy. Dead cavalrymen, riflemen and infantrymen of many regiments lay thick on these hills of such importance to the British, and most now were inside the German lines.

Rawlinson had received a visit from the Tiger, Clemenceau, as battle raged on the 30th, and had complained to him that the French were not taking their share of the fighting. Foch arrived next day, and by April 3rd Debeney's troops had taken over the line as far as the Luce again, including the village of Hangard, on its northern banks. It was very kind of the Boche, Rawlinson remarked, not to interfere. Yet there were signs that they were about to make another big attack and to meet it he had to rely on the hard-worn 18th and 14th Divisions, who held the line on right and left, with one Australian battalion between them. There were ample guns and ample reserves of a sort, but nothing fit for counter-attack except the remainder of

the 9th Australian Brigade. The drooping yet dauntless Watts
was still the operational corps commander in charge.

It rained all night on the 3rd/4th and after briefly giving way
to morning mist the rain continued all through the day. The
shells began to fall, hideously and lavishly but somewhat haphazardly, at 5.15 a.m., and at 6.30 the storm groups came in
with dense supporting waves awaiting their chance behind
them. Seventeen German divisions were committed, five from
Marwitz's Second Army against the British XIX Corps, twelve
from Hutier's Eighteenth against the French.

The first break occurred on Watts's left wing. Hardest hammered of all divisions on March 21st, the 14th could not withstand another pounding not far removed in ferocity from the
one that day. They fell back out of Hamel and across its
surrounding open slopes in such confusion that one brigade
commander stayed at his headquarters as a despairing example
and was swiftly captured, dying soon afterwards from a stray
bullet through the head. But shells fell on the Germans almost
as fast as the rain, at one point from guns of the 16th Irish
brought forward to fire over open sights and also, with great
effect, from guns of the 3rd Australian Division on the high
ground north of the Somme. The 6th Cavalry Brigade came
forward and took up position dismounted, leaving one trooper
out of four behind as horseholders. The Germans were stopped
—there were many regulars among these cavalrymen, thanks
to their higher survival rate, and they were expert with their
rifles and Hotchkiss machine-guns. More Australians arrived to
support their one battalion in the line, who being outflanked on
the left fell back to within a mile due east of Villers Bretonneux.

This town stands on the rim of the plateau, controlling
observation of Amiens, and had to be held. It had many strong
buildings, including a chateau and a small factory, and normally
contained a population that had sunk in number since the
Franco-Prussian War to 4,600. On this day it was turned, in
the words of F. M. Cutlack, a hardened Australian war
correspondent, to "a most horrible ruin, a revolting sight of
torn and gutted houses and littered streets, littered too with
dead here and there among the splintered glass, smouldering
beams, and heaps of brick". It became a matter of honour for

the Australians that the enemy should never have the chance to gloat over these charred, awful, very moving remains.

The 18th Division on the right were so thinly spread that one battalion—the 11th Royal Fusiliers—had been called from billets in reserve during the night to make a hazardous compass march, checked by torchlight on soaking maps, across clinging plough and occupy a gap that had been discovered just to the south of Villers Bretonneux. The division repelled their attackers in the morning. Their trial came in the afternoon, when they came under furious bombardment, followed by mass attack. There was great misery in the mud and rain, with many a rifle bolt jamming and the production of fire from a Lewis gun turned to a high art—although one private of the 7th Buffs fired 2,000 rounds from his. Some cohesion was retained on the left and a controlled withdrawal made, but on the right, where the ground sloped in folds gently down to the Luce, there was desperation, if not despair. The Germans came squelching through Hangard Wood and up the slopes on towards Gentelles. Then the 8th Royal Berkshire leapt up from their reserve position and after firing a withering volley, as in some old style battle, drove the Germans back; their commanding officer, Lieutenant-Colonel R. E. Dewing, one of the heroes of March 21st, was mortally wounded at the moment of triumph, and by the end of the day the Berkshires were down to a strength of fifty-eight. The line rallied, and soon another counter-attack came in, launched from Villers Bretonneux by parts of two Australian battalions and the 7th Queen's. It gained quick initial success. The Germans fell back wearily, across ground strewn with their dead, and concentrated on holding what was left of their gains.

The French meanwhile had been forced back from the remaining foothold on the cherished high ground above Moreuil and driven back over the Avre after some hard fighting. On their extreme left they fought defiantly for Hangard village. They lost it in the late afternoon, but at dusk regained most of the village in conjunction with a counter-attack by the 6th Northamptonshire, which regained part of Hangard Wood. There were to be further shocks for the Germans. Twice during the night Australians came dashing at them through the mud and forced them further back from the approaches to Villers Bretonneux. Not since the offensive opened had a day's attacking ended like this.

North of the Somme the 4th Australian Division emerged triumphant from a hectic day's fighting near Albert. Next day, April 5th, more widespread attacks were made on the Third Army, combined with desultory efforts south of the Somme, and all were repulsed. Rawlinson learned this day that the whole of Birdwood's Australian Corps were to be transferred to his command, with a frontage up to Albert. "Hurrah!" he wrote in his journal. There was further reason to shout hurrah if he but knew it. As more worn and weary troops of the Fourth Army (as they had now become) relieved gasping defenders and patched up the line, Ludendorff decided that his great Michael offensive had reached its end.

7

REFLECTIONS AND RECRIMINATIONS

(April 6–9)

Although he had made enormous territorial gains, the prizes Ludendorff had aimed to gather from his Michael offensive remained tantalisingly out of reach. The flank of the British had not been turned, far less rolled up; their bastion of Arras had scarcely been dented; Amiens was within range only of his heaviest guns; and so far from diverging, the French now stood firmer at the side of their allies than ever before. He had merely worn down his opponents, just as they had worn down his resources on the Somme and at Ypres, and it now remained to be seen whether they had been sufficiently weakened to succumb to the subsequent assaults that Ludendorff planned more as despairing afterthoughts than as components of a master plan. The British Official History concludes, after careful investigation, that the German and Allied losses were about the same, around 250,000 each. The British contribution (from March 21st to April 5th) was 177,739, with the heaviest sufferers the 36th, 16th and 66th Divisions (in that order), each with over 7,000, whereas only one other division, the 59th, exceeded 6,000. Half the British casualties came under the heading 'missing', which normally meant captured, but it transpired that ten per cent of them were stragglers who rejoined their units. But the Germans had lost fewer men for good, with a much smaller prisoner rate, and their transient preponderance in manpower had been slightly increased. Mathematically they still had a chance.

Morale, of course, mattered more than numbers, and in this less determinable sphere the British had defied the rules and stolen the lead. The Germans started with all the advantages. They had gained victory in Russia, which many of the assault divisions had experienced; they were rested, excellently trained, and fired with enthusiasm for a new offensive technique well suited to the wave of optimism on which they rode; the fog gave them the break they needed and soon they were waging glorious open warfare, finding it so easy to turn the flanks of a foe who had every reason to be on the verge of despair under the unrelenting momentum of the assault. Yet the despair never revealed itself in the mass surrenders to be expected, and instead of softening the resistance became stiffer, the going harder. Maddeningly perverse as ever, the British seemed to be gaining in confidence the further they retreated. It was on the German side that signs of despair appeared. Hands were apt to go up under no great constraint, the arrogance was gone, and prisoners told their captors tales of self-pity, of how they had been driven onwards day after day without even knowing the objective, of lack of food and rest, and of the loss of so many dear comrades.

Much has been made of the effect on the German troops of finding the English back areas "a land flowing with milk and honey" when they had themselves been told that the U-boat campaign had brought Britain to starvation. The biblical phrase appears in the diary of the poet and novelist, Rudolf Binding, who was on a divisional headquarter staff in von der Marwitz's army. He used it on March 27th to describe the glee with which his soldiers had equipped themselves with English jerkins, water-proofs, boots, "or some other beautiful things". On March 28th he recorded that "the advance of our infantry suddenly stopped near Albert. Nobody could understand why". He was sent into Albert to find out and discovered "strange figures, which looked very little like soldiers", engaged on the collection of all manner of loot, from cows to writing paper, or staggering around with bottles of wine in hand and under arm. "The advance was held up, and there was no way of getting it going again for hours."

Binding notes that his division was fresh and "our way seemed entirely clear". This shows that he was under a false impression, and one should therefore be wary of his interpretation of the situation. The advance had stopped on the morning of the 26th, hard upon the German's entry into Albert, and it had been stopped by something more potent than the intoxicant of loot and wine: the weapons of the newly-arrived 12th Division. Probably knowledge of the damage wrought by these weapons gave the cows and the wine their enticement. The alternative was not a clear road ahead but one of daunting peril.

It is a recurring theme of the retreat that while newly committed British divisions, such as the 8th, the 35th and the 12th, gave great boost to the defence, fresh German ones were of little avail in reviving the momentum of the offensive, as in the example quoted by Binding. An endemic flaw in the German system may account for this. Their divisions were graded and there was further selection within them, the best forming the stormtroopers, and the best divisions, specially selected and specially equipped, opened the assault, led by the best men. Their cult was initiative. This gave the offensive tremendous impetus at the start, but as the best men fell and the best divisions became worn out the impetus subsided and initiative was apt to be diverted to other directions than the defeat of the enemy. In face of the disillusion and gnawing awareness of want caused by the revelation of the enemy's plenty, and in the grim, eerie, desperately depressing wastes, back to which their endeavours had brought them, morale could be maintained only by confidence in final victory or by the rigid enforcement of discipline. Their own inability to go on was emaciating the one and the cult of initiative was an impediment to the other.

The fortitude shown by the British, specially by those men of the Fifth Army who had to hold on for eight, nine, or ten days without proper rest, seems all the more amazing now that passions have subsided and examination can be less partisan. Obviously there were blemishes. Some battalions allowed themselves to be very speedily gobbled up when the great blow fell, and once the retreat began the mere sight of some men falling back could be sufficient to set off others. Yet there were many acts of collective heroism, of which a few have already been described and many others are on record in seldom opened pages of regimental histories, those conscientiously compiled works that do not have to disclose every fact but seldom make vain or boastful claim. To take two random examples from books by professional historians, C. T. Atkinson describes the spirit of the 8th Royal West Kent (24th Division) as "really extraordinary", tells how "badly wounded men insisted on keeping with their companies" and quotes an officer as saying, "Every man was putting out the greatest he had in him". Similarly, Everard Wyrall quotes the commanding officer of the 2nd Middlesex (8th Division): "The fighting spirit was as high on the tenth day as on the first. The pride of all ranks in the Regiment grew from day to day".

Herbert Read's essay previously quoted—he of the Green Howards—gives more of the reality of the retreat than is to be found in any regimental history, and it is interesting to note from this how morale declined once battalions became inter-mixed and split into heterogeneous groups. Arbitrary groupings of men, whether organised under an officer or mere stragglers, were often made by unknown staff officers who imperiously waylaid them as they stumped along a road and sent some off to hold one feature, some another. Read was separated from his friends and divorced from his brigade in this manner, and when the shells began to fall among his half-dug trenches he did not wait for orders from he knew not whom before con-tinuing the withdrawal. Yet demoralised though they became, his men were willing enough to run fearful risks to avoid capture, just as they had been when flung from their redoubt at Roupy. A young North Country subaltern, whom Read encountered as fellow flotsam of the retreat, had a similar story to tell. His men were hopelessly trapped in a sunken road, swept at either end by German machine-guns. He put it to the vote whether they should surrender or run for it. They unanimously opted for the run, and it cost half of them their lives.

If such spirit could be shown in despair and isolation, it becomes easier to understand what could be achieved by those battalions that were able to maintain unity and cohesion and remain under commanders and staff they knew. As the battle progressed sense of achievement strengthened the bond of fellowship, with some aid from the peculiar conditions prevailing, most notably a growing reduction in the weight of artillery fire the Germans could bring down. And sometimes there were odd moments of uplift, such as never entered the set battles of the preceding years. The sight of the people, some so old, some so young, trailing away from their homes roused the compassion even of the most weary soldier and turned his mind from pity of himself—but not from enjoyment of the eggs, chicken and coffee left behind in their houses, which formed a marvellous variant to the demoralising and debilitating monotony of cold bully beef. There were other diversions of a less material kind. Sheltering in a church at Vrely, for instance, before the Battle of Rosières, men of the 3rd Rifle Brigade were refreshed by an organ recital played by their orderly-room sergeant.

Perhaps the factor that sustained the British most strongly—in contrast with both the Germans and French—was their bland conviction, amounting almost to assumption, that they would win in the end, and once the initial shock of the opening onslaught had subsided this conviction grew stronger day by day. There was touching faith in the high command, whatever may have been said in hospital beds; indeed, according to Captain G. H. F. Nichols (Quex), the historian of the 18th Division, the belief was prevalent that the retreat had the definite aim of making the enemy vulnerable to a great counter-stroke that Haig was planning further north. (He did, in fact, have such a scheme in mind but lacked the resources for it.) Optimism, of course, was part of the British heritage—the country had always won before and it just did not occur to the soldiers, the majority of whom were there by their own choosing, that the habit might be broken—and whereas it might be inarticulate among the lower reaches, it stemmed in higher places from the far seeing conclusion of the G.H.Q. Intelligence Branch : "If Germany attacks and fails she will be ruined". Thus we find Congreve, commander of VII Corps, writing to his mother on March 27th, when fortunes might have appeared at their nadir, to say, "I don't feel a bit depressed by this blow of the Boche, and no one hereabouts seems to be". And on the same day Malcolm, Gough's former C.G.S. removed to the command of the ill-fated 66th Division, when asked the situation by a liaison officer at crisis point of the Battle of Rosières, quietly replied : "It is quite good : we have won the war". A very different view was being taken in London.

The generals may not always have anticipated events with the clarity that is so easily acquired in retrospect, and there were times when extrication crises could have been avoided by more imaginative staff planning. But their steadfast determination never sagged, in the face of nightmarish difficulties of communication, and without it there would have been no determination at battalion level. That the men were not without appreciation of their higher commanders is touchingly illustrated by the action of four volunteers who for four miles carried the body of their dead brigadier—R. Barnett Barker of 99 Brigade—rather than that it should rot in the keeping of the enemy, during the most gruelling day of the retreat from the Flesquières salient.

As for Gough, no more is known of the complaints made by men in hospital than Lord Derby's assertion. Derby, of course, was pursuing a long hunted hare, and with the wily Wilson on his side, eager for the removal of Rawlinson from Versailles, it would have been easy enough to obtain the answers required to some tilted questions, nor would any hospital ward ever lack its critics of the high command. It is a mark of the distortions in circulation that Lloyd George should have condemned Gough for failing to blow up the Somme bridges : he was in fact blaming him for the limitations of dynamite, for apart from those entrusted to the French railway authorities all bridges were destroyed but could still be crossed on foot. It seems certain enough that Gough's corps commanders, who alone were fully qualified to comment on his fitness for command, would have refuted with disgust the charges whining round London.

Technically, Gough might be criticised for his dispositions to meet the initial onslaught. Thirty-six battalions were spread along his forward zone and they were devoured almost complete. Some inflicted great destruction, which would have been all the greater if they had not been blinded by fog, but they were doomed from the start, because they were too far apart to support each other and their orders did not envisage a retirement. Also 381 guns were lost on this opening day, the majority because they were placed far forward to give moral support to the infantry. Battalions, guns, machine-guns—so much might have been preserved if plans had been more elastic.

Yet Gough was carrying out his orders. G.H.Q. had expressly changed the term "outpost zone" to "forward zone" and ordered that the troops holding it "do all in their power to maintain their ground against every attack". The generals could not be blamed for interpreting this order literally, and it consequently made nonsense of the specific order to Gough to "protect at all costs the important centre of Peronne". Haig unintentionally acknowledged this when he said, "You can't fight without men, Hubert". They had been expended holding ground of no vital importance, and there were insufficient behind them to perform more than temporary patch-work. Peronne might have been saved if the 35th Division had arrived earlier, but it was in Belgium when orders for its despatch were issued at 11.15 p.m. on the 21st, which was eighteen hours after the attack started, and its infantry were not out of their trucks, twenty miles behind the front line, until 6.30 p.m. on the 23rd, that is one hour after Peronne had fallen. This was the cost, as Lloyd George shrieks from his War Memoirs, of Haig's absorption with the Ypres sector and of his disdain for the project of the Allied central reserve. It also points to the one palpable cause of failure attributable to Gough, lack of influence.

Gough had three handicaps—the harm done to his reputation during the Ypres offensive, his comparative youth, and his lack of inches—and there is endless scope for speculation on the effect they had on the course of the battle and on the degree to which his successor owed the results he achieved to the influence that flowed with such ease and confidence from a reputation firmly established and made the more imposing by maturity, charm of manner, and physical stature to match. By his own testimony, which there is no reason to doubt, Gough was treated like a child by Haig's Chief of Staff, Lawrence, who was ten years his senior but his junior in military rank. He was reproved for wanting to move his reserves forward before battle and patronisingly soothed, with implied reproach for being an alarmist, when he reported the effect of the onslaught. Haig had no time to listen to him at any length when he paid him his one visit, and it is perhaps not so surprising that when he was put under the French he should be ignored by his immediate superior, Fayolle, slandered by Pétain, and accorded a delinquent's treatment by Foch. In proportion to the slights cast on its brave and indomitable commander, so was the Fifth Army neglected.

With Rawlinson's arrival the change was immediate. He

wrote at once to Foch. Back came the divisions of III Corps, for which Gough had been vainly agitating, and Byng was obliged to hand over an Australian infantry brigade. Even Clemenceau, whom a fortnight earlier Rawlinson had accompanied to London for a particularly fruitless meeting of the Supreme War Council, came to pay his respects, and Rawlinson was able to make amends for Gough's humiliation by expressing his dissatisfaction with the French.

It was Gough's misfortune that his removal happened to suit the ambition of a man of influence whom he heartily despised, his fellow Irishman, Henry Wilson. Being himself a man of no influence, he had no option but to go. Yet if fate was cruel to him, it was kind to his country. For whereas Rawlinson could have done no more than Gough to halt the German advance— at any rate once it had begun—there can be no doubt that he was much better equipped, with both temperament and ability, to conduct the ensuing battles through which the army in front of Amiens would retain its crucial rôle. Rawlinson's arrival was to prove quite as significant as a better publicised arrival in more recent years, that of Lieutenant-General B. L. Montgomery to take command of the Eighth Army in August 1942. Both were occasioned by disastrous events outside the control of the men they replaced. Both were in due course to be followed by shattering defeat for the Germans.

And while military developments bustled along towards their next stage of revelation, Lloyd George was busy manning his defences in Parliament. He had made a great personal effort, as soon as the weight of the German offensive became known, to procure and despatch reinforcements to France. Galvanising the War Office and the Shipping Controller, he managed to get some 150,000 across the Channel by April 7th, at more than double the normal capacity rate for transit. Some of these had been on leave, some employed in industry or agriculture, and about 50,000 were six or less months short of their nineteenth birthdays, the age limit having been reduced by order of the War Cabinet. The rate somewhat slowed down subsequently, and it took four months for the reinforcement figure to pass the 449,000 that had allegedly been available for drafting in January, before the lowering of the age limit under nineteen.

Above, gun teams move forward against a background of burning stores and wire at Homiecourt, Third Army sector north-west of Bapaume, on March 24th; *below*, men of the 17th Northern Division in reserve on March 26th after the five-day retreat from the Flesquières salient

Above, an isolated section of 5th Gordon Highlanders of the 61st Division on the Plain of Santerre, near Nesle, shortly before the town was taken; *below*, German prisoners near Albert on March 31st

Above, British and French troops round up abandoned cattle behind the line near Boves; *below*, a scene in Amiens on April 3rd, when the city was still in peril of capture

Above, a German view of Villers Bretonneux, from the south-east; *below*, Australian officers and men just relieved from positions defending the town

Above, left, General Sir Hubert Gough, Commander of the Fifth
Army; right, General Sir Henry Wilson, C.I.G.S.; *below*, General
Sir Henry Rawlinson at Fourth Army Headquarters

Lieut.-General Sir John Monash, Commander of the Australian Corps; *below*, Commander of the Canadian Corps, Lieut.-General Sir Arthur Currie, right, with his predecessor, General the Hon. Sir Julian Byng, promoted to the command of the Third Army in June 1917

Above, Canadian infantry, guns and cavalry en route to the front in the early morning of August 8th. Passing them are German prisoners under escort from Hangard; *below*, Headquarters 3rd Canadian Division as the attack was resumed on August 9th

Above, a combined infantry and tank attack near the railway line during the Australians' advance on Lihons on August 9th; *below*, a diminished Australian platoon being briefed for an attack

Royal visit to France in August. *Above*, General Rawlinson and Field-Marshal Haig with King George V; *below*, at Flixécourt, Fourth Army Headquarters. Front row, left to right, General Rawlinson; General Debeney; Marshal Foch; H.M. King George V; Field-Marshal Haig; General Pétain; General Fayolle. Second row, left to right, General Weygand (C.G.S. to Foch); Lieut.-Gen. Lawrence (C.G.S. to Haig); Maj.-Gen. Holman (D.A. and Q.M.G. Fourth Army); Maj.-Gen. Buckland (C.E. Fourth Army); Sir Derek Keppel (Equerry). Hatless on steps, Maj.-General Budworth (C.R.A. Fourth Army) and Maj.-Gen. Montgomery (C.G.S. Fourth Army)

Above, two men of the 5th Australian Division who did not get through the wire round Anvil Wood, a strong point adjacent to Mont St. Quentin, reduced on September 1st; *below*, members of the 12th Division in a newly-won position at Epéhy on September 18th

Above, men of the Australian 5th Division, moving forward on September 29th, find the Americans held up around Bellicourt, above the St. Quentin Canal tunnel. The tanks in the background, except for the longer Mark V Star, are equipped with 'cribs' for crossing ditches; *below*, the Band of the Staffordshire Brigade playing amid the ruins of Bellenglise

Men of the Staffordshire Brigade at the St. Quentin Canal, scene of
their triumph on September 29th. They are returning from an address
by their Brigadier three days later

Orders were also issued for the despatch of a second division back from Italy, the first having returned just before the offensive began, and two from Palestine.

The energy of Lloyd George was a great asset at a time of crisis, but he was not going to extend aid to praise when he was himself held responsible for the crisis by many, because he had starved the B.E.F. of men. In the debate introducing the Man-power Bill on April 9th his criticism of Haig was cryptic but scathing. He implied that he had been forced into retreat by a weaker army and even claimed that "the Army in France was considerably stronger on January 1st 1918, than on January 1st, 1917". There were gasps of disbelief, of bewilderment, dismay. The statement was dishonest : in infantry the B.E.F. was 70,000 weaker, and the overall increase was caused by the arrival of an extra 375,000 men of the labour corps for work on the lines of communication. But much as he would have liked to, Lloyd George dared not open direct fire on Haig, and he therefore made Gough his target, again not directly—"all recriminations at this hour must be shut out"—but by stinging implication.

Twice he strayed far from indisputable truth in making his flank attack. The Third Army was praised for "never giving way 100 yards to the attack of the enemy", and Brigadier-General Carey was dramatically extolled as the sole saviour of Amiens, he who "gathered signalmen, engineers, and labour battalions, odds and ends of machine-gunners, everybody he could find, and threw them into the line and held up the German Army and closed the gap on the way to Amiens for about six days". It was immaterial that the force had been formed and put in position long before Carey's arrival : the enrobement of a hero was an essential accompaniment to the sacrifice of the scapegoat. As for the latter : "Until the whole of the circumstances which led to the retirement of Fifth Army and its failure to hold the line of the Somme at least till the Germans brought up their guns and perhaps the failure adequately to destroy the bridges—until all these are explained it would be unfair to censure the General in command of the Army—General Gough. But until these circumstances are cleared up it would be equally unfair to retain his services in the field".

The prisoner had been arrested and charged. His trial never came : there was no formal enquiry. Gough eventually received word from Lord Milner, who succeeded Derby as War Minister, that he was eligible for re-appointment to an active command, but the public were not to know that his dismissal was not fully justified—until his accuser published the fifth volume of his War Memoirs in 1936. Here Haig is indicted as the villain, tendentiously, tediously, and vindictively (although he was then dead), and Gough is acquitted : "He could not be blamed for the fact that at the end of a full week of hard fighting the Germans still possessed that overwhelming superiority on the battle front. . . . Nevertheless, Gough's sacrifice has pointed the finger of censure at him. That was unfair—nay it was shabby". How true.

8

BACKS TO THE WALL

(April 9–29)

While Lloyd George attacked his soldiers in the Commons, they were in retreat again in France. Ludendorff had let loose the offensive that had originally been considered as an alternative to St. Michael, had then been put in pickle as a possible complement to the ill-fated Mars, and had finally come to fruition in such diminished form that its code name was altered from the grandiose St. George to the derisory Georgette. It was directed at Hazebrouck, the capture of which would split the B.E.F. roughly at the junction between Plumer's Second Army and Horne's First, and was to be followed by flanking blows against the Ypres Salient designed to make this prop both of the morale and supply line of the British collapse. The strategy was sound in that most of the British divisions originally holding this sector had been exchanged with mutilated ones from south of Arras, but the change of code name throws penetrating light on the declining confidence of the high command and must, as Winston Churchill would realise, have had a poor psychological effect. Ludendorff implies in his Memoirs that his expectations were not high. The fourteen divisions of von Quast's Sixth Army selected for the opening assault (of which six were in second line) were all fresh, but they suffered from the complexes of inferior grading, being 'trench' divisions as opposed to 'Storm'.

None the less they made a triumphant start. They attacked on a twelve-mile frontage south of Armentières, preceded by the standard bombardment, which burst forth in the pre-dawn darkness of this Tuesday, April 9th, the heavies having lumbered up like a travelling circus from their last performance in front of Arras. Within three hours the Germans had plunged three miles into the defences with negligible casualties. This was because over half the line under attack was held by the augmented 2nd Portuguese Division and they had run. "They bolted helter-skelter", Haig reported in his diary after seeing Sir Richard Haking, the corps commander concerned, who had just returned from Italy. "Some even took their boots off to run the quicker, and others stole the bicycles of the Corps Cyclists who were sent forward to hold La Couture and vicinity". At least it gave the British something to laugh about, and veterans were still gleefully recalling the occasion when the Second World War began.

It was known that the Portuguese troops were bad. There had been revolution at home, officers were allowed home leave

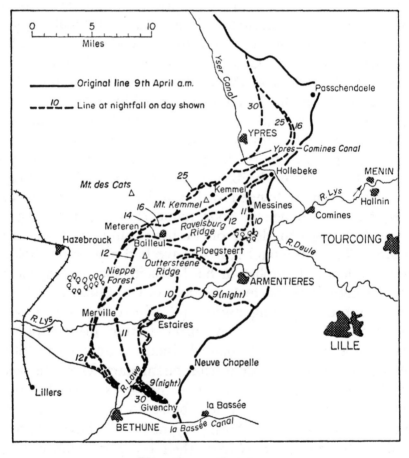

The Lys offensive

and the men denied it, and they had had a beastly winter in the cold and wet. Indeed, one of their divisions had been removed, leaving the other one with an extra brigade and an enormous frontage to hold. But it was across boggy land, which necessitated the construction of breastworks, and it was regarded as a 'safe' area until May—even though it included Neuve Chapelle, where in March 1915 the British had carried out their first experiment in offensive action. Suddenly this sector held by the Portuguese did not seem safe at all. The drought during February and March had dried the ground to a degree never before experienced earlier than summer, and all the ominous preliminaries to an attack had been detected, which British Intelligence foresaw as a holding attack preparatory to a double-pronged assault on Vimy Ridge. Arrangements were hastily made to relieve the Portuguese, but the Germans forestalled them by twenty-four hours. It was ironic that having been thwarted the previous autumn by an abnormal abundance of rain, Haig's plans should now be thrown into confusion by an abnormal shortage of it.

So swift was the flight of the Portuguese that plans to meet such an emergency somewhat miscarried. The 11th Cyclist Battalion and the 1st King Edward's Horse made prompt and brave intervention, but the 50th Northumbrian Division (on the left) and the 51st Highland were committed piecemeal and were soon at full stretch trying to hold the line of the River Lys on a frontage almost double that originally held by the Portuguese. These two famous territorial divisions, who were again to fight side by side in the Second World War, had been restocked with raw material during a week's recuperation from their mighty exertions in March. On their left another convalescent from the March offensive, the 40th Division, were already in the line and were enveloped and badly mauled by this new onslaught, but on their right there was a division that had had respite since the Battle of Cambrai, the 55th North Lancashire, and they repulsed the Germans with magnificent vigour and blocked the road to Bethune and its precious mines. The divisional policy was to employ every battalion on the defence of the battle zone, either in position or by immediate counter-attack, and it was most effective.

Next day, the 10th, the Germans extended the frontage of the attack northwards, the Fourth Army storming the Messines Ridge with the aid (once again) of early mist. It had been in the keeping of the Australians, but was now thinly held by three more convalescent divisions, one of which was the 9th Scottish, late of Congreve's Corps, with the South African Brigade resurrected but pitifully short of experience. Generous as ever, Plumer had already sent the 29th Division and another infantry brigade to help Horne stem the penetration along the marshy and closely-hedged country by the Lys, and he could give nothing but his fatherly encouragement to the divisions holding the exposed slopes around Messines, the masterful capture of which the previous June had brought such joy to the British nation and to the troops in the Ypres Salient released thereby from enemy observation. Despite a brave counter-attack by the South African innocents, the village of Messines was lost and some, but not all, of the ridge. Armentières, which lay between the two German thrusts, had to be hastily evacuated, the 34th Division, who had fought so well for the Third Army in the opening days of the March offensive, narrowly evading encirclement.

Meanwhile the German drive towards Hazebrouck caused mounting alarm. On April 10th the 50th and 51st Divisions had been pushed back beyond the line of the Lawe and Lys rivers and had fallen slowly, doggedly back on either side of the Lys, where it runs due west. On the 11th the 51st were saved from complete destruction by the arrival of another Territorial division that had borne a tremendous burden during the March retreat, the 61st. North of the Lys XV Corps, which from midday on the 11th was transferred from Horne's to Plumer's command, had to contend with the strongest pressure of all. Every scratch reserve had to be summoned to thicken up the remains of the 50th and 40th Divisions, the 29th and newly arrived but far from fresh 31st Divisions, in a line that became ever longer as ground was given to the bustling, insidious attackers. Further north, however, there was some successful withdrawing from hazardous salients and no cause for immediate alarm.

It was on this night, Thursday, April 11th, that Haig made his one dramatic gesture of the war. He issued his famous order of the day "To all Ranks of the British Forces in France", and it is such a model of dignified exhortation that it is worth quoting in full:

> Three weeks ago the Enemy began his terrific attacks against us on a 50-mile front. His objects are to separate us from the French, to take the Channel ports and destroy the British Army.
>
> In spite of throwing already 106 divisions into the battle and enduring the most reckless sacrifice of human life, he has as yet made little progress towards his chosen goals.
>
> We owe this to the determined fighting and self-sacrifice of our troops. Words fail me to express the admiration which I feel for the splendid resistance offered by all ranks of our Army under the most trying circumstances.
>
> Many among us are now tired. To those I would say that victory will belong to the side that holds out the longest. The French Army is moving rapidly and in great force to our support.
>
> There is no other course open to us but to fight it out! Every position must be held to the last man: there must be no retirement. With our backs to the wall, and believing in the justice of our cause, each one of us must fight on to the end. The safety of our homes and the freedom of mankind alike depend on the conduct of each one of us at this critical moment.
>
> D. Haig, F.M.

Haig must have known that his order would cause alarm at home and surprise in many parts of the B.E.F., since barely a fifth of its divisions were at that time under assault. In fact it caused amusement in the quieter sectors and no doubt drew grunts of cynicism from those hardest beset. He must also have appreciated that, unlike his divisions, an appeal of this nature could be used only once. Presumably it was meant most of all for those unfortunates who had been removed from the fire of one battle to be thrown into that of another, and his basic philosophy of war is expressed by the words "Victory will belong to the side which holds out the longest." His diary entries show his anxiety about lack of reserves to defend the precious Channel ports, but are as full and matter-of-fact as ever and contain no hint of despair nor even mention of the need to issue an order of the day. They more than hint, however, that it was not addressed to the British troops alone.

Haig had, in fact, been becoming increasingly exasperated with Foch. No one better appreciated than Haig himself the need to husband reserves and that its corollary was to demand the maximum in endurance from the troops already committed; he realised that the art of defence is the art of thrift and had shown himself master of it. Foch also practised the art—and to such a degree that Haig brooded darkly about his motives. All he had offered up to the Wednesday night, April 10th, was four French divisions to come into reserve west of Amiens, where they would greatly inconvenience the administration of Rawlinson's army. "Most selfish and obstinate" Haig called him in his diary on the 9th with all the pique of a man sagging beneath a burden that his friends disdain to share. But an imploring letter from him next day brought Foch to Montreuil on the night of the 10th, where he (Foch) agreed that the Germans had singled out the British Army for destruction and promised to despatch four French infantry divisions and three of cavalry to Haig's aid. Haig's entry that night shows that pique still smouldered and was fanned by suspicion : "I am glad that the French at last are beginning to realise the object of the Germans. The French losses in this battle are about 20,000 to 25,000."[75,000 would have been nearer the true figure.] "Ours are 160,000 and will be more. This shows their share in the fight so far! But, personally, I have come to the conclusion that Foch is afraid to put any French Division into the battle, and that he won't do so until force of circumstances as a last resort compel him." He wrote his celebrated order of the day twenty-four hours later, and one of its aims must surely have been to add force to circumstances.

The 12th was a day of agonised crisis for the British on either side of the Lys, but it subsided in their favour with the arrival of three divisions that had already done plenty of travelling in response to emergency calls. The first was the 5th Division, one of the two that had struck the first blow at Mons. After Third Ypres they had been rushed off to Italy, only to find the line stabilised and quiet on arrival, and in March they had been rushed back to France, again finding the line stabilised on joining Byng's Third Army. Now transferred to Horne's First Army, still twelve infantry battalions strong, they were sent through the Forest of Nieppe, north of the Lys on the extreme left of the Army line, where the situation was exceptionally fluid. They soon ejected the Germans from the forest and stabilised a line beyond its eastern fringe, and from now on the First Army stood firm on either side of the Lys. Alone of the army commanders, Horne evaded the inconvenience and humiliation of having to move his headquarters back.

On the immediate left of the 5th Division, but in Plumer's army, the 1st Australian Division played the saviour's rôle. The last Australians to leave Second Army and the only ones to return, they had an adventurous trip back. Big shells crashed around the station at Amiens as they crowded on to their trains on the evening of the 11th, causing the prolonged disappearance of all railway officials, and aircraft tormented them all the way to Hazebrouck, causing greater delay than casualties. Meanwhile bombs had forced Plumer out of his headquarters at Cassel, and in front of Strazeele, five miles from Hazebrouck, a medley of dutymen and students from his headquarters strove to plug gaps in a line near bursting point. The four hours required to repair a bombed railway bridge postponed the arrival of the first Australians until the late afternoon of the 12th. "Oh! those four hours," wrote the Chief of Staff, Harington, in his life of Plumer, his beloved chief. "I was at Hazebrouck when the trains at last arrived. I can see the Australians detraining and advancing towards Strazeele. Glorious fellows and so were the servants and grooms they relieved."

Other glorious fellows—the 33rd Division—had also rejoined the Second Army after a brief stay with the Third and were now showing their mettle at Meteren, a few miles north-east of Strazeele. The Germans suffered appalling losses from the weapons of the new arrivals. They gained Meteren and its adjacent ridge, but no more. Like that other great communications centre, Amiens, Hazebrouck remained tantalisingly out of reach, at the even shorter distance of six miles.

Further north they strengthened their hold on the Messines

Ridge and enforced the slow, carefully planned withdrawal of the British from Passchendaele right back to the very outskirts of Ypres and the line of the Yser Canal. The decision almost broke Plumer's heart after the terrible price he had paid for those awful miles of mud, but he more than halved the line to be held by the weak and tired divisions in this sector and undoubtedly saved them from a fate worse than that which befell the holders of the Flesquières salient.

None the less there was still a salient, though smaller than the Germans imagined, and on April 17th they sought to engulf it by launching great converging attacks with their Fourth Army from the north and their Sixth from the south. Both failed disastrously. The Belgians on the left of the British triumphantly repulsed the Fourth Army, and the attack by the Sixth crumpled beneath the machine-guns mainly of the 19th Division before Mount Kemmel, the most easterly of the steep and incongruous peaks running in a row down the centre of the Second Army's sector. It was a surprise for the Germans to find a defence so well organised on a line hastily occupied after the loss of the Messines Ridge, and another cause of discomfiture to them was some very effective bombing and machine-gunning by the R.A.F. Near the end of the day the French took over certain positions and by the 19th they had fully relieved the British on a frontage of some nine miles in the centre of the Second Army line. No longer did Plumer's men have that backs-to-the-wall feeling.

Rawlinson had to contend with the next crisis. He had reorganised his line, but without fresh troops, since April 4th. Butler had relieved the exhausted Watts and now had his III Corps headquarters at Dury, Rawlinson having moved his to Flixécourt, north-west of Amiens, on the extension of his front to Albert. Butler had two divisions in the line. Released at last from their long involvement with the French—they had held their original positions south of the Oise until the end of the first week of April—the 58th London were on the right, next to the French in Hangard. The 8th were on the left covering Villers Bretonneux. The hardy 18th were in reserve, having been involved in yet more fighting on April 12th, when they helped the French to win an out-and-back battle for Hangard. The Australian Corps, whose divisions were still twelve battalions strong, held the line from north of Villers Bretonneux up to the Somme with the 5th Australian Division and from the Somme to Albert with the 2nd and 3rd. The 4th were in reserve, with one brigade, the 13th, frozen as Army reserve.

Rawlinson had now received some tanks. One of the old Fifth Army battalions had been partially re-equipped with Mark IVs, those heroes of Cambrai which in theory were obsolescent, and he also had some Whippets. These had much lower tracks and mounted a towering turret well forward, with four Hotchkiss machine-guns covering all directions; they had a crew of three. Despite their name, they could attain their advertised maximum of 8 m.p.h. only on a good road, but had done well on their two appearances in action and much was expected of them by the tank men.

The infantry of Butler's divisions had been made up to strength with new and young reinforcements who far out-numbered the men with battle experience. There was a touching enthusiasm about them that could be turned to good account by seasoned officers, but of all commodities none was scarcer than the latter. On April 17th a fierce bombardment of Villers Bretonneux and its surrounds, by high explosive, phosgene and mustard gas, gave the "children"—as Rawlinson termed them— a particularly horrid and debilitating initiation. The mustard gas was the worst. 8,000 shells of it were counted down in the course of five hours, leaving poisonous, blistering liquid to lie for days, and the torment they caused was aggravated by the fact that the British could not retaliate in kind.

Butler's other great worry concerned his right flank. From the high ground beyond the Luce the Germans could stare upon the British line from its right rear, and the French, ensconced far behind the Avre, did not seem even to care. Repeated pleas from Rawlinson at last stirred them to attack on April 18th. They did not get as far as the line of the Avre. Amiens was still in danger. Haig suspected that the Flanders offensive was intended as a diversionary preliminary to a further assault against Arras and Amiens, and there were signs that a fresh blow was about to fall.

Warning of it came from prisoners—always a fluent source, such was the waning loyalty of many Germans, but sometimes an inaccurate one—and was confirmed by air reports, and sure enough at 3.45 a.m. on Wednesday, April 24th, gas and high explosive shells pounded the gun lines in front of Amiens, followed by a torrent of high explosive on the forward positions. But the sector under deluge was short. The German Second Army could muster sufficient storm divisions to make only Villers Bretonneux and Hangard their objectives. Four, of which one was fresh from Russia and the others refurbished after a hammering in March, attacked the two holding the front of the British III Corps and one the French at Hangard, with a further three in reserve. Yet the weaving forms of the storm-troopers were not the first to emerge from the fiendishly persistent mist when the shells stopped falling among the forward British trenches at 6 a.m. To their horror the young soldiers found great slabs of iron on top of them. Carefully assembled without detection from the air and brought forward while their drone was drowned by the crash of shells, German tanks were making their first full-scale attack. Great hefty brutes they were, with tracks obscured by mighty skirts of steel; each had a 6-pounder gun, six machine-guns and a crew of eighteen jammed together like sardines in a tin.

Ludendorff had little use for tanks. Judging from his memoirs, the demise of the British offensive at Cambrai made a greater impression on him than its opening. He persuaded himself that "The best weapons against tanks were good nerves, discipline and intrepidity," and the inference is that he regarded his enemies as well endowed with these qualities, for he did not give the production of tanks high priority. His scepticism had the usual result: the attack was on too small a scale to achieve decisive results. For this the British had good reason to be thankful when on this bleak April morning the underprivileged founder members of the German Panzer Corps took their chance to smite the enemy with his own invention. Only thirteen tanks lumbered into the attack, and yet they speedily carved a three-mile gap in the British line. Having no anti-tank weapons, the men of the hitherto so valiant 8th Division ran or surrendered as the monsters bestrode their trenches and pumped bullets into them. The Londoners stood firmer, thanks largely to the collapse of a tank down a quarry, and their right wing, being unmolested by tanks, repeatedly repulsed the German infantry.

The tanks shepherded the infantry into Villers Bretonneux and gained them, when the mist lifted, their first view of a long-promised land, the Somme valley at its junction with the Ancre and the rooftops and towering cathedral of Amiens, ten miles away. Further southwards a historic encounter took place, the first between tank and tank. As the leading German tank rumbled up the spur towards the village of Cachy it came under fire from two British ones on its right flank. The latter were 'females', armed only with machine-guns, and were holed by the German gun and forced into retreat. But the third member of this forward section was a 'male', with a 6-pounder gun on either side, and it happened to be No. 1 Tank of No. 1 Section, A Company, 1st Battalion, Tank Corps. Its first hit made the German slew and overturn. Two other German tanks appeared. The fire of Britain's No. 1 was too much for them. One trundled off smoking and the other emitted its crew.

Soon after this contest an airman spotted a force of German infantry, estimated at two battalions, concentrated in this same area north-east of Cachy, presumably in readiness to attack the village. He dropped a message on the headquarters of the Whippet battalion, and seven of them roared off, under command of Captain T. R. Price. Although they had over three miles to travel, they found the enemy force still in position, spread across a hollow, and they swept down upon them in line. The Germans had no cover except shell-holes and they unwisely sought refuge in them. The Whippets crunched and slaughtered them hole by hole, turned round and made a second awful run. They returned "covered in blood and human remains" (to quote their officer's report) leaving behind them three tanks disabled and successfully evacuated and a fourth in flames, hit by a shell. The two frizzled bodies inside it were the only British among German ones who, it was claimed, could not possibly number less than 400, all felled by one enterprising officer and fourteen men.

The tanks had played their part. Such as were still running on the German side took shelter, and no further opportunity

came the way of the British. The German infantry meanwhile
had swarmed down the slope from Villers Bretonneux and into
the woods between Cachy and the main road. Here they were
vigorously halted by the reserve brigade of the 8th Divisions
and one of the 18th.

Rawlinson's reaction to the crisis was to demand that Villers
Bretonneux be retaken at once. It was found that the Germans
were too well established, with good fields of fire for their
machine-guns from the Villers Bretonneux ridge, and he therefore resolved on a night attack, to be launched as a pincer
movement by his Army reserve, the 13th Australian Brigade,
and a brigade from the division on the right of the Australian
line, the 5th Division, who had already made an important
contribution by standing firm in their positions to the north-east
of Villers Bretonneux rather than making the customary conforming movement to trim the edge of the dent. On the right of
the pincer a composite brigade of III Corps were to enlarge the
frontage of the attack to include Hangard Wood. At 2 p.m.
Rawlinson rang up Butler and explained exactly how the attack
was to be carried out. He stressed the importance of getting
reconnaissances started at once and ordered that all troops in
the attack, who belonged to five divisions, must have a single
commander. The one chosen was Major-General W. C. G.
Heneker, who as commander of the 8th Division had closest
knowledge of the situation. Rawlinson sent one of his staff officers
to remain with him and make sure that there was no alteration
to his (Rawlinson's) orders.

Haig arrived and approved the plans, and at 3.45 there was
a visit from Foch's envoy, Lieutenant-General Sir John Du
Cane, who had been taken from command of a corps in the
thick of the fighting by the Lys to be the senior British
representative on the Generalissimo's staff. He brought a
message, written by Foch's hand, which began almost as if in
jest, *"L'importance de Villers Bretonneux qui domine Amiens
ne peut échapper au Genl. Rawlinson"*, and urged him to
launch a counter-attack *"comme celle le Genl. Debeney a montée
dès ce matin 10 heures"*. This was too much. So far from having
already made an attack, Debeney had told Rawlinson that he
could not co-operate with him that night, but might attempt

something next day (which he did not); "Debeney is no good—cannot fight," wrote Rawlinson in his diary on the 25th. He was so cross with Foch that he told a staff officer to tear up the message, but the latter kept it and it journeyed eventually to the Public Record Office in London.

The plan was daring. The two Australian brigades had to advance two miles in the moonlight, on either side of Villers Bretonneux, with their inner flanks exposed to enfilade fire; there was little information as to where the enemy was and little time for assembly. The 13th Australian Brigade had to come from across the Somme and they met many youngsters put to flight by the tanks. The memory stuck vividly in one Australian mind of how they talked to these men and persuaded several of them, in a friendly manner, to come back with them and throw out the Germans.

The British brigade on the right, formed by the 18th Division with a battalion of Londoners under command, were the only ones able to cross the start-line on time, and they were soon in trouble from enemy posts that had evaded the fixed, brief concentrations fired by the guns. But they made plucky progress, especially in the case of the 7th Bedfordshire on the left, who were reduced during the night to a few makeshift platoons under the overall command of 2nd Lieutenant W. Tysoe, the only officer left. The Germans tried without success to obtain his capitulation by persuasion through a sergeant-major emissary who naively pointed out that he would win the Iron Cross, First Class, if only the Bedfords would surrender!

The 13th Australian Brigade got badly entangled by British wire as they began their advance round the right side of Villers Bretonneux. Then they nearly had a battle with troops of the 8th Division still holding out near the edge of the town. When at last the Germans opened up the Australians charged with typical gusto and so amazed them by their disregard of enfilade fire that they sowed panic in their ranks. But at the far, southeast corner, just outside the town, they met stiffer opposition around the Monument (which commemorates a stand in the Franco-Prussian War) and its adjacent farm. The 13th were held here, just short of their objective, unable to envelop the town.

The assembly of the 15th Brigade, of the 5th Australian Division, was badly upset by the need to avoid patches of mustard gas and they did not start their attack until midnight, two hours too late to take advantage of a barrage that could not be repeated and with clouds now obscuring the moon, greatly aggravating problems of navigation. By all normal rules their attack should have been a flop. Yet so far from being dispirited by the breakdown of their time-table, the Australians dashed forward with a mighty cheer as soon as fire was opened at them. The nerve of the Germans could not stand the strain; they fired as wildly as they were charged and scuffled out of their captured trenches, leaving it to the Australians to wage dispute among themselves as to which positions they should occupy. They settled for a trench line north-east of Villers Bretonneux, from which their patrols tried in vain to link up with the 13th Brigade across the east flank of the town.

When it was light, various parties entered the gas-contaminated hulks of Villers Bretonneux, the 8th Division from the west, the 15th Australians from the north-west. The latter found they had been forestalled. Two hundred of their comrades, who were thought to have been casualties, were found in the cellars sampling the wine. They had some Germans with them. Others were still at large, but were soon rounded up, the total haul coming to 472 prisoners and sixty machine-guns. The day, April 25th, was the third anniversary of Anzac Day, and the date today is as firmly associated with 'Villers Bret' as with Gallipoli. Not only were the Australians to remain from now on as guardians of the shattered town but were to make great financial contribution, when the war ended, to its rebuilding.

At 3.45 a.m. on the 26th the 13th at last linked up with the 15th, although still held up at the Monument, and at dawn another long-awaited event took place: the French made an attack on Hangard (which they had lost on the 24th) and on Hangard Wood, the edge of which was held by hard-pressing elements of the 58th and 18th Divisions. It was carried out by the famous Moroccan Division with great panache, the sounding of trumpets and beating of drums, terrible losses and hardly any territorial gain. None the less they relieved the British, linking up with the Australians just to the south of the Monument, and another slice of line was taken over by the French from their unappreciative allies. Butler's III Corps was once again removed from the line. It might have been eliminated if Hutier had been able to co-operate in strength with Marwitz's rather footling but thoroughly alarming last attempt on Amiens.

A day of joy at Villers Bretonneux, April 25th was one of deepest gloom for the Allies further north. There were four French divisions now in the line, holding the central nine miles of the British Second Army's front, with three cavalry ones in reserve. They formed General Mitry's Détachment d'Armée du Nord, which consisted of two corps, the left-hand one being Robillot's II Cavalry Corps, whose notion of co-operation had caused Maxse such distress. This corps held Mount Kemmel, the seemingly impregnable boulder that provided a unique view of the German line almost from Ypres to Bailleul.

The German Alpine Corps attacked at 7 a.m. on this eventful Thursday, April 25th, and in the course of a mere half hour made themselves masters of the Mount. Their gunners had paved the way with that terrible dosage of gas and high explosive so well known to the British but not previously administered at full strength to the French. The gas shells put almost all the French artillery out of action, and the subsequent concentrations on the forward positions, tremendous both in weight and accuracy, had particularly deadly effect because of the very density of the troops packed into the trenches. Many of the survivors fled, even before they were attacked. It was a fearful humiliation, most of all for poor Robillot, who had freely and dogmatically given advice on the defence of this fortress peak long before he had taken it over.

French generals had always tended to take a superior attitude as the representatives of a great land power. It had not been lowered, rather the reverse, by the fact that the British had borne far the heavier burden during the last ten months. Gough and his generals had been patronised or snubbed during the March retreat, and at the Doullens conference the French had been willing enough to exaggerate British shortcomings in order to conceal their own. There could be no hiding responsibility for the present disaster, and however alarming the consequences it portended not every British general was so sorry that it had happened. For Haig it was the fulfilment of his fears. "What Allies to fight with!" he wrote in his diary.

As if bemused by their success, the Germans were slow to deepen the breach. Thanks largely to the exertions of the battered brigades of the 9th Division, who were on the left of the French, a line was patched up some two miles in rear. Next day a joint counter-attack was attempted, but, as had happened before, the British—in the persons of the 25th Division—were the only starters. But Foch was quick to send Mitry fresh divisions, and when the Germans renewed the attack in earnest on April 29th they were surprised and depressed by the weight of fire they encountered from undetected positions. Five divisions, with four in second line, were launched against the sector held by one French and two British. Some gains of no great importance were made against the French, none against the British. French honour was redeemed.

It was Georgette's dying kick, not that this was yet apparent to troops striving to make newly occupied trenches habitable in the face of shelling, rainfall and, especially round Ypres, a steady deluge of mustard gas. Further back, men of the Labour Corps were hard at work on emergency lines covering Dunkirk, St. Omer, and Boulogne, and as the slush flopped from their shovels, Ludendorff was planning preliminaries to a fresh assault against the Channel ports. The first was to be an attack against the French line north of Paris, designed to bring their reserves back from Flanders. The second was to be a repetition of St. Michael, named New Michael, but with a diversionary rôle. The knock-out was to follow in June: New George.

But his armies had now suffered 348,300 casualties since March 21st and an emaciating drain had been made on their zest by the despairing efforts they had been called upon to make to break a line that would only bend. The British casualties now came to 239,793, not counting returned stragglers, and the French to about 110,000. They were the most bloody forty days of the war.

9

NO REFUGE

(May–June)

Once again a lull in the fighting was followed by an eruption
on the political front. Lloyd George's speech on April 9th had
further embittered the relationship between Government and
G.H.Q. There was anger in particular at his statement that the
B.E.F. was "considerably stronger" at the start of 1918 than of
1917. Indeed, it caused a sense of outrage among men who had
seen and protested against the disbandment of one infantry
battalion out of every four, and now casualties had so outnumbered reinforcements that eight divisions had to be reduced
to mere cadres to bring the others up to fighting strength. The
soldiers felt tricked and betrayed.

This led to an extraordinary intervention by their self-
appointed champion, Major-General Sir Frederick Maurice.
As Director of Military Operations at the War Office, he was
responsible for providing the Prime Minister with information
on fighting strengths. He neither heard nor read his speech on
the 9th but learned of the anger it roused when he visited France
soon afterwards. He aso learned (to quote his publication,
Intrigues of The War) "that a scheme for removing Haig from
supreme command was rapidly coming to a head." By now
(since April 22nd) he had been relieved of his duties as D.M.O.,
having (according to Lloyd George) lost the confidence of
Wilson. He was waiting, though apparently without definite
promise, for an appointment in France, presumably to the command of a division. He decided that in the nation's interest he
should sacrifice his career for Haig's and therefore sent a letter
to *The Times* and *Morning Post* in which he described the
Prime Minister's statement as "not correct" and also refuted one

made by Bonar Law. Having satisfied themselves that he was aware of the risk to himself—"it is a small thing compared to the risk of our losing the war," H. W. Gwynne of the *Morning Post* was assured—these papers published the letter on May 7th. In it Maurice justified himself as follows:

> My reasons for taking the very grave step of writing this letter are that the statements quoted above are known to a large number of soldiers to be incorrect, and this knowledge is breeding such distrust of the Government as can only end in impairing the splendid morale of our troops at a time when everything possible should be done to raise it.
>
> I have therefore decided, fully realising the consequences to myself, that my duty as a citizen must override my duty as a soldier.

Asquith, as Leader of the Opposition, tabled a motion demanding an enquiry and Lloyd George utterly routed him by quoting information provided by Maurice's department and pouring ridicule on Maurice. (The information had been provided but had been altered by an amendment which was ignored and remained ignored even when Lloyd George wrote his Memoirs, although its existence had subsequently been brought to his notice.) Maurice had meanwhile gone into retreat, far removed from contact with any politician, and there was in any case nothing he could do to substantiate his charge. He was duly retired on half pay and cast aside more widely derided than applauded, but on the testimony of his daughter he was sustained by the lasting conviction that he had upset the scheme to remove Haig from command. If he did, in fact, achieve that, these pages will in due course show that he might reasonably claim to have shortened the war.

The only other hint of any such 'scheme' at this particular time would appear to be confined to a diary entry made by Wilson on May 11th, two days after the Maurice debate, about a discussion on the appointment of a new C.-in-C. Home Forces in succession to French. "I could not get Milner" (who had now succeeded Derby as War Minister) "or Lloyd George to make up their minds. On the whole I advised Haig being brought home. But Lloyd George and Milner would not decide." The rôles had changed; in former days it would have been as extraordinary for the C.I.G.S. to make such a suggestion as for the Prime Minister to demur. Maurice's letter at least drove home the message that in the trenches there was no confidence in the Government, whatever the feeling in Westminster, and it might well account for the absence from letters and diaries of any further mention of the question of replacing Haig. Haig, typically, felt no gratitude to Maurice for his self-sacrifice. "This is a grave mistake," he wrote in a letter to his wife. "No one can be both a soldier and a politician at the same time."

A shaft of light was thrown on the Maurice affair with the publication in 1956 of Lord Beaverbrook's *Men and Power: 1917–18*. In it he quotes an extract from the diary of Lloyd George's widow and former secretary in which she described how the ignored amendment was discovered by a colleague at the bottom of a despatch box and thrown in the fire, before Maurice had written his letter. Controversy flared again, but from the military angle the interest in the case lies not so much in the question of who was deceiving whom as in the heat of the passions aroused. It is forgotten sometimes that all were trying their hardest to win the war, and the strange thing is that Lloyd George may unconsciously have been contributing towards that end by slandering the B.E.F. in the House. It was much better for the morale of the soldiers that they should be able to lay the blame for the retreats they had endured on the wicked machinations of politicians rather than on any short-comings on the part of their generals.

Meanwhile evidence kept arriving that the morale of the battered divisions was standing the strain remarkably well. Haig was not the man to wait passively for the enemy to strike his next blow, nor for that matter was Foch. A series of local attacks was delivered all along the line to deter the withdrawal of good German divisions for offensive preparations, and Haig also instructed his army commanders to prepare plans for more ambitious offensives on certain sectors. Among the attacks to be considered was one from Villers Bretonneux, to be prepared by Rawlinson in conjunction with Debeney.

The Australian Corps played an important part in these minor operations and in the process reduced the enemy to a highly satisfactory state of jumpiness. They made their attacks at night. On May 2nd/3rd the 4th Division struck from Villers Bretonneux in conjunction with the French and gained a strip of ground which brought five enemy divisions into action to recover it. Two nights later the 3rd Division fell on the enemy round Morlancourt, on the other side of the Somme, and took permanent possession of his forward trench lines, netting 150 prisoners. On May 18th/19th it was the turn of the 2nd Division, on the left of the 3rd. They crossed the Ancre to capture Ville-sur-Ancre and drove two miles beyond it. Some 400 prisoners were taken in this most successful and heartening operation. The following night the French chimed in with an attack near Kemmel which yielded 300 prisoners.

In exchange for the aid of these French divisions south of Ypres, Haig had agreed to send five of his battle-worn divisions to release fresh French ones in a quiet sector of the French line. It was a system that Foch termed *'roulement'* (a word first coined by Pétain at Verdun) and asked to be implemented on a larger scale, much to the consternation of Wilson, the former Francophile now so insular in his office in Whitehall. He suspected Foch of megalomania, but Haig had shown himself able to subdue any such tendency, if it existed, and after the crisis in April his relationship with his Generalissimo showed steady improvement. He made it clear that the loan of these divisions could only be temporary, and without delay they were put into the line to hold the right-hand portion of a narrow ridge northwest of Reims along which ran a famous highway, the Chemin des Dames. It had been captured from the Germans the previous October in a limited operation prepared with clinical efficiency by Pétain as a tonic for the French Army and nation and as a somewhat belated irritant to aid the British Passchendaele offensive. The Germans had displayed no urge to regain the Chemin des Dames.

Three British divisions were put in the front-line, and all were 'old boys' of the Fifth Army. On the left were the 50th Northumbrian, who had arrived first, only a fortnight after being hacked to pieces by the banks of the Lys. In the centre were the 8th, hastily stitched together again after being ripped wide open by the tanks at Villers Bretonneux on April 24th. On the right, holding lower, marshy ground, were the 21st, the product of Leicestershire, Lincolnshire, and counties northwards that had fought so well on March 21st, in the centre of Congreve's corps, and later been transferred to the Messines Ridge, there to receive a second hammering. They now belonged to Sir Alexander Gordon's IX Corps, whose other two divisions, in reserve, were ex-Third Army relics of the March and April fighting, the 19th and 25th.

'Quiet sector' were joke words in British terminology, but now they really seemed true. "For three weeks," wrote an officer of the 50th Division, "in trenches shadowed by green trees and the Boise de Beau Marais gay with flowers and singing birds, the war bore a different aspect. Here surely was that hitherto phantom sector all had some day hoped to find."

Unfortunately there were as many woods on the enemy side, great big woods in which soldiers could trample the flowers and scare the birds in their thousands with little risk of detection by prying eyes. But nocturnal noises of assembly, especially of the guns, sent their messages to ears that had heard it all before. Little heed was paid to their warnings. In the great quiz games so ardently played at the various Allied headquarters the sector Arras–Albert was regarded as the most likely target for the next onslaught, for which the Germans were known to have sixty-two divisions fit for attack, and as evidence of activity accumulated opposite the Chemin des Dames it was thought likely to prelude a diversionary attack. And this is what Ludendorff intended it to be.

The guns opened at 1 a.m. on May 27th and in greater density than in any previous undertaking, each mile of the twenty-four chosen for attack being pummelled by 35.6 batteries, as opposed to 26.6 on March 21st. Every target received simultaneous drenching to a depth of twelve miles, with a liberal lacing of gas in this latest recipe of master-cook Bruckmüller, and extra-heavy concentrations were directed on the centre of the ridge, where the 50th disintegrated amid heaving earth and crashing branches. When the German infantry swarmed in at dawn, obscured as usual by mist, they quickly isolated and overwhelmed the few brave groups that fired at them from among the dismembered or groaning forms of their comrades.

One or two better organised stands were made further back, including a famous one by the 2nd Devonshire of 8 Division, who for three hours waylaid a whole division without aid from artillery, all of which had been destroyed. The French honoured the Devons with a collective Croix de Guerre.

By noon the Germans were over the Aisne, which ran behind the ridge at a distance of three to four miles from the original front line, and the 8th and 50th Divisions, with all their artillery, had been all but wiped out. The 21st, who held the line of the Aisne–Marne Canal below the wooded slopes, fared rather better. Nearly a third of their infantry were lost forward of the canal, but on the swamps beyond the canal the Germans were held, and later the 21st skilfully wheeled back so as not to be outflanked, hingeing on their right, where touch was maintained with the French. Meanwhile the 25th Division had belatedly been released from Army reserve and divided between the three others as token replacements for their losses. No sooner had they arrived in their stop-gap positions than the three brigades of this division were outflanked and forced back. By the end of the day the Germans had pushed the British back eight miles and the French, in one place, twelve.

They owed their staggering gain in part to the unequalled performance of Bruckmüller and his artillery—"all were united in astonishment at what it had done," wrote the historian of one German division—and in part to the co-operative way in which General Duchêne, commander of the French Sixth Army, had insisted on making the front line his main one in defiance of the policy laid down by Pétain, who was an advocate of elasticity. It was the old emotional outlook versus the practical, and the emotional, although discredited, counted Foch among its adherents—indeed, his directions contradicted Pétain's—and had another in the Prime Minister, Clemenceau. Pétain had a supporter in Gordon, the British corps commander, who had good reason to know how much the Germans relied on their opening bombardment; but when he protested to his army commander, Duchêne, against having his men and guns made easy targets, he was quelled with an abrupt, *"J'ai dit."*

The ironic thing is that despite—or rather because of—the ghastly and almost total sacrifices made by the 50th and 8th

Divisions and the two French ones on their left, Duchêne may well have contributed more to the allied cause than would a man with less rigid ideas on defending French soil. For once again Ludendorff allowed himself to be lured off his intended course by success. His troops had broken through on the sector nearest Paris, with a completeness never achieved in March, and had presented opportunity far too enticing for the restless old opportunist to resist. Fresh divisions were brought up, earmarked originally to renew the assault on the muddy, shell-torn, gas-infested line in Flanders, to hold which the British still relied on grudging aid from the French. The advance continued beyond the Aisne, beyond the Vesle, and on May 30th as far as the banks of the Marne, a penetration of almost thirty miles, as the crow flies, in four days. There was consternation in Paris, fifty-six miles from the German spearhead; after four terrible years of trial and sacrifice the situation once again screamed for a miracle of deliverance. In the characteristic manner of frightened men, the politicians bayed for blood. They demanded the dismissal of Duchêne and with greater vehemence that of the man whose directions he had flouted, the Commander-in-Chief, General Pétain.

Fortunately for them it was impossible to remove Pétain with any speed—General Guillaumat, Clemenceau's choice, had first to be recalled from Salonika—and he remained to apply the cool and sensible measures required. Instead of rushing his reserves into battle, he placed them in an arc of long-stop positions barring the route to Paris along the northern bank of the Marne. As usual the German effort dwindled as their preponderance in artillery declined, the heavies being outranged and in any case earmarked for another task. Near Reims, the Germans hammered in vain against the eastern side of their narrow wedge to the Marne. In company with some dauntless, assorted survivors of the other divisions of IX Corps, the 19th Division fought with distinction here—a counter-attack by the 4th King's Shropshire Light Infantry, 200 strong and led by a subaltern, won them the Croix de Guerre—and such was the impression they made that when all other commanders from that of Army Group downwards were sacrificed to the howling mob a special request was made to the British that Gordon and his corps might remain. On the west side of the bulge the Germans forced the French out of Château Thierry, on the Marne, during the course of June 1st–3rd, and made some gains further north, but were then brought to a halt.

A significant event, heartening to the French, depressing to the Germans, occurred on June 2nd: the American 2nd Division took over the defence of the route to Paris from Château Thierry. It was graduation from the 'quiet sector' rôle agreed by Pershing on March 25th, and the doughboys showed themselves more than worthy of their new responsibilities, for on the 6th they dashed into the attack, recapturing the village of Bouresches and half of Belleau Wood. But the 1st Division had forestalled them by over a week. Holding part of the French line near Mont-didier, they had gone into the attack on May 28th and success-fully eliminated a salient in the German line, capturing the village of Cantigny. Not surprisingly, means of speeding up the despatch of American troops had top place on the agenda of an emergency meeting of the Supreme War Council in Paris on June 1st. There were now twelve divisions of them in France, each twelve large battalions strong, and of these four were available for operations anywhere, five were undergoing training with the British, and three with the French. Pershing had agreed that infantry should come over ahead of the guns, and now it was urged that a further 310,000 be shipped across during the next two months, with Britain supplying the ships and hoping for use of the men. As crisis mounted for his hard pressed allies, so did Pershing's dear prospect of commanding his army in the field recede.

By June 6th it had become clear that the Germans had shelved their ambitions by the Marne for the time being and were preparing a fresh blow some forty miles to the west, between Noyon and Montdidier. These two towns, it will be remembered, were the furthest gains made by the redoubtable von Hutier and his Eighteenth Army in March, but now his preparations were so blatant that it appeared either that he was losing his touch or else was staging a bluff. Prisoners made it clear that if the French were being misled then so were they, and so many were prepared to run the risk of desertion that it became clear enough that something very unpleasant for the front-liners was about to occur. A touch of fever had smitten the German General Staff. Speed was now the prime essential, at the price even of surprise, and such was the haste to keep the enemy reeling that the guns were clumsily assembled and the troops inadequately fired with that precious ardour that was becoming harder to generate with the demise of each successive offensive. Yet despite the haste, the day had to be postponed until June 9th, such were the problems of transporting the all-important heavies from one engagement to the next.

Our old friend General Humbert and his Third Army were to be the recipients of this latest onslaught. He had his troops well forward in compliance with Foch's doctrine that "any retirement, even a very limited one, plays the game of the adversary" and also in the belief that he was himself soon to launch an attack. Pétain and his Army Group commander, Fayolle, managed to prevail upon him to make some hasty adjustments to his dispositions, and the Germans, attacking with fifteen divisions on an eighteen-mile front, made greater gains in ground (to the extent of six miles) than in guns and men. None the less they crossed the Matz and seriously disabled three divisions. But Humbert could cushion the blow, having as many as five infantry and three cavalry divisions in reserve and Fayolle could use his reserves on a counter-attack against the Germans' right flank. It was entrusted to a rugged fighting general, one of the few to survive Nivelle's offensive, the square-jawed Mangin. With great alacrity he assembled a force of five divisions, backed by some tanks, to which he gave the rôle of following up and passing through the infantry after aircraft had provided the latter with their initial fire support. Put in on the morning of the 11th, the attack achieved considerable though by no means spectacular success. It was sufficient to bring von Hutier's last offensive to an end.

Pétain's prestige was rightly restored. He, quite as much as Foch, was an advocate of the employment of reserves for a flanking counter-attack rather than for frontal defence. It was a fairly obvious ploy and it may seem strange that it was so long before either of the allies had been able to give it effect. The answer is that it required the availability and correct positioning of ample reserves, and this in turn called for an

accurate forecast of the course of events. For the first time
these requisites had been met.

First the British and then the French had shown their capacity
for survival, but both armies had been stretched to their limit
and each of the Commanders-in-Chief now had that grieved
feeling that he was carrying rather a larger burden than the
other. Foch might have been a judge in the bankruptcy court.
He kept asking Haig for divisions to form a general reserve, and
Haig, having first expressed "my firm resolve to do all I can to
assist General Foch *short* of imperilling the British Army",
became so concerned about the cost of compliance that he asked
Milner formally to modify the clause of his mandate under
which he was responsible for the safety of his forces. Pétain,
complaining on June 11th that "I have at my disposal only one
division fit to be called a reserve", implored Foch a week later
to make the British take over a larger part of the line so that
the French could be "ready to resist a new shock in the direction
of Paris which cannot fail to materialise". But Foch was not
impressed. He knew that the bulk of the German reserves—"a
mass of thirty-five to forty divisions, of which thirty are reconstituted or fresh"—was north of the Somme and he agreed
with Haig that they presented a greater menace than the smaller
reserves opposite Paris. The humiliation of the Chemin des
Dames had at least raised the prestige of the British Army. The
Generalissimo listened with increasing respect to the views of the
English Field-Marshal and with thinly concealed irritation to
those of his compatriot and temperamental opposite, the canny
and gloomy Pétain.

10

THE PROTOTYPES

(July)

November 1st, 1917, is a famous date in the annals of the Australian Army, and May 30th more so. On the first of these the five Australian divisions in France were brought together to form the Australian Corps, whereas previously they had been split into two corps, one of which was a hybrid. On the second, the commander of this corps, the British but none the less popular Sir William Birdwood, was appointed to the command of the resuscitated Fifth Army, and in his place an Australian was raised to the command of the Australian Corps, with promotion to lieutenant-general: Sir John Monash, commander of the most newly arrived division and the last to turn up the left sides of their hats, the 3rd.

The Australians thus gained parity with the Canadians, who had been under command of one of their nationals, Sir Arthur Currie, since Byng's appointment to the Third Army in June 1917. But there was the difference that whereas the Australian divisions were made available for emergency errands and had patched tottering lines for other commanders, the Canadian Government allowed no such dispersal of their troops and while the Germans made their great attacks, first on one side of them and then the other, Canada's four divisions stayed together around Vimy Ridge, snarling like a pride of lions over their kill. Monash meanwhile turned covetous but unavailing thoughts towards his 1st Division, those saviours of Hazebrouck who still formed an essential prop in the defences of Plumer's Second Army.

The Australians had had some chastening experiences since their arrival in France in May 1916. The fury of the Somme made the Gallipoli beaches tranquil in memory, and there were so many flaws in planning that the insular Haig was driven to make the scathing diary comment: "Some of their divisional commanders are so ignorant and (like many Colonials) so conceited, that they cannot be trusted to work out unaided the plans of attack." In April of the following year the 4th Division in particular had a gruesome taste of British inefficiency, when their army commander, Gough, put great faith in some tanks allotted them for an attack on Bullecourt and the tanks failed even to reach the start-line. But under the more careful planning of Plumer, Australian dash and initiative at last paid good dividends in some fine successes, little publicised today, that preceded the final agony of Passchendaele. They spent the winter scourged by high explosive and gas on the exposed slopes of the Messines Ridge and in the quagmire below, yearning for the chance to get in among their tormentors again.

It was a great fortune for the British cause that the Australians escaped bludgeon assault when the Germans struck. When summoned, they could make the most of opportunities to topple tiring attackers in conditions of open warfare, which gave such scope to the adventurous spirit that had inspired emigration in the first place and had then drawn so many men in from wild and remote bush stations to enlist for service in a far, far distant land. Mention has been made of some of the successes they gained after the exhaustion of the German effort on either side of the Somme. They established such dominance that the mere entry of two or three Australians into a trench was sufficient to send all German hands into the air quaking, and a number of positions were won by this system of 'peaceful penetration' as they termed it. The diggers had a sublime contempt for Fritz—they preferred this nickname to the heavier 'Boche' or 'Hun' favoured by the British. For the run-of-the-mill surrenderer they felt a sort of amused affection, but there was little chance of mercy for the man who stopped firing and put his hands up in one motion. Documents later captured showed how very worried von der Marwitz was becoming about the moral ascendancy the Australians had gained over his men. Little could be achieved by censure. With rations short and dreary and hope fast receding, the conscripts of the 'trench' divisions were easy meat for intimidation by the volunteer soldiers opposite them, so many of whom depended for their peacetime livelihood on their wits, daring and physical prowess.

The officers of such men had to lead by example, without aid from the mystique that a commission conferred on a British officer, and the majority owed their position to the fact that they were more resourceful, more daring, more contemptuous of danger than their men. Fortunately Mr. Monash—as he was respectfully called by his highly unmilitaristic men—had other qualities besides. Like Currie, the Canadian, he had never been a professional soldier, and it shows that Haig was not such an encrusted reactionary that he should have supported the promotion of these two men. Monash was an engineer by profession and a German Jew by descent, his parents having emigrated to Australia before his birth to escape the petty persecution inflicted on their race. He had a heavy jowl and a curving nose. He also had great acumen. His approach was radical, his method thorough. He believed in consultation with his subordinates, but once a plan was made and the final orders issued, he insisted that there must be no alteration whatever. He regarded the smooth co-operation between all arms as the most essential ingredient of success, and indeed in his book, *The Australian Victories in France in 1918,* he likens the preparation of a battle plan to that of an orchestral composition, with each instrument allotted its harmonious task. His approach, in other words, was similar to Rawlinson's and it is hard to say which of them deserves the greater credit for the tactics they so successfully evolved. While claiming a large part of it, Monash acknowledges in his book how helpful he found Rawlinson's "charming and sympathetic personality".

Soon after he had taken command of the Australian Corps Monash proposed the operation that was to become the overture to the grand opera of August. The need for it was obvious enough. In capturing Hamel on April 4th the Germans had made a dent in the British line between Villers Bretonneux and the Somme, and from it they had good observation of the Australian positions north of the river. Much was to be gained from removing the dent, and Rawlinson agreed to a full-scale divisional attack supported by tanks and aircraft.

The main task was allotted to the 4th Australian Division, and
the first essential was to restore their confidence in tanks, which
had stood at zero minus ever since the Battle of Bullecourt. At
last some Mark V tanks were available. Although similar in shape
to the Mark IV, they were much improved mechanically, being
drivable by one man instead of three, with a commander and six
gunners forming the remainder of the crew. Most were males,
carrying two 6-pounder guns and four Hotchkiss machine-guns,
and the remainder females with six machine-guns. Their despatch
from England had been delayed because, like Ludendorff, G.H.Q.
had given higher priority to the provision of other commodities,
but thanks partly to the influence of the Minister of Munitions,
Winston Churchill, the Mark Vs were at last beginning to arrive
in strength, and Rawlinson was able to allot Monash two
battalions (seventy-two fighting tanks) for the Hamel attack. The
Australians went to meet them, each battalion making an outing
by bus. They climbed over them, explored their interiors, took joy
rides on them and practised battle drills, watching with glee as
a tank slewed round to crush an imaginary enemy post indicated
by a real grenade despatched from the discharger cup of a rifle.
This was pioneer work in the art of co-operation and was the
start of a happy fraternity between the Tank and Australian
Corps, which never again suffered blemish.

An amazing feature of the plan was that eight battalions were
to be employed in the attack on a frontage of almost 6,000 yards,
for which the normal German assault allotment would be four
or five divisions. Furthermore, the objectives were held by more
battalions than would be attacking, that is by three regiments,
each of three battalions in three tiers of defence, and unbeknown
to the Australians two of these regiments would belong to one
of the storm divisions of the March offensive, brought in after
a long period of rest and replenishment to bolster the crumbling
morale. Sixty tanks were assigned to the assault battalions, and
it is a mark of the confidence placed in them that there should
be such economy in infantry. There were to be two new methods
for their employment. One was that they were to advance behind
a creeping barrage in line with the infantry and unheralded by
any set bombardment; this placed on the infantry the onus of
cutting their own paths through the wire, but the entanglements

were not thick. The other was that the tanks came under command of their infantry battalion commanders, which was reasonable, since their task was to help them, but a notable concession all the same.

Reinforcing the eight Australian battalions there were to be four companies of infantry (each 250 strong) from the American division affiliated for training, the 33rd. This was to be the first time they were to fight side by side with Haig's men, and it was no mere coincidence that the date chosen for the attack should be Independence Day, July 4th. All accounts agree that the Americans in training with the British—the infantry of five divisions—were most humble pupils, avid for every piece of advice the veterans could give them, and pathetically eager to prove themselves worthy. The battalion commander of these men in the long gaiters detailed to accompany the Australians is reported to have addressed them as follows: "I just want to tell you boys that you are going into a good keen fight among the Australians and you're going to give the Huns hell. . . . Now you're going into action with some mighty celebrated troops guaranteed to win, and you've got to get up to their level and stay with them. There'll be a whole heap of people looking on at you, who won't be on the spot, and you've got to make good." As Cutlack, the war correspondent, observed: "This extraordinary oration, which would probably have left a British battalion stone-cold and aroused an Australian one to rebellion, put the American heart exactly right."

With less than twelve hours to zero hour, and with the Americans already distributed by platoons to the Australian companies with which they were to fight, a sickening order reached Monash from Rawlinson: the Americans were not to be used. Pershing, whom a fortnight earlier Rawlinson had described as "stupid and obstinate", had ruled that their employment in the attack could not be classified as training and had therefore vetoed it, much to the indignation of the commmander of his 33rd Division, Major-General G. Bell, and his men. Monash would not accept this. He himself forbade any change in a subordinate's plan at such an hour and he told Rawlinson, who came to the headquarters of the 4th Division to meet him, that if there were to be no Americans there would be no attack. Rawlinson opted for the attack, told Monash to go ahead with his original plans and passed his decision on to G.H.Q. for confirmation. Haig was out visiting; he was eventually intercepted and countermanded Pershing's order. It was now a case of "let battle commence", with confidence in its outcome restored by Monash's firm resistance to interference.

The objective was a spur, a typically long, clean-curved spur with corn growing on it in places, which ran north-eastwards from the Villers Bretonneux plateau to the Somme. The village of Hamel was sprawled up its forward slope, as viewed by the Australians, and about a mile to the right the distorted trees of Vaire Wood could be seen running along the top of the slope. Both were known to be strongly fortified, but the Germans had done little else during their three months' sojourn. There was only one continuous trench line and no great amount of wire.

Certain noises had for some time nightly disturbed the Germans holding these positions, the drone of aircraft on their way to bomb billeting areas, the crump, crump, crump of harassing shells, and nearer dawn the more hollow burst of gas shell. They did so again on this Wednesday night, July 3rd, successfully drowning the rumbling and spluttering of the sixty tanks. At the first, barely perceptible approach of daybreak on the Thursday morning, the harassing fire grew in volume, until suddenly it burst forth into a mighty torrent of shells, stretching far to left and far to right, falling equally on the infantry in front and the gunners behind, and augmented by the vicious ceaseless crack of bullets from over a hundred Vickers machine-guns. There was the plop of gas shell, too. It was in fact smoke, which served to send heads into gas masks but performed no other useful function for the attackers, since once again a mist had unexpectedly arisen—and it was the Germans' turn now to gape into it in fear and bewilderment.

After only four minutes' pounding the barrage lifted from the forward positions, and Australians, Americans and the iron monsters manned by the British burst simultaneously upon their gas-masked, pumpkin-helmeted foe, most of whom were cowering in makeshift shelters or lying prostrate. Some fought well none the less, especially on a downward spur from the Australian line towards Hamel, where navigational errors prevented the tanks from giving the aid intended. But every lift of the barrage was accompanied by a fresh rush of infantry and tanks, and the attack never fell behind schedule, across the valley, round the sides of Hamel and of Vaire Wood, and across the top of the spur, with the mopping-up of village and wood left as a speedily accomplished last task. Within little more than ninety minutes the whole of the feature had been won, constituting an advance of more than a mile all along the line, and the tanks were coming back laden with cheering wounded and with such words of praise chalked on their hulks as "Dinkum Chum" and "Humdinger". The mist had now been replaced by a great dust cloud, affording just as effective a cloak for the concealment of the tanks. As a final phrase of the symphony, aircraft flew in and dropped ammunition by parachute for the most forward machine-guns, thus relieving the infantry of one of their most dangerous and unpleasant tasks in an attack, porterage.

Some 1,500 Germans, with 171 machine-guns, were captured in this little attack and hundreds killed. Its most significant feature, emphasising the stunning effect of surprise and speed combined, was the complete absence of any counter-stroke, either in the form of attack or fire alone. For the first time the tanks were able to rally and withdraw virtually unscathed after reaching the objective; only five were knocked out, one of them by its own barrage. The Australians suffered 776 casualties, a large number of whom were walking wounded, and the Americans 134. This was indeed a low figure for the results achieved and was very cheering to Rawlinson, who attributed it to the daringly large frontage over which the battalions had been spread. It had been a day of experiment, with stimulating results.

The Australians were not alone in their glory. The British 5th and 31st Divisions, of Horne's First Army, had in fact forestalled them. On June 28th they errupted from the outskirts of the Forest of Nieppe behind a creeping barrage preceded by no warning bombardment, and they took all their objectives in an advance of over a mile. But the casualties were less heavily tilted in their favour, nor did the terrain and the state of the enemy's defences offer such prospect of larger developments as on the Villers Bretonneux sector.

Rawlinson proposed another attack at an army commanders'

conference on July 5th. But Haig was wary; he had not the troops to hold the salient that would be formed. He none the less instructed Rawlinson to study the problem further and draw up a plan of greater scope, working on the assumption that he would in due course receive more troops.

Anxious eyes were meanwhile being kept on the German preparations for their next assault. Both British and French Intelligence claimed that groups of thirty-five or more divisions were being assembled for attacks upon their lines, and both were right. Ludendorff had decided that his May and June offensives had not sufficiently achieved their function of drawing troops away from Flanders, where he still planned to strike the decisive blow. He therefore prepared another diversion in the Marne sector, aimed at securing Reims and thus greatly facilitating communication problems, and this was to be followed with minimum delay by a knock-out delivered with his right, smashing through between Ypres and Hazebrouck. This sector was in fact more vulnerable than he realised, for the French Army of the North was in the process of dissolution, maintaining the fiction of its presence by wireless messages and a thin line of covering troops ahead of the British. The remains of Gordon's XI Corps had been returned by the French in exchange.

The signs of activity opposite the French became so conclusive that on July 12th Foch yielded to agitation from Pétain, and on returning from leave on July 14th Haig found that four of his divisions had been ordered to the French sector. There was also an urgent request from the Generalissimo that the British should launch a diversionary attack near the Lys, as previously called for in a directive. Haig thought only of the attack against his own line which was so obviously in course of preparation. He appealed to Foch for the return of his four divisions and the two men met next day, July 15th. But by now forty-one German divisions, of which seven were entirely fresh and the remainder refurbished, had answered the beckoning of Bruckmüller's mighty guns on either side of Reims.

It had been easier for Pétain, since the disaster on the Chemin des Dames, to teach his army commanders how to combat the German battering ram, and on the east side of Reims the measures taken by General Gouraud, commanding the French

Fourth Army, were a model of elasticity in defence and made this convert to the Pétain doctrine a great hero of the French people. Thanks to their superiority in the air and a certain defeatist lethargy displayed by their enemies, the French obtained detailed notice of the coming assault, and by the process of depriving a prisoner of his gas-mask they were able to discover the exact hour the bombardment was due to open on the 15th. Shells tossed and crumpled the stormtroopers as they moved into their assembly areas, and when their own guns burst forth with their familiar crash of unison most of their shells landed on positions recently emptied of guns and infantry. After a bewildered advance of two or three miles, amid much shellfire, the Friedensturm—or Peace Assault—came to a painful end for the twenty-two divisions attacking on this side of Reims.

West of Reims, along the slant formed by the bulge made in May, there was less confidence among the French in an elastic defence, partly through a natural desire to hold the banks of the Marne, which formed the bottom lining of the bulge. The Germans swept across the river with great dash and skill and also made a dangerous salient eastwards, north of the river, threatening the one road that connected Reims with the rest of unoccupied France. But the French had sufficient local reserves available to drain the momentum of the first alarming rush after it had gained a depth of nearly six miles, and their aircraft, with British aid, made the task of supply and reinforcement across the raft bridges over the Marne one of horror and despair. The R.A.F. contributed nine squadrons, equipped with Sopwith fighters or de Havilland bombers, and in helping to isolate the six German divisions in the Marne bridgehead they performed a task (at a cost of fifteen aircraft) of greater value than the ambitious strategic bombing on which other squadrons were engaged.

As usual the 'heavies' had set off for their next engagement soon after firing their opening salvoes. The Crown Prince Rupprecht had suffered many frustrations in the planning of his offensive, called Hagen, against the British Second Army. The number of his storm divisions had been whittled down from thirty-two to twenty-four and many gaps in their ranks had recently been opened by an influenza epidemic, which hit both sides but caused the greater destruction among the ill-nourished Germans. However, now at last the guns were arriving, and Ludendorff himself turned up to make the final arrangements in conference at Mons. It was here, on November 11th, 1917, that decision was taken on the opening of the great spring offensive. And here, on July 18th, just as discussion had begun on the next great blow, scheduled for the start of August, news arrived that led to the dissolution of all further plans for the offensive by the German Army. The French had launched a great counter-attack.

It was a deliberate stroke, long prepared, directed at the western flank of the great bulge to the Marne, with the main object of recapturing the town of Soissons, through which all supplies and reinforcements for the forward German divisions had to pass. Execution was entrusted to the dynamic General Mangin, now commanding the French Tenth Army, and it was pure chance—and very fortunate chance—that the Germans should have plunged deeper into the bulge before he was ready. The assembly of the assault troops and the 225 tanks supporting them was skilfully concealed, and their impact was dramatic, bringing great kudos to Foch in particular for what appeared to be masterly opportunism. The 1st and 2nd American Divisions, still raw and impetuous, formed the spearhead of the twenty-two divisions employed, with the Moroccan Division in between them. Attacking behind a creeping barrage that crashed down without warning and with the Renault tanks behind them in support, they advanced four miles on this opening day, July 18th, carving myriad channels through the standing corn. Mangin was warm in praise of his Americans. "You rushed into the fight as to a fête", he said in a congratulatory order.

Various German officers have left their descriptions of the jangled bundle of nerves that had taken the place of the decisive Ludendorff on his return to his headquarters at Avesnes. Field-Marshal von Hindenburg, the revered father figure and titular Chief of the General Staff of the Field Army, suggested a counter-attack when they discussed the situation that night. This produced (according to Foerster) an expression of rage on Ludendorff's face and his departure from the room spluttering a word that sounded like "Madness!" But if a counter-attack were not feasible, the Germans could still preserve remarkably good order. Reserve divisions, earmarked originally for Prince Rupprecht, slowed down Mangin's tanks and men, and although the bulge had to be evacuated and a withdrawal made of some twenty miles, back to the Vesle, the task was performed with all the old professionalism and an absence of haste. The four British divisions summoned by Foch, all veterans of the Third Army, were brought in to speed their departure, the 51st Highland and 62nd West Riding attacking from the east, the 15th Scottish and the 34th (the latter now containing five battalions from Palestine) from the west. They fused relief and advance into one operation, but had to fight doggedly for every mile won. None the less a great victory had been achieved, and Parisians could celebrate their most thrilling piece of news since that first miracle of the Marne almost four years earlier.

While Ludendorff writhed in the grip of indecision, forced to give up his Hagen offensive but refusing to admit that the only alternative was to go on the defensive, and tormented by growing signs of his troops' demoralisation, which he attributed to the Government's weakness in allowing the dissemination of socialist propaganda and to their recalling, after allowing long leave, ex-prisoners of the Russians—while Ludendorff was in turmoil, Haig saw the future with fresh clarity and with optimism, if not exuberance, to match even that of his Generalissimo. All through this last offensive by his enemies, plans for his own had been crystallising. July 16th was the day of revelation to the principal participant, and others received instructions too. Plumer had a visit from Lawrence and was warned to expect an attack by Prince Rupprecht's group at an early date, and so confident was Haig in its outcome that he wanted Plumer to make plans for the recapture of Mount Kemmel as a counter-blow to be delivered when the German attack subsided in exhaustion. It is significant that while these matters of defence were entrusted to the Chief of Staff, Haig himself did the briefing for attack. At the headquarters of the Third Army he saw both Byng and Horne and instructed them to prepare plans for an attack in the vicinity of Arras. He then had Rawlinson to lunch at G.H.Q., Montreuil, and confided that the other attacks were intended as diversions. His was to be the main one.

Rawlinson's version of this meeting is illuminating. "Had lunch with DH", he wrote in his journal. "I proposed offensive east of Villers Bretonneux, if he would give me the Canadians. To my surprise and delight, I find he has already decided to do this. . . . I gave him my proposed objectives. . . . He seemed to think that the Germans would not, or could not, continue fighting during the winter, and that they would do their utmost to come to terms in the autumn, especially if they failed in Champagne, as now seems probable."

Thus the attack mooted by Haig in early May and recommended by Rawlinson, with illustration, in early July took a leap nearer realisation, and since the land around Villers Bretonneux was the least shell-pocked on the entire battle-front, gave every facility for the assembly and employment of tanks, and aroused no great defensive effort on the part of the enemy, it is no less surprising that Haig should have appreciated its possibilities than that Rawlinson should have stressed them. It is more remarkable that Haig should even at this stage have forecast the end. His view was consistent with the prediction made in January by his Intelligence branch : "If Germany attacks and fails she will be ruined." But it was brave—Lloyd George would have said mad—to expect its speedy fulfilment at a time when the Germans had as yet lost scarcely a mile of their enormous territorial gains, when they still had upwards of fifty divisions in reserve, and when 1919 was without dispute regarded as the year of hope by the British, French and American Governments, and even by Haig's peer as an optimist, Generalissimo Foch.

Haig sent his proposals to Foch in a memorandum despatched on July 17th. He expressed disenchantment with the project, previously pressed by Foch, of attacking across "the flat and wet country" of Northern France and suggested instead "a combined French and British operation east and south-east of Amiens so as to disengage that town and the railway line". Two days later, that is on the 19th, an important local attack was made on Plumer's front to dissuade the Germans of Haig's disenchantment and gain a feature of equal value for attack and defence, the village of Meteren and its commanding ridge. The twice ravaged 9th Scottish Division were entrusted with the task and carried it out with great verve, Major-General Tudor rushing up on a bicycle to congratulate his men the moment success was reported.

It took Rawlinson only a day to submit his detailed proposals to Haig, and on the 21st he expounded them to his four corps commanders—Butler of III, Monash of the Australian, Currie of the Canadian, and Sir Charles Kavanagh of the Cavalry Corps—to his tank and air commanders, and to senior officers of his own headquarters. It was as much conference as order group, and Rawlinson's affable and so approachable nature provided the oil required for the smooth settlement of difficulties, the most important of which was the concealment of all preparations for the attack. From Monash we learn that "details were discussed at great length in the light of the views held by each corps commander" and he was himself well pleased with the concessions made to him. It was fortunate none the less that no spy lurking in the village of Flixécourt was able to detect and note the significance of the flag of Canada on the bonnet of one of the staff cars that passed up the main street on that sunlit afternoon.

Rawlinson had one request to make to Haig, bred from experience dating back to the first Battle of the Somme and certainly not weakened by recent events: that the French should have no share in the attack beyond allowing the British to extend their front. But Haig had already suggested a combined attack, and the idea appealed to Foch, who had long been contemplating an operation to regain Montdidier. Debeney took a step towards it on July 23rd and showed that there was some fight in his First Army. Making a surprise attack between Moreuil and Montdidier, he drove the Germans back over the Avre with aid from—but heavy casualties to—a battalion of British tanks.

It was finally settled that there should be a combined attack by the British Fourth and French First Armies when Foch held a conference on July 24th at Chateau Bombon, the new home of his expanding but still relatively miniature headquarters. This was the famous 'turning-point' attended by the three Commanders-in-Chief, at which Foch's Chief of Staff, General Weygand, read out a memorandum proclaiming that "The moment has come to abandon the general defensive attitude . . . and to pass to the offensive" and listing "a programme of offensive operations to be executed without delay". They aimed, however, at nothing more ambitious than the freeing of communication centres. According to Foch the response was not over-enthusiastic. Haig described the British Army as "far from re-established" and Pétain the French one as "worn out, bled white, anaemic". Both, no doubt, were wary of the schemes of the impetuous Generalissimo. Pershing said of the American Army that it "asks no better than to fight, but it has not yet been formed". This deficiency, borne so feelingly as the price paid for giving aid at the hour of need, could at last be remedied. Over a million American troops were now in France.

On the 26th Foch held another conference, this time at Sarcus, where he previously resided, and attended by Haig, Rawlinson, and Debeney. The plan of attack was discussed and its date agreed, August 10th. Then on the 28th Foch intervened again. He wanted the date advanced, to harry the German withdrawal from the Marne, and he asked Haig to take the French First Army under his command. This was the highest honour yet paid the British Commander-in-Chief by a Frenchman. Haig accepted and, in exchange for the return of his four divisions, agreed to advance the date and thus confer fame on August 8th.

11

SURPRISE COMPLETE

(August 1–8)

Neither side had yet succeeded in launching a great attack that caught the other entirely unawares. Plumer at Messines and Byng at Cambrai had gained surprise by using unexpected tactics, but in both cases the Germans had more than an inkling that an attack was in the offing. Similarly the Germans had stunned their opponents by the weight of their onslaughts in March, April and May, but had been unable to conceal their final preparations.

There had been no subtlety whatever about Rawlinson's previous attempt to turn the baffling key on that disastrous opening day, July 1st, 1916, although he had subsequently redeemed his reputation for deft generalship. He had a difficult problem now. Thousands of men and hundreds of machines had to be brought forward through the bottle-neck of Amiens without detection, and the time in which to complete their assembly had since July 28th been reduced by two days: sure cause of aggravation if not of confusion. But his headquarters contained many trusted men of great experience and with enthusiasm revived by the long break from operations and the subsequent reunion. There was the added spur of the possession of unrivalled material, the nine magnificent divisions of the Australian and Canadian Corps, battlewise, confident and unimpaired by the great losses nearly all the other divisions had suffered, and eleven battalions of the Tank Corps, equipped with new machines that they were itching to use. It is amazing that there should be such an abundant blend of experience and enthusiasm as the war entered its fifth year.

Conversely, there was no enthusiasm left in the ranks of the

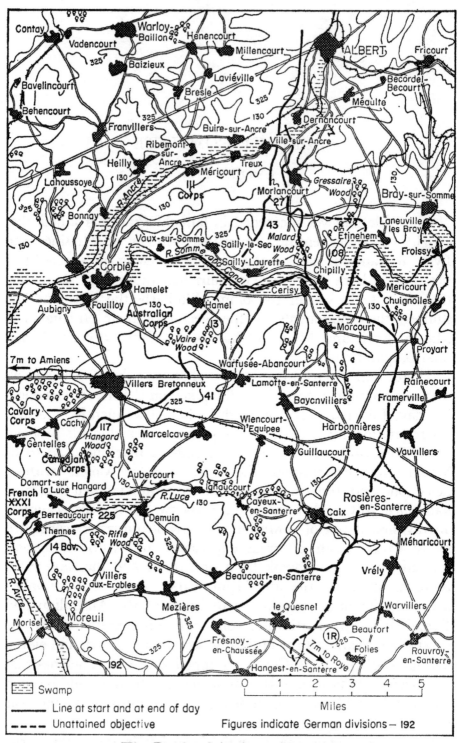

The Battle of Amiens, August 8

German Army, although it was still held together by a sullen streak of pride. While there were desertions in the front line and acts of mutiny in rear areas, the ordinary loyal German revealed his disillusion—perhaps too his lack of nourishment—in a strangely uncharacteristic, almost nonchalant, indolence. At staff level maps would be displayed showing elaborate fortifications, but all too often the work had been ordered and not carried out, and no one troubled to see that it was done. In the trenches, as the Australians had discovered, corpses lay unburied and latrine arrangements were ignored. A change had come over the once industrious Hun.

Rawlinson's primary task, as laid down by Foch, was merely "to disengege Amiens and the Paris-Amiens railway" and the objective assigned by Haig was a line of villages, which formed the old French front line, known as the Amiens defence line, at a maximum distance of seven miles from the existing front line. They ran across the great plain of Santerre from Mericourt, on the south bank of the Somme, to Hangest, a mile to the south of the Amiens-Roye road. This line was to be consolidated, and the British were then to "press the enemy in the direction of Chaulnes" while the French were similarly to press him in the direction of Roye. As a preliminary to the operation the British were to extend their line by some four miles to include the Amiens-Roye road, which was to be their right boundary. It will be noticed that this straight, poplar-lined, Napoleonic road ran aslant across the British and French sectors and would eventually have to be taken over by the French.

The Australians and the Canadians were to make the main assault, with the left flank of the former resting on the Somme and that of the latter on the railway line running east-south-east from Villers Bretonneux. Their objectives extended to some four miles into the German defences, and the Cavalry Corps were then to pass through and seize the remaining two or three miles as far as the old French front line, which they were to hold until relieved by the infantry of the two asault corps. III Corps, now on the left of the Fourth Army line, were to make a conforming advance north of the Somme, standing firm around Albert. The French XXXI Corps had a similar task on the right. They were to attack from across the Avre, capture Moreuil and in the process outflank the Montdidier defences.

The Australian and Canadian Corps were each to employ four divisions, with a separate allotment for their first and second objectives, and in reserve, further back, the Australians could call on their 1st Division, due at last to be returned by the Second Army, and the Canadians on the British 32nd Division, also from Second Army and held back under G.H.Q. control. Each of these two corps were allotted a brigade of four battalions of tanks, consisting of 108 Mark Vs, thirty-six Mark V Stars (a longer tank capable of crossing wider obstacles and carrying infantry Lewis-gun teams) and twenty-four carrying tanks, the much appreciated servants either of the infantry or fighting tanks; the total therefore being 168 tanks per corps. The Australians also had a battalion of armoured cars. The Cavalry Corps consisted of three cavalry divisions, nine mounted regiments in each, and had an allotment of two battalions of Whippet tanks, forty-eight in each. The other (eleventh) battalion of tanks was allotted to III Corps and was armed with Mark Vs. The Australian and Canadian Corps also had a combined allotment of 490 guns, ranging from 8-inch howitzers to 60-pounder guns, in addition to the standard forty-eight guns with each division; bringing their total to 922. All this—artillery, tanks, the men and horses of eight infantry and three cavalry divisions, and the mighty stock of ammunition they needed—had to be squeezed into the triangle east of Amiens formed by the Somme, the front line and the Avre, each arm measuring some six or seven miles. There was no great scope for concealment on these rolling uplands. Much of the ground was under direct observation from the enemy-held hills south of the Luce, and in the ground dead to their vision activity sent out its warning message by the dust cloud it produced. If von der Marwitz could deduce what was afoot it would be easy for him to scotch the offensive as it had been for General Gouraud and his French Fourth Army on July 15th.

To achieve his great design Rawlinson concocted a nicely balanced blend of bluff and secrecy well in keeping with the reputation that had long ago won him the epithet of fox. There were two complementary sides to the bluff. One was to transmit indications that the Canadian Corps, whose movements were such an obvious guide to Haig's offensive intentions, had been transferred to the Second Army for an attack on the objective that the British could be presumed to covet the most dearly, Mount Kemmel. To this end two Canadian battalions were actually put in the line in this sector; the corps wireless link opened up behind them and two casualty-clearing stations arrived in the administrative area, that favourite hunting ground of spies. None of the men had any notion that their function was illusory, and their movement was enshrouded by sufficient secrecy to make it convincing. The Royal Air Force also made contribution to the great pretence, both by activity over Kemmel and the construction of dummy airfields.

The other side of the bluff concerned the extension of the Fourth Army line as far as the Amiens-Roye road. This was the sector on which the Canadians were to attack and it might have been feasible to have kept the French in the line until the attack. Rawlinson chose instead to side-step the Australians. They were relieved of their remaining commitments north of the Somme by III Corps before dawn on August 1st, and by dawn next morning a single Australian brigade had taken over the twisting four miles of trenches held by the French south of Villers Breton-neux. There was a plausible enough reason for this awaiting deduction by German Intelligence. The French were still heavily involved in eliminating the bulge to the Marne and would obviously want the British to relieve them of commitments elsewhere. The knowledge that the Australians were being employed on this apparently defensive task could bring nothing but comfort to the German mind concerned with larger issues than front-line skirmishing; and as a form of insurance the rumour was deliberately put into circulation, on the first clandestine appearance of a Canadian around Amiens, that after their great endeavours on this sector the Australians were at last to be relieved for a rest.

The attainment of secrecy, the twin of overt deception, depended very largely on the energy of the staffs and the discipline of the troops involved. In Major-General Montgomery, his Chief of General Staff, and Major-General H. C. Holman, his administrative chief, Rawlinson had two zealots for detailed

planning, and they proved themselves equal to the gigantic task
of feeding the loads of almost 300 special trains filled with troops,
guns and ammunition, together with endless road convoys, into
their battle positions without detection. Practically all movements
were made at night and delayed as long as possible to reduce
to the minimum the time spent in assembly areas. The last nights
had therefore to be the busiest, straining to the limit the traffic
capacity of the three routes available to the Australians and
Canadians. As noise reducers, roads were strewn with sand or
straw and wheels were wound with rope or sacking, and it was
successfully impressed on every man that he had a part to play
as important as that of the planners, a part demanding wariness
and patience. It was an undoubted aid to this great feat of
organisation that the troops themselves were successfully inspired,
however hardened, with that sense of occasion preluding great
happenings. Other, more easily visible aids took the form of a
spell of cloudy weather, which much hampered aerial reconnaissance, and lay in the fact that Amiens had for several months
been emptied of its inhabitants by order of the French Government, with consequent loss of opportunity for German spies.

As for Rawlinson's air arm, this had been increased to 800
planes, divided into eight squadrons of fighters, three of bombers
and six for close co-operation work. It was a mighty array, which
posed its own problems in the matter of airfield concealment.

Before handing over their sector north of the Somme on the
night of July 31st/August 1st, the 5th Australian Division
achieved one further exploit of 'peaceful penetration', driving
the enemy back some 500 yards by boldly sneaking into his
trenches at various points. This was fine, but it complicated the
problems of the relieving units, since the line was not clearly
charted, haphazardly overlapped German positions and in places
was unfortified. Two divisions, earmarked for the attack on the
8th, were due to come in here, and just as Butler's III Corps
was the only survivor of the Fifth Army still with the Fourth,
so these two were the only surviving divisions, and they were to
hold the same position on the corps front as on March 21st, the
58th London on the extreme right, the 18th Eastern on their left.

These two hard-wearing divisions had had a fortnight out of
the line to freshen them up for the coming battle. But they were

far from fully trained. Few battalions had more than two or three officers with experience of an offensive—and like as not it had been a hideous one gained in the sludge around Poelcapelle or on the shell-tossed wastes so near to their present location by the Somme. The majority of the men were young and raw, with some rough knowledge of battlecraft gleaned from being plunged straight into the line. In the rush for reinforcements many had joined battalions that had no connection whatever with their parent regiments, in violation of a system that had once been conscientiously maintained. The 7th Buffs (East Kent Regiment) of 18 Division, for instance, had received a large draft of North Countrymen, most of them miners. Yet the system was strong enough to withstand such shocks. Battalions, and divisions too, had their traditions and their individual forms of asprit de corps, and 'foreigners' quickly became as proud of 'our mob' as the veteran who had won the same cap badge all his service. Such were the intangible threads of loyalty that sustained these divisions from buffeting to buffeting.

Also in III Corps, by strange coincidence, were sister divisions of both the 58th and 18th. The 47th London, composed of first line Territorial battalions, held the slopes behind Albert, near where their retreat from the Flesquières salient had ended. The 12th Eastern, most of whose battalions, like those of the 18th, were from regiments south of London, stood between the 47th and 18th. They had been instrumental in stopping the Germans at Albert and had escaped crippling loss, but had been hard-used all the same. Bell's 33rd American Division were also in this corps. They had graduated beyond the kindergarten stage of being split by platoons among their teachers, as in the Hamel battle, and were now held in reserve, ready to put complete regiments into battle but not yet equipped with their own artillery and other components required for a divisional battle. It was heartening for the British to have these grave and ardent troops in their midst, and the deference paid them by the Americans was both flattering and challenging.

On August 4th Ludendorff issued an order of the day, which began : "I am under the impression that, in many quarters, the possibility of an enemy offensive is viewed with a certain degree of apprehension. There is nothing to justify this apprehension,

163

provided our troops are vigilant and do their duty." As if in immediate compliance with this instruction a raid was made that very night on a post in the line south of Villers Bretonneux, just taken over from the French by the 13th Australian Brigade and very thinly held. The five occupants of the post were captured. It suited Rawlinson's purpose well enough that the Germans should know that the Australians were there, but there was none the less considerable anxiety as to what these men might tell their captors. It proved in the event to be unfounded: the Australians were so reticent that their behaviour was extolled as a model for prisoners by German Intelligence.

A night later there was a bigger and altogether more disturbing scare. On this night the 58th Division came into the line by the Somme, taking over from a brigade of the 18th who in turn were to relieve another brigade of their own division as a prelude to the attack. This second relief had just begun when, in the early hours of the 6th, a ferocious bombardment fell upon the tired and fretting men of these divisions as they peered around their shallow trenches or laboured along them through the all too familiar mud brought into being by recent rainfall. The bombardment lifted, and through the pre-dawn gloom came waves of determined attackers, spread over a frontage of 4,000 yards split between that of the 58th and 18th Division. With the lines to their guns cut, Londoners, Bedfordshires, Northamptonshires and East Surreys fell fighting, submitted, or dodged back as best they could. Soon the Germans had entered a quarry where a great battle headquarters was under construction for the 8th. A brisk counter-attack drove them out, but they retained gains to a depth of half a mile, with abundant ammunition all round them providing clues to what was being planned. Over two hundred men of the two British divisions were meanwhile being chivvied back towards the German lines, stunned by the suddenness of it all. Their captors belonged to the 27th Wurtemberg Division, a storm division of some distinction refreshed by a three months' rest from the line and intensive training for this task of reprisal (as they imagined) against the insolent Australians.

Strict orders had been issued in III Corps witholding knowledge of the coming attack from all but a few selected officers below the level of battalion commander, and although there had been dumping of ammunition the guns had not yet been brought to their forward positions for the attack. None the less there were a number of gunners among the prisoners, who would normally have had no business so near the front line, and it was suspicious, too, that men of two divisions should be found in a sector previously occupied by one. Inevitably most of the prisoners were aware that something was afoot. . . . But the preparations were allowed to go on unimpeded, and when German accounts were published it was confirmed that not a word had been said about any coming attack.

By daybreak on Wednesday, August 7th, the main assault force was fully assembled within two or three miles of the enemy lines. Many trench lines had been dug by the Australians, as indication to the enemy of their preoccupation with the defence of Amiens, and these were now crammed with the infantry of four divisions, with those with the furthest objectives nearest the front line. Three Canadian divisions had during the night marched forward to occupy trenches vacated by the French close behind the Australian brigade holding their line, and a fourth was further back, out of observation by the enemy. The tanks had meanwhile been gradually fed into copses or ruined farm houses two to three miles behind the line, their movement being synchronised with raids by Handley Page bombers made an hour before dawn as a matter of routine, and with the coming of daylight reconnaissance aircraft of the R.A.F. made their routine flights to check on the camouflage arrangements of the new arrivals, tanks, infantry and guns. Just as close a watch was kept over the enemy, especially his gun lines. Counter-battery officers noted many changes of position, but fire was still directed on the old, empty positions as a further refinement in the art of 'foxing Fritz'.

The scene around Villers Bretonneux on this eve of battle seemed weirdly quiet and deserted. Monash had even forbidden reconnaissances, telling his officers to rely on excellent air photographs in place of inspecting the ground, and when he made his final inspection of the forward area he was glad to see no sign of life. In his own words, "It was only when the explosion of a stray enemy shell would cause hundreds of heads to peer out from trenches, gun-pits, and underground shelters, that one became aware that the whole country was really packed thick with a teeming population carefully hidden away." But across the river there was activity enough. The 18th Division, with some but not complete success, were bombing the Wurtem-burgers back from the positions they had won the previous day. In the afternoon the Australians had a sudden, literal flare-up in their midst. A chance shell hit a carrying tank laden with petrol on the slopes behind Villers Bretonneux and the resultant smoke drew a deluge of shells which destroyed a further fourteen of these tanks and their valuable loads, making an enormous blaze. Many finger-nails were bitten in anticipation of an extension of this so fruitful bombardment.

But quiet returned, and when darkness fell the final movements were made undisturbed. In Amiens there was a continual, muffled 'clip-clop-clip' as the three divisions of cavalry—containing all but five of the twenty-eight regular regiments of the Cavalry of the Line—marched eastward along the sand-strewn road to assemble alongside their Whippet tanks and rows of guns stripped of their camouflage garnets for action. Further eastwards patrols crept out of the trenches to cover the forming up in no-man's land. They were followed by officers carrying rolls of white tape which they spread into rectangles facing the enemy lines and some 200 yards from them at the nearest. Then came the guides, each to be shown the tape line for his company, and finally the assault troops, grouped in ten phalanxes spread across ten miles of frontage but with each man visible through the pitch darkness only to those within a few yards of him and feeling naked and lone. In silence so tense that every clink or gulp sounded like a bang, the men sunk to the ground alongside their tapes and tried to suppress that chill shiver within them by thoughts of practical things of the positioning of the rifle, the fixity of bayonet, the accessibility of the two grenades and the 150 rounds of ammunition strewn around waist and chest, or by more baleful thoughts of all the other things they carried, sandbags, shaving gear, iron rations, field dressing, mess tin, ground sheet, entrenching tool and water bottle (or if an Australian, two water bottles).

Each phalanx consisted of a brigade. The battalions lay side

by side at a depth of four waves, a company in each, and ammunition carriers and stretcher bearers formed a fifth wave, the
whole phalanx forming a square about 400 yards wide and deep.
Tapes were laid out behind them for the guidance of the tanks,
and at around 2 a.m. the familiar drone of aircraft was heard
overhead. It was made by a single Handley Page bomber, which
flew to and fro for three hours, for thick mist made it too
hazardous to send up more aircraft; but the sound of tank and
bomber was very similar and the approach of the one merely
seemed to increase the volume of the other. At 4.20 a.m., as the
faintest glimmer in the east signalled the approach of dawn, the
sky was lit as by sheet lightning to a distance of six miles on
either side of Amiens and the missiles from 3,532 British and
French guns (of which 1,500 were medium or heavy) screeched
into the German positions to announce the start of what was to
be named by the British the Battle of Amiens and more dramatically tagged by Ludendorff the Black Day of the German
Army.

The opening was an enlargement, almost exact, of the Hamel
model. After only three minutes on the forward line the barrage
made a lift of a hundred yards and the men of seven divisions
of the Fourth Army—three Canadian, two Australian, and two
British—fell upon those of six German divisions, all of Marwitz's
Second Army, from just beyond the Luce on the right to the
ridge north of the Somme on the left, a distance of ten miles
without taking every curve into acount. Another three divisions,
one Canadian and two Australian, waited to pass through, and
although the Germans had six divisions in reserve within a three-
hour march of the final Allied objective they had none in immediate support of the forward divisions, which were sited in depth
on the three-tier system. The French meanwhile prepared to
assault two German divisions with six, a much more conventional ratio. Marwitz's divisions were weak in numbers and
morale, but were well supplied with artillery, machine-guns, and
anti-tank weapons. Theoretically, they had every chance of with-
standing the British Fourth Army's assault, being outnumbered
by only ten to six. Nor should the Fourth Army's preponderance
in tanks have given them crushing advantage, although the total
available to them was 435. Their task was infantry support, not

massed attack on the Cambrai model, which had relied on surprise for its effect and been proved vulnerable to coolly applied gunfire. Rawlinson based his plans on the distribution of six tanks across every 1,000 yards on his main front of attack, and when sub-allotted for the two phases this was the rough capacity of the four battalions (each of thirty-six fighting tanks) with each of the two corps attacking with four divisions on a frontage of four miles and to a depth of four miles plus. The tanks could hardly be expected, on this basis, to achieve shock results against a well-organised defence.

Yet their impact was devastating, for despite their experience at Hamel the Germans were taken completely by surprise and once again, by extraordinary coincidence, there was a thick layer of ground mist. This upset plans for infantry and tank cooperation, and indeed some tanks strayed hopelessly off course, but it blinded the German gunners and made the noise and sudden apparition of the lurching, belching monsters more terrifying than would otherwise have been the case. Just as devastating, and without debt to the mist, was the mighty, paralysing strike of shells falling alike on infantry, field gunners, heavy gunners and headquarters staffs, hitting targets that the Germans imagined to be concealed and landing at a density for which they had no notion that their enemies had either the guns or ammunition. Major-General C. E. D. Budworth, Rawlinson's artillery chief, proved himself this day the match of Bruckmüller. It was a triumph for the industry he inspired that so many pieces should be assembled unnoticed and a triumph of craftsmanship that registration of targets could either be concealed or else completely dispensed with, thanks to the careful calibration of every individual gun on the ranges. It was also a triumph of allied co-operation, in particular for the co-ordination achieved by Haig's staff, that the French contribution should be as effective and unsuspected as the British.

The Australians, as so often, had the easiest passage. Their assault waves crept up so close behind the barrage that they were through the wire and upon their foe the moment it lifted. Every three minutes the process was repeated, with the line of shell bursts, straight and even across the well-cropped plateau, dropping back a hundred yards and a fresh wave of cheering men rushing in at once, closely attended by their rumbling, lumbering tanks, looming out of the mist like ghosts. Here and there machine-gun posts, sited in depth, gave trouble, but none survived long against the deadly combination of bayonet, grenade, bullet and iron. A group of four guns, well wired-in with a complete company to protect them south of the main Roman road, submitted to a solo assault by Lieutenant A. E. Gaby, of the 28th Battalion, who alone could find a gap through the wire. The fact that he (who was killed displaying similar valour three days later) was the only Australian to win the V.C. on this famous day bespeaks the shortage of opportunity that came the way of the others.

Well before 7 a.m. the two assault divisions, the 2nd on the right and the 3rd on the left, had advanced the two miles to their objective and were spread along a four-mile line from the railway line to the Somme. Just behind them was the valley containing the joint villages of Warfusée-Lamotte, along which the Germans had made their alarming penetration on March 27th. A stroll through the mist and smoke that now clogged this valley would have revealed many guns pointing towards the British lines or tilted in weird contortion. The crews of some were sprawled around them, slain by Budsworth's guns, while those of others had been retrieved alive, often in their gas masks, and shepherded along to the villages to swell the columns of bemused Germans, some in pyjamas under their greatcoats, awaiting permission to march further into France. On the other side of the railway similar scenes were being enacted around Marcelcave, with the look of bemusement on the more intelligent German face made the starker by the realisation that their captors were Canadian.

For news of the progress of his men Monash had to rely on the pigeons that came homing back to their bus-lofts from the forward headquarters, on reports dropped with streamers from reconnaissance aircraft—an effective system once (but not until) the mist had lifted—or on news from staff officers who ventured forth on horseback or motor-bike. It was a slow process building up information in this manner—lamp signal, the quickest means, could of course not yet be used—but the columns of prisoners marching back, often with no escort but wounded in need of their assistance, and the remarkable scarcity of hostile shelling conveyed a reassuring message. Preparations for the next phase went ahead long before the full success of the first was confirmed. Gun teams cantered up and snatched away the artillery of the 4th and 5th Australian Divisions the moment they had completed their part in the programme that nursed the 2nd and 3rd Divisions on to their objectives, engineers helped to bring forward the tanks of these two divisions, and a whole battalion of pioneers set to work on bridging the trenches astride the main St. Quentin road and removing fallen trees so that the armoured cars could pass through.

The two follow-up divisions crossed their start-line punctually to schedule, that is at 8.20, and as they did so the mist began to disperse under the heat of the August sun. It was the sort of scene of which generals had been dreaming ever since 1914. Ahead went a long line of lithe skirmishers, unpresaged by any barrage. Tanks were liberally distributed among them, some of the first lot joining the second, and there were more infantry behind them, spread wide and deep in their section groups, followed by field guns fully limbered, ready to drop trails into action on call, and overlapping the gunners, spread between the railway and the road, came files of cavalry, jingling, expectant, tossing, and bobbing in and out of dips, trenches and shell holes.

The 5th Australian Division marched on the right and the 4th on the left, the latter with a brigade of the 1st Division in place of their 13th Brigade, who had held the line for the Canadians. They had more than half the tanks, forty-two being allotted each division, with others released after duty for phase one. The 4th Division made the slower progress, for they had to comb the loops, re-entrants, and catacombed embankment by the Somme. The 5th could fan out across flat, unhedged fields of corn or roots, broken a mile ahead by an island of trees surrounding the village of Bayonvillers. There were some ferocious whizz-bangs as they topped the rise out of the valley beyond the start-line. Three batteries of field guns and howitzers had opened up point-blank between the main road and railway. The tanks and infantry went bald-headed at them, and soon the gun crews, such as survived, were being booted back along with the many other little queues of Germans that kept emerging from various warrens, but eight tanks had been set ablaze or otherwise disabled. None the less the tanks now drew ahead of the infantry, blasting out machine-gun nests here and there, and although three more were knocked out before the men of a battery by Bayonvillers were bolted, the main impediment was the shells from Budworth's heavy guns, which instead of speeding the retreat were now slowing the advance, so far had progress exceeded expectation.

Soon after 9 a.m. the cavalry made their first effective intervention in the rôle for which their horses had for years been provided with bountiful keep, at the cost of such effort in terms of supply and transportation. The honour fell to a squadron of the Queen's Bays, of the 1st Cavalry Brigade. With the flash of their sabres making strange contrast with the squat inelegance of their steel helmets, they swung right-handed past the tanks and infantrymen that had surrounded Bayonvillers and, undaunted by the forbidding crackle of bullets, swept down upon a column of transport trying to escape to the south. It was captured complete. The Bays now tried to enter Harbonnières, two miles on from Bayonvillers, but reserves had been mustered to hold it; the Bays were forced to take cover and the Whippet tanks that came to their aid were also held up. The Australians eventually forced an entry and flew the Dominion flag from the church tower, but before they did so a squadron of the 5th Dragoon Guards galloped past the northern side of the village and became the first to reach the final objective, the Amiens defence line. The time was 10 a.m. and the penetration one of six miles in five hours and forty minutes, surely a record for the Great War. And as the 5th took occupation of the empty, overgrown trenches and sent troopers out to gather in prisoners like sheep, they noticed a column of smoke coming from a train half a mile further on. Two squadrons rode off and gained possession of two trains, both of which had been wrecked by the R.A.F., and three more batteries of guns. One of these trains had just arrived with 600 leave details or reinforcements on board, who were all captured or killed, and the other contained an 11-inch railway gun, used for bombarding Amiens, whose crew had been wiped out by a bomb in the act of firing.

Before these adventures of the 5th were over, cars of the 12th

Armoured Car Battalion came humming along the main road, further to the north, after tanks had removed the final obstacles blocking their route. There were twelve (or sixteen, versions differ) of them, each capable of 20 m.p.h. either backwards or forwards, and mounted with two tall turrets, each of which contained a Hotchkiss machine-gun. They had a glorious time. In a valley short of the final infantry objective, running towards the Somme, they put to flight or death a mass of Germans trying to contend with Australians approaching them from the other flank. They then went on beyond the final line and split into three. One section went northwards and shot up headquarter men sitting at their dinner in the village of Proyart and caught others in their billets in Chuignolles. One section travelled a further four miles up the main road, shot up dumps, sent back prisoners and had a fight with some guns at Foucaucourt, in which one car was lost. The third section went southwards to Framerville, which contained the headquarters of a German corps, whose commander made his getaway just in time. In the words of the commanding officer, Lieutenant-Colonel E. J. Carter, "They found all the Boche horse transport and many lorries drawn up in the main road ready to move off. Head of column tried to bolt in one direction and other vehicles in another. Complete confusion. Our men killed the lot (using 3,000 rounds) and left them there; four staff officers on horseback shot also. The cars then ran down to the east side of Harbonnières . . . and met there a number of steam wagons; fired into their boilers causing an impassable block." Like most of the others, the Colonel's car broke down before the day's excitements were over. He was towed homewards across the Amiens line by prisoners he had taken.

For another raider there was a different ending. The commander of a Whippet tank, Lieutenant C. B. Arnold, had such good shooting into German columns clearing off beyond Harbonnières that he drew far ahead of his comrades, both tanks and cavalry. Eventually, having caused horrific destruction, his tank was set on fire. One of his crew was killed and he and the other had to run through blazing grass and roll to extinguish flames on themselves. Then the Germans arrived, and Arnold was bayoneted through the arm, knocked out by a rifle butt and jerked back to consciousness again by multiple, brutal blows from the boots of raving Huns.

Alone of the Australian divisions, the 4th suffered some tribulation on this great day of elation. They had the amusement of flushing many stragglers from the dug-outs along the embankment by the Somme and the thrill of unearthing a good haul of loot. But in a tough fight for Cerisy and the next little riverside village, Morcourt, they came under unpleasantly hot fire from the Chipilly spur, that long, steep-sided intruder from the northern side of the river in between two lower spurs on the south side. Six tanks were among the casualties suffered in securing these villages and instead of going on to his final objective, the village of Mericourt, on the far side of the spur, Major-General E. G. Sinclair-Maclagan, the divisional commander, halted his men on the high ground above it and formed a defensive flank.

Possession of this spur had enabled the Germans to force Gough's army into painful contortion on March 27th–28th, and once again the men on the south bank could lay the blame for their plight on failure by their comrades on the other side. Chipilly spur was the final objective of the 58th Division. A report had reached the Australians that it had been captured and there can be no doubt that some rude things were said about the 58th Division, maybe of British soldiers in general, when realisation came, in most damaging form, that the report was not true. None the less the Londoners had come the better part of two miles, which at the start of most offensives would be regarded as a triumph.

It had not been so easy for the assault brigades of III Corps, quite apart from the fact that neither their recent experiences nor their innate characteristics kindled inside them the fire that made the 'Colonials'—the volunteer soldiers of the new-born nations of Canada and Australia—such irresistible attackers in this year of ebbing strength and spirit, 1918. The German attack on August 6th enforced hasty revision of plan, which included the summoning of a brigade of the 12th Division to take the place of the worst hit one of the 18th, and it also showed sensitivity to intrusion in this area which was in sharp contrast with the reaction to the Hamel attack a month earlier. Furthermore, the allotment of only one battalion of tanks to the whole corps stressed the subsidiary nature of the part assigned the British infantry and gave them the status of poor relations.

The Germans gave further display of their sensitivity by plastering the assembly and rear areas with high explosive and gas shells all through the night preceding the attack, and there were, in fact, as many Germans waiting for the attack to come in, in anticipation of a resumption of the counter-attack begun on the 7th, as there were British forming up to make it. However, the sudden bombardment at 4.20 had devastating effect, especially on the German batteries crowding the wooded valleys by the Somme, and the six London or Home Counties battalions that made the initial assault successfully groped through the mist in their gas masks to evict the Germans from their newly won trenches and make many of them prisoner, even though few of their tanks managed to reach their rendezvous. While one battalion of Londoners hounded the Germans out the village of Sailly-Laurette by the swamps of the Somme, a brigade of them followed the advance of the barrage over dales and ridges as far as the Corps' first objective, more than a mile and a half from their start-line, leaving many posts behind them to be mopped up. On their left the 9th Royal Fusiliers and 7th Royal Sussex of 12 Division, hastily briefed and gassed in transit, found the going tough once they had recaptured the recently lost trenches, and the 10th Essex, of 18 Division, had to be prematurely committed to secure the first objective, which lay on the road to Bray.

Yet further left the 7th Queen's, who had the task of securing a defensive flank overlooking Morlancourt, ran into swarms of determined Wurtembergers and were counter-attacked with stick grenades. There was grim grappling in the mist, with the tanks astray and the barrage receding, and as he sauntered above the trench line bringing cheer to his men and shepherding a tank to their aid, Lieutenant-Colonel Bushell, that hero of March 23rd, fell shot through the neck. His runner dragged him to shelter but could not save his life. A beacon of courage, which provided light for the entire division, had been snuffed out, to become just another corpse. The calm, indestructible Ransome of the 7th Buffs was called upon to "clear up the situation", a task in which he was well practised. Amazingly, he fought in every big battle (with the exception of Loos) from Mons to the Armistice, never further from danger than brigade headquarters, and the Germans did not hit him once.

It was in the second phase that the plans of III Corps began to go seriously awry. A fresh brigade of Londoners passed through to capture Chipilly spur, but they had to make a steep descent, followed by an even steeper ascent, and could not keep up with their barrage. Machine-guns ripped them, fired by men of a division, the 108th, which was in process of relieving the one in the line, the 43rd. Even so, airmen reported that British troops were on the spur. This served both to anger the Australians and impede further attempts. The unfortunate 2nd/2nd London, sent in as first reserve, were deprived of the bombardment hastily planned for them, only to be mown down by a hail of bullets from the village and slopes said to be held by their comrades. The reserve brigade, summoned for an attempt at dusk, also failed, largely because their barrage fell almost a mile too far ahead.

As for the 18th Division, the remnant of the 10th Essex, less than a hundred strong, advanced 1,000 yards towards the second objective in weird isolation, and when suddenly the mist lifted they captured the crews of two German batteries taking their ease on the edge of Gressaire Wood. A company of the 7th Royal West Kent joined them with two tanks, but the Germans brought reinforcements to the scene in much larger number and forced the disjointed groups of the 18th Division back through the trampled cornfields to their first objective in mounting haste. Probably the divisions of III Corps would have fared better if they had had a longer pause on the first objective, in order to mop up many little pockets of resistance and marshal men and tanks for a better co-ordinated assault. There were problems in this sudden switch from defensive to offensive beyond the experience of junior commanders and most of the staff, and in this instance they were made all the more acute by the unexpected activity of the enemy.

On the Australians' other flank the Canadians were also confronted with tougher problems than they were themselves. As one example, they had to attack over unfamiliar ground with cramping restrictions on reconnaissance, both as regards time and movement; as another, their front line contained many awkward bends and salients; and as a third, they had the obstacle of the Luce stream and its swampy water-cress bed, which was just within their front line on the right and from there ran obliquely across their line of advance. But there was no shortage of experience here. In no other army had such a corps of four crack divisions been preserved unblemished all through the tumultuous months of the German offensive.

Sir Arthur Currie, their big, well-built commander, whose military bearing belied his civilian background, was not able to make his plan as simple and symmetrical as Monash's. South of the railway line, where the country was open save for the occasional wood or village, he put in two divisions, the 1st (on the right) and the 2nd, each to advance on a frontage of one brigade with the other two brigades ready to leap-frog through on the capture of successive objectives. On their right the 3rd Division had a more complicated task. Their objectives included the oft-disputed ruins of Hangard on the north bank of the Luce, the orchard-screened village of Demuin on the south bank a mile further east, and most important of all the high ground south-west of Demuin, across which ran the road to Roye. This was the hill for which the 20th Light Division had fought so bravely at the end of March, and the little wood on its forward slope and on the right of the road (as viewed by the Canadians) had retained the name of Rifle Wood. It dominated the valley of the Luce and the country far beyond.

The sector taken over from the French south of the Luce extended only half a mile on either side of the Roye road and was little more than a hundred yards deep. Yet into it were squeezed an assault brigade—and there were still four battalions to a brigade in the Canadian and Australian Corps—together with a company of fourteen tanks. By courtesy of the French the latter came in from the right flank over a bridge in their sector, for though the main road bridge was intact it was noisy to cross and a certain target for defensive fire. This daring feat of assembly was successfully accomplished, except for the ditching of those of the tanks, and when the barrage smote the hill at 4.20 the 43rd (Manitoba) Battalion crept close to it to assault the hill from the north-west, where the curves of the slope gave best shelter for their approach, while two other battalions followed the course of the poplar-lined river-bed eastwards, the one to loop right-handed round the other shoulder of the hill, the other to assault Demuin. The tanks merely blundered towards the falling shells through mist that was at its thickest here in the Luce valley.

It was an intricate manoeuvre skilfully executed, and though the Germans of the 225th Division fought well, especially the machine-gunners, there could be no stopping these tough and seasoned Canadians and they were soon on the edge of Rifle Wood. Meanwhile a thunderous bombardment rocked the broad spur on their right, on the top of which were the wizened trees of Moreuil Wood. At 5.5 a.m.—that is after forty-five minutes—the fire lifted from the German front line and in came two divisions of Frenchmen on a frontage of a mere two miles. Debeney required the longer bombardment because he was not employing tanks, except for two battalions of light Renaults with a follow-up rôle, and it was a nasty blow to von der Marwitz to hear of this extension of the assault just as the reserves of the divisions here had been ordered to the aid of their tottering partners on their right. With greater weight of heavy artillery than the British, the French made good initial progress, although always lagging behind the Canadians. A third division of their XXXI Corps came across the Luce to join the others for the assault on Moreuil Wood and a fourth, coming in at right angles, crossed the Avre and set about combing the ruins of Moreuil. Later the frontage was further widened when two more divisions, one of them colonial, attacked across the Avre south of Moreuil. Haig, visiting Debeney, found him "almost in tears because three battalions of his Colonial Infantry had bolted before a German machine-gun", but though the British had made the running they had no cause for the complaints of apathy and lack of co-operation on the part of their allies that had been so rife in this area for the greater part of the year.

The Canadians meanwhile were enjoying almost, but not quite, as successful a day as the Australians. They put rather more tanks into the initial assault, thirty-six with the 3rd Division, twenty-one with the 1st and seventeen with the 2nd, and their fortunes were roughly proportionate to their distance from the Luce. Of the twenty-eight that crossed the river, fourteen of them over the main road bridge as soon as the leading company had gone on, eight were knocked out by gunfire and eight fell prey to accidents. One tank, topping the mist-clad hill beyond Rifle Wood, was blasted by a 5.9-inch howitzer at fifteen yards range, with the destruction of both tank and howitzer and of their two crews. On the more open ground north of the river the tanks forged ahead of the infantry and sowed great terror, but in the mist they by-passed a number of machine-gun nests that were fought very pluckily, specially in Hangard Wood and copses beyond, where the battle ranged over a great depth. Two V.C.s were won here by men of the 13th (Royal Highlanders) Battalion of the 1st Division, Corporal H. J. Good and Private J. B. Croak, whose separate acts of heroism wrested no less than seven troublesome machine-guns and three howitzers from the enemy, at the cost of Croak's life. There was also stiff resistance in Demuin, and here three amazing feats of single-handed assault, undaunted by a bad wound received earlier, won a posthumous V.C. for Corporal H. G. B. Miner of the 58th (Ontario) Battalion of the 3rd Division. Later on, Lieutenant J. E. Tait, 78th Nova Scotia Highlanders of the 4th Division (who was subsequently killed), won the Canadians their fourth V.C. of the day, sure indication not only of the tremendous spirit of the attackers but of the stubbornness of the defenders too.

By 11 a.m. the follow-up brigades of the three divisions had all gained their second objectives, or red line, and their men were preparing defensive positions, chivvying Germans out of dug-outs, inspecting items of captured equipment, looking around for loot, patching up wounded friend or foe or merely basking in the sunlight that had replaced the mist and watching the aeroplanes stream overhead on their way to harry the assembly of von der Marwitz's reserves. On the right Brutinel's Independent Force of motorised machine-gunners and cyclists had come roaring up the Roye road and taken up position to protect the right flank and help the French forward. Across the downs to their left the Canadian Cavalry Brigade, of Harman's 3rd Cavalry Division, were trotting past corpse-strewn gun lines, disabled tanks and their own waving infantry, and behind them came the 4th Canadian Division, marching along in extended formation to come through and take the final objective over from the cavalry, seven miles beyond the bridge over the Luce. The cavalrymen cantered on past the forward line into glorious open country, with Whippet tanks following, outpaced. Squadrons fanned out and one clattered into the village of Beaucourt to catch 300 Germans in the act of marching off, but horses and men were sent reeling by hot fire when they tried to advance beyond the village. It came from Beaucourt Wood, two miles short of the final objective, and there were found to be too many field guns and machine-guns for the cavalry and light tanks to quell on their own.

On the extreme left there was no such impediment. Perhaps an hour after the 5th Dragoon Guards had gone through past the Australians on the other side of the railway, it was the turn of the 15th Hussars, with the 19th coming up on their right flank, to make a glorious dash past cheering Canadians in Guillacourt. The two great waves of horsemen, each 300-400 strong, galloped for over a mile past cowering Germans, crumpled guns and tempting items of loot. Bullets and shells made some horses overturn and some riders sway helplessly, but the great majority reached the fringe of the old trench line, where three troopers out of four leapt off, seized their rifles from their 'buckets', and jumped into the shaggy trenches, having driven out a few Germans here and there. The horses meanwhile were trotted back to find cover in a friendly dip. Intermittent shelling caused the Hussars some casualties as they waited for the Canadian infantry to relieve them, and patrols that tried to enter the straggly village of Rosières, over a mile further on, were stopped by machine-gun fire. Elsewhere large numbers of Germans were to be seen drifting back. The cavalrymen merely sped them on their way with bullets and laughed at the vain efforts made by German officers to bring their men back.

In the centre of the Canadian front the 7th Dragoon Guards fought a furious battle in the wood beyond Cayeux. Many of their horses were felled by machine-gun fire, but by combining mounted and dismounted tactics the regiment hacked their way through the wood, cursing the Whippets—which could scarcely keep pace with a man across country, far less a horse—for not

179

being there to help them but emerging triumphant with twelve machine-guns and a battery of guns yielded to their sabres. There were still two miles to be crossed to the old trench line on this sector, up slopes amid which the village of Caix nestled, but the course was now clear and other members of the 1st and 3rd Cavalry Divisions rode up to take possession with only a few horses roaming wild-eyed and riderless among them or cast in helpless, pathetic convulsions behind.

Further to the right, where the Canadian cavalrymen had been checked, the way was still barred. the 1st Reserve Division, of von Hutier's Eighteenth Army, had come forward from the direction of Roye and occupied two villages astride the main road, Fresnoy on the south side, which the Canadian cavalry had previously found empty, and on the north the larger Le Quesnel, which was behind Beaucourt Wood within the final Canadian objective. The 4th Canadian Division arrived and deployed thirty Mark V Star tanks, each containing three detachments of infantry Lewis-gunners who sat in the most stifling part of the interior and had no cause to enjoy this early experiment in the armoured conveyance of troops. These long, slow, cumbersome tanks chugged forward well ahead of the infantry, as conspicuous as battleships at sea. Nine of them were soon ablaze, hit by cleverly camouflaged guns guarding the approach to Le Quesnel, and eleven others were disabled in other parts. A few reached the final line round the left flank but were too isolated to remain. Three more tanks were knocked out trying to help the infantry into Beaucourt Wood. It was bravely rushed at about 4.30 p.m. by enterprising groups from three Ontario battalions and more gains were made further leftwards, for his contribution to which Lieutenant Tait won his V.C. But Le Quesnel held out and it was decided to postpone further attempts until the early morning, when better co-ordinated artillery support would be available. The French on the right came up to, but not into, Fresnoy.

Thus only on the flanks had Haig's attack failed to achieve all the ambitious gains planned. No other had made more ground in a single day except for Ludendorff's against the Chemin des Dames position on May 27th, but of much greater importance was the overwhelming nature of the victory. In the words of the official German Monograph, "As the sun set on August 8th on the battlefield the greatest defeat which the German Army had suffered since the beginning of the war was an accomplished fact." It admits that the five divisions between the Avre and the Somme "were nearly completely annihilated". The qualifying 'nearly' referred to the third battalion of each regiment of these divisions. The first two, in front line and support, had been caught beneath the creeping barrage and in many cases had not had time to emerge from their shelters before the Canadians and Australians were upon them; they had been demolished, in many cases complete with regimental staffs. The third battalions, at rest, had been scattered but some had been rallied. As the Hussars had observed, the response was mixed. Some officers, according to Ludendorff, were told, "You're prolonging the war," when they tried to stay a flight, and reinforcements coming up were treated to jeers of "Blacklegs!" The material loss for the day, as estimated by the Monograph, was 650 to 700 officers and 26,000 to 27,000 other ranks (which would not include wounded likely to return "within a reasonable time") and more than 400 guns.

The Australians had sent back 7,920 prisoners—out of a total Allied haul of 15,750—to pass the message abroad, in its most vivid and exhilarating form, that a great victory had been won, and it had cost them a mere 652 casualties, of whom only eighty-three were killed; surely the cheapest victory ever gained. The Canadians took 5,030 prisoners, and the cost to them was 3,868 casualties, of whom 1,038 were killed. The latter now lie in rural graveyards adjacent to where they fell, giving vivid indication of the sweep of the battle and the price paid for each objective. The Australian dead on the other hand lie side by side under the shadow of their monument on the commanding ground just to the north of Villers 'Bret'—their Vimy Ridge.

The Tank Corps paid dearly for a contribution that was at its most effective when they were supposedly at greatest disadvantage, that is when the mist lay thick. It appears that over a hundred tanks were knocked out by German guns or anti-tank rifles, and out of 415 that went into battle only 145 were available to continue the fight next day. The Cavalry may have lost a thousand horses. 1,800 is the figure given for the period August 7th-13th, the 8th being far the heaviest day of action.

The Royal Air Force also suffered heavy losses. During the morning their planes caused great fear and havoc, according to German reports, by attacking troops in transit on roads and railways close to the front, but around noon an all-out effort was ordered against the bridges over the Somme Canal with the ambitious object of completely isolating von de Marwitz's remaining troops. The German reaction was brisk and fierce. Every obtainable fighter, including Captain Hermann Goering's famous Richtofen squadron, was rushed in to cram the adjacent aerodromes, and the British bombers and fighters, the latter laden with 25-lb. bombs, ran into more enemy planes than had ever been seen, among them the new Fokker D.VII, which had a speed of 125 m.p.h. and a great rate of climb. Yet the Germans were still outnumbered. They fought with a new, despairing recklessness, and in some terrific battles they saved the Somme bridges from destruction, though at ruinous cost to themselves. Forty-four British planes were brought down during the day and a further fifty-two damaged beyond local repair. If August 8th was the black day of the German Army the same could not be said of the Luftwaffe.

Ludendorff had yet to offer his 'black day' phrase for coinage and only in retrospect, when the war was over, could a sober assessment be made of the moral effect of what in terms of the entire battle front might have been regarded as a local affair of no strategic importance. Yet sufficient had been revealed to plunge him into a morbid state of defeatism and to convince him that the only thing that could save the German Army now was speedy negotiation to bring the war to an end. As an aid towards this end, he offered his resignation to Hindenburg. It was refused, and the Kaiser too showed that he would not countenance the jettisoning of a faithful servant as a means of slipping from the entwining grasp of darkness. The First Quartermaster-General stayed at his post, a restless, jumpy, indecisive caricature of his former bustling self.

As for Haig, there is an endearing note of wonderment in his diary entry for the 8th: "The situation had developed more favourably for us than I, optimist though I am, had dared even to hope. *The enemy were completely surprised.*" There was slightly more to it than that. The Germans had first been stunned by the unexpected fury of the opening blow and then knocked flat, morally and physically, by the speed with which succeeding waves had passed through. This was due, above all else, to imaginative and meticulous planning at army, corps and divisional level, to the superb prowess of the eight Canadian and Australian divisions, and to the magnificent co-operation given them by the Tank Corps, Royal Artillery, Cavalry Corps and Royal Air Force. And behind the achievement lurks the inspiration of Rawlinson, that apostle of co-operation with flair for making newcomers happy members of his team. The key had been turned at last, at any rate of the outer door.

12

COMPLEMENTARY SUCCESS

(August 8–15)

The plans for exploiting success had always been somewhat vague. Originally little more was aimed at than the capture of the Amiens line, and in any case there were insufficient reserves available to attempt a breakthrough on the German scale. But with nostrils quivering with the whiff of victory near the Marne, Foch had summoned Haig five days before the battle began to tell him he wanted no delay on the Amiens line and to explain his plans for extending the offensive southwards, with the French Third Army joining in. Rawlinson had as a result issued orders that on capture of the Amiens line the Cavalry Corps were "to push forward with the least possible delay towards the line Roye-Chaulnes" (i.e., south-eastwards) with the Canadian and Australian Corps cast in supporting rôles, the latter "pivoting on the Somme" while swinging their right forward. Debeney, meanwhile, was told that in addition to covering the flank of the British he was to form "a mass of manoeuvre" ready to strike on the other side of Montdidier, while Humbert's Third Army prepared "a great coup de main" further to the right.

The 2nd Cavalry Division did make a wary attempt to pass through in exploitation soon after the other two divisions had reached the Amiens line, but machine-gunners in the houses of Vrely and Rosières made it sickeningly clear that cavalrymen were desperately vulnerable in twentieth-century warfare, however successful they may have been in charges against weak and disorganised opposition. Senior members of the Tank Corps, in particular Colonel F. J. C. Fuller, its Chief of Staff, were meanwhile racked by frustration. In the absence of his chief, Major-General H. J. Elles, Fuller had proposed to Rawlinson, at a pre-

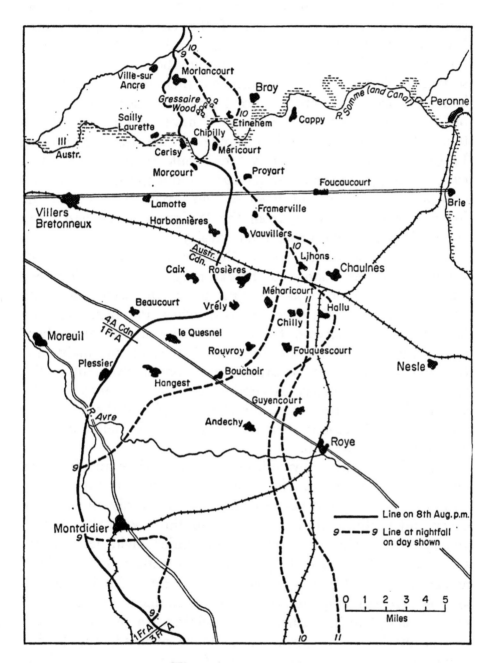

The advance on Roye

battle conference, that the ninety-six Whippets should be used in mass to crash through beyond the Amiens line and swing right-handed against the flank of the Germans opposite the French. But tradition had prevailed, and the Whippets were forced into scattered, unhappy subordination to the faster but so vulnerable horses. It is obvious that there would have been a better chance of a complete breakthrough under Fuller's plan, but less certain that the results would have been as dramatic as the protagonists of the tank still imagine. The Germans around Le Quesnel showed how easily tanks could be picked off when caught unsupported in broad daylight, and it would have needed only a few guns around Rosières and Vrely to have sent the funereal smoke billowing from the Whippets. They had losses enough in their support rôle to the cavalry.

Typically, the sector where German confusion was at its greatest, and the chance of breakthrough therefore brightest, was the one intended as the firm pivot, the sector next the Somme astride the St. Quentin road, where the armoured cars had reaped their harvest. There were plenty of Australians here in fit state to carry on the advance all through the night, but Rawlinson was not to be drawn into rash involvement in the exhilaration of victory. Accepting the shortcomings of the cavalry, he decided to assign the Canadian Corps the main rôle for the 9th and drove to their headquarters at Gentelles, arriving at 4.30 p.m. (on the 8th).

Until that morning this village had been a close and frequent target for enemy guns. Now there was none left uncaptured within range of it, and where men had crept warily all was now cheer and bustle, making the sultry air throb with the beat of victory and giving the Army Commander vivid feel of his achievement. He was met by the chief of staff, a British officer named Brigadier-General N. W. Webber, since Currie was out visiting. Webber emphasised that the Canadians, especially the 3rd Division, had had a hard day's fighting. Rawlinson, as ever, was sympathetic. He promised to make available the British 32nd Division, which was still under G.H.Q. control and whose men were being brought up by bus to the neighbourhood of Gentelles. With this division replacing the Canadian 3rd on the right of the 1st and 2nd, an advance towards Roye was to begin half an hour after the 4th Division's attack on Le Quesnel at first light. The Cavalry Corps were to operate on the right flank, keeping touch with the French, and the Australians were to conform with the Canadians under their own arrangements.

Communications had suddenly presented problems of stifling perplexity. It had been so easy during the preliminaries, when all movements had been carefully regulated and messages could instantly be passed right down to company commanders by well-secured telephone lines. But now the roads were choked with prisoners and wounded going back and with reinforcements and supply columns coming up, and local telephone lines were being snapped by tanks, limbers, and horses as soon as laid. Even between army and corps headquarters morse telegraph and despatch rider were the only means of message transmission.

At 6.30 p.m. a telegram reached Headquarters Canadian Corps to the effect that the 32nd Division could not after all be released and that Webber, the B.G.S., was to ring up for instructions, which meant driving ten miles, for the nearest telephone to Army headquarters was at Dury. So blocked was the road, mainly by this unavailable division, that the journey took two hours, and the unfortunate Webber (according to his account) was then rebuked by Montgomery, who said he was "very irate with the Army Commander for daring to give away the 32nd Division and with myself for aiding and abetting". It was not the first time that Rawlinson had been obliged to withdraw an undertaking, made with impulsive affability in the course of a visit, after returning to his headquarters and being confronted with emphatic and dogmatic argument by his chief of staff. It appears that the latter's self-confidence was inflated by the great personal contribution he had made to victory, and he presumably invoked the doctrine preached as ardently by Foch and Ludendorff as by the British General Staff, the doctrine that reserves should not be committed until the divisions in the line have given their all. It demanded a further effort from the 3rd Canadian. Possibly Rawlinson consulted G.H.Q. before agreeing. All that is on record, in the log of either headquarters, is that the 32nd remained under G.H.Q. control.

It was a self-defeating triumph for doctrine, purchased in the currency the Germans needed most, time. Webber had first to return to his own headquarters at the same exasperating crawl and then make complete revision of plan, for whereas the 32nd Division could have advanced on a front of two brigades the 3rd were too weak to commit more than one and consequently the frontages allotted the 1st and 2nd had to be enlarged. Detailed written orders for the operation had to be produced, and just as devotion to this practice had prevented the divisions of Watts's corps from making their escape in darkness on Gough's last morning in command of the Fifth Army, so now it allowed the Germans ample respite for recovery. Four and a half divisions, which had always been handily placed, completed occupation of a line covering the gap caused by the collapse of the five south of the Somme, some of whose reserve battalions and oddments could still play a part in the type of repair work they had so often forced on their opponents in the days, recent yet far-off, of their own offensives. Meanwhile on the British side infantrymen slept in their new, foul-smelling dug-outs, tank men tended and refuelled their overstrained machines, cavalrymen rode in relays to the Luce stream to water their tired and thirsty horses, and gunners joined the queue for more forward positions or began the task of removing the captured guns beyond reach of counter-attack—for the Battle of Cambrai was still fresh in mind, in none more so than in Rawlinson's.

Only in Gentelles was there strenuous activity all through the night. The orders for the Canadian attack were not finished until after 4 a.m. and had then to be distributed either by motor-bike or car. As Webber had given warning over the telephone, zero hour for the main attack had had to be postponed from 5 to 10 a.m.

However, the 4th Division were ready, and at 4.30 they duly made their assault on Le Quesnel. There was a marked lack of that precision which had been such a decisive feature of the fighting on the previous day. No shells landed, because a despatch rider had lost his way, but the infantry went bravely in with a tank or two, unmasked this time by mist, and in the course of an hour bombed and bayoneted the Germans out of the village. There was tough opposition in an adjoining wood, where the Germans held out until after noon. The main attack should by now have been well under way, but tiresome problems of assembly were accentuated by some accurate shelling, enforcing a further postponement of zero hour to 11. In the event only one brigade out of the five involved succeeded in crossing their start-line on time, the 6th Brigade of the 2nd Division on the extreme left, and that without such tanks as were still available. Their neighbouring brigade entered the fight piecemeal, company by company as they came up, and the 1st Division on their right did not start until 1 p.m., the artillery being late in getting into position. It was 2 p.m. before the forward brigade of the 3rd Division—two battalions, each accompanied by seven tanks —passed through the 4th beyond Le Quesnel. The staff machinery, it seems, was encumbered by a certain 'morning after' stiffness.

Lack of co-ordination would have been of no importance twenty-four hours earlier, when the Germans were in disarray. But they had made good use of the respite and as many troops were now deployed in defence as there were attackers. Their positions were poorly fortified but were of considerable natural strength. Five villages were strewn across the path of the Canadians with others beyond them, being for the most part mere centralised groups of farm buildings standing a mile apart from each other. Except for two woods and the odd copse, the ground was open between them and the machine-gunners in the houses could peer down their sights on glorious long sweeps of high standing corn, from which there could be no escape for the unwary. The Canadians came across this ground with sketchy support from their guns and only spasmodic help, though sometimes highly effective, from their Mark V and Whippet tanks, while the cavalry dallied in rear, occasionally making a brave but hopeless attempt to pierce a gap. The infantrymen had to rely on their infantry skills, and these they did not lack.

By advancing in short rushes, under cover of their machine-guns, and by making full use of every ditch, dip, or manure heap, these Canadians gradually forced an entry into the villages and silenced the chattering guns. The 2nd Division won Rosières at 4.30, after two hours of toil and turmoil in its straggly streets, in the course of which four of the five supporting tanks were knocked out, and others of this division pushed two miles beyond this village, up a flanking valley, to capture Méharicourt.

The 22nd French Canadians were to the fore here and owed much to the dash and valour of the thrice-wounded Lieutenant J. Brilliant, which won him the V.C. Three V.C.s were won by the 1st Division in a three-mile advance as far as Rouvroy, which included the capture of three other villages. Two went to men of the same battalion, Corporal F. G. Coppings and Lance-Corporal A. Brereton, of the 8th (Manitoba) Battalion, both of whom rushed troublesome machine-gun posts on their own. Yet despite such exploits, around 425 officers and men of this battalion lay dead or wounded when the survivors sunk down in the twilight and dug themselves in along the road connecting Rouvroy and Méharicourt. On the right the 3rd Division made some amends for their tardy start by advancing up the main road as far as Bouchoir, but they were still six miles short of Roye, instead of the four intended.

The Australians did rather more than merely conform to the Canadian advance. The 5th Division, south of the St. Quentin road, had this task initially, and they suffered losses as they exposed their left flank to fire from the villages through which the armoured cars had spread destruction the day before; at Vauvillers, a mile beyond Harbonnières, a single anti-tank gun picked off all six of the tanks allotted one brigade. The 5th gained Vauvillers after a tough fight, and at 1.45 the 1st Australian Division passed through to celebrate their return to the Corps by carrying the advance as far as the gently sloped but commanding ridge of Lihons, which brought them in line with the Canadians.

The task was entrusted to two battalions that had already marched ten miles and now went a further three across downland, spread in open formation with seven tanks ahead of each. As they came to the foot of the ridge shells fell fast among them and machine-guns jabbered in increasing number. Tanks shuddered with sickening clang and crumpled beneath the crash of steel, and more and more infantrymen were sent spinning. It was torment for these Australians to be caught on the bare open slopes after coming so far. They struggled on, some making dashes while others fired from the cover of meagre bumps in the ground. Private R. M. Beatham, of the 8th Battalion, attacked four machine-guns with one assistant and, despite being early shot through the leg, gained them all, killing ten Germans with bayonet and grenade and making another ten prisoner. At last the objective, another old trench line, was reached and the men leapt in, but still some Germans fought. Again Beatham charged a machine-gun post. He was riddled with bullets but as a dying gesture hurled a grenade that killed his killers. His comrades set upon those Germans still holding out and speedily finished them off under the inspiration of having seen a V.C. well won. There were twice as many Australian casualties this day as on the 8th, and barely half as many battalions went into the attack.

General Butler of III Corps, who was far from well, called on the 131st Regiment of the American 33rd Division to aid the 58th London in the renewal of their efforts against Chipilly Spur and the hillside Gressaire Wood further to the north. Because of the distance the Americans had to come zero hour had to be postponed from dawn to 5.30 p.m. The main attack was aimed at the thin neck of the spur, and as a preliminary to it a very weak battalion of Londoners, with impromptu aid from another, tried to get into the riverside village of Chipilly. They were stopped by hot fire from the steep-sided bank of the spur above the village. A patrol of six men of the 1st Australian Battalion, commanded by C.Q.M.S. Haynes, slipped over the river to join the Londoners and shepherded them one by one into Chipilly, by dint of superb fieldcraft, having first discovered that it was empty. They then showed them how to wipe out the various machine-gun nests embedded in the spur on either side. Americans came across to help and by 8 p.m. 200 prisoners and twelve machine-guns had been rounded up without harm to the amazing six Australians.

In the main assault, launched at 5.30 under a creeping barrage three miles wide, two weakened brigades of Londoners went in with the three-battalion regiment of Americans in between them, and by midnight they had won their objectives. It was tough going up and down the wooded slopes and by the end of it some of the London battalions were down to sixty men. The Americans had a rush to get to their start-line in time, in spite of the postponement, and left behind rations, ammunition and even weapons that they should have brought with them. They suffered heavy losses from machine-gun fire in the early stages

and especially from the right before Chipilly Spur had been sub-
dued, but their spirit was as inspiring as news of the great victory
on the other side of the river, and by moral support as much as
physical Londoners and Americans helped each other on against
strong, newly-reinforced opposition.

In extension of this attack, with the same zero hour and barrage, a brigade of the 12th Division attacked the slopes of the
basin in which the village of Morlancourt stands. There were
many machine-guns hidden among the crops above this large
village and they were tackled with fine spirit, for which inspiration on the left wing was provided by Lieutenant-Colonel
W. R. A. Dawson, of the 6th Royal West Kent, who led his
battalion mounted, his daring undimmed by the six wounds he
had received since August 1914; he would receive his seventh on
October 23rd, and it would prove mortal. Sergeant T. J. Harris
of his battalion, a veteran who held the Military Medal, without
any prompting stormed three posts that were causing much
damage. Over the first two he triumphed, but in the third
attempt he was killed. The Royal West Kents battled on and
gained their objectives, as also did the 6th Queen's next to them
and on the right the 6th Buffs, who had started the attack at
dawn before recall orders reached them. The 1st Cambridgeshire efficiently mopped up the village. There was to be a posthumous V.C. for Harris, and further to emphasise that the
Colonials had not done all the fighting III Corps could claim
the passage of all but 3,000 prisoners through their cage over
the two days.

On the other flank the divisions of Debeney's First Army had
not shown themselves in the mood for heroics; indeed, the
volatile French soldier was never at his most dashing best on this
particular sector. Throughout the morning of the 9th Debeney
was peppered with exhortations from Foch, which by-passed the
operational commander, Haigh, urging him "*move fast,* march
hard, manoeuvre to the front, *reinforce firmly from the rear*
with all the troops you have until the desired *result has been
obtained*", and a little later, "push forward the XXXI Corps
drums beating on Roye, *without losing a minute,* beating down
all hesitation and delay". The lugubrious Debeney visited his
corps commanders to pass on, perhaps with a shrug, the

Generalissimo's instructions. Some progress was made, rather less and later than by the Canadians. Then at 4 p.m. Debeney's right wing leapt to life and by nightfall his XXXV Corps had driven a $2\frac{1}{2}$-mile wedge into the German line on the other side of Montdidier. The Germans were in danger of being caught in a pocket within a pocket, the inner one formed by the wings of Debeney's army, the larger one by the shoulders of the British Fourth and the French Third Armies, the one already barging heavily, the other showing marked signs of preparation for a spring.

Von Hutier, of the Eighteenth Army, was in command here, and he made plans for extrication with typical vigour, while his army group commander, Prince Rupprecht—the Eighteenth had been transferred from Prince Willie's Group in July—dragged from a reluctant Ludendorff permission for a general withdrawal by this army, so that it might free its flanks from exposure. It was an anxious night for the Germans. The Canadians in particular had inflicted heavy loss, virtually routing two of the divisions brought in from reserve. In and around the newly captured villages wounded Germans lay groaning all night, disturbing the Canadians more than the bombers that also plagued them. Many comrades of these abandoned, wounded wretches were streaming back with tales of horror, their tongues loosened by drink, and flinging taunts of 'war-prolongers!' on the fresh troops that emerged from train or lorry to gasp at the disordered scene of fleeing soldiers, loose horses and hopeless blocks of vehicles. Fifteen divisions had been ordered up from various parts of the front, but only four arrived, without their artillery, during the night in order to prop a line that was at its flimsiest by the junction between von der Marwitz and von Hutier. A night attack could have wrought chaos, but such a project had even less appeal to the methodical British than to the Germans during their offensives, and again the night was used by both sides for reorganisation. Certainly the Germans did not waste it. As new arrivals marched to the new gaps von Hutier's divisions came back, as much as nine miles at the furthest point, leaving much equipment behind them and the town of Montdidier in a state of devastation as shattering for its inhabitants as no doubt it was satisfying for those charged with the final demolitions.

Rawlinson's plan for Saturday, August 10th, was much the same as for the 9th, namely to press on steadily on a wide front-age with the Canadian Corps still cast as spearhead. Again the Canadians got off to a good start, the 3rd Division capturing Le Quesnoy, near the main road beyond Bouchoir, in a dawn attack. The 32nd Division had at last been released by G.H.Q., to become the second fresh division committed by the Fourth Army since the 8th, against ten thrown in opposite them. The 32nd were a New Army division, drawn from either side of the Scottish border and with a regular battalion now forming part of each brigade; they had fought under Rawlinson on the Somme, followed him to the Channel sector in 1917 and seen the extinc-tion of the German March offensive with the Third Army. Now, fresh to battle, they strode in vigorously behind a few tanks, the leading brigades passing through the 3rd Canadian at 8 a.m. They gained two woods but were counter-attacked out of the second. The opposition had stiffened, and the going had become unexpectedly difficult too. It had been forgotten that across the next three miles the last battles of the Somme offensive had been fought. The farmers had been too daunted even to attempt removal of the dereliction. There were many strands of rusted wire, plenty of trench lines, and shell holes large enough to gobble up Whippet tanks and ensnare Mark Vs, and over them all grass and brambles rampaged, providing excellent conceal-ment for machine-guns and making the obstacles undetectable at a distance.

Starting later than the 32nd, the 4th Canadian on their left also began well, each forward brigade having sixteen tanks, thanks to the release of a fresh battalion of them, and such was the progress made that cavalry patrols, following the infantry, reported back to Headquarters Cavalry Corps that a break-through could be made. The 3rd (on the right) and 2nd Cavalry Divisions were ordered forward, the former with the Canadian brigade leading. A squadron of the Fort Garry Horse trotted past gaping and hard-beset infantrymen, scouted forward to find the way barred by machine-gun bullets, veered right-handed across the main Roye road and galloped through bursting shells, jumping wire strands and trenches, to pound into the village of Andrechy. Here they captured an enormous supply depot, which lay inside the French sector of attack and had regretfully to be handed over when French infantry appeared on the scene. Another squadron made a charge against the German entrenchments on the British side of the road. It met with predictable disaster, as did an attempt by the 2nd Cavalry Division further to the left. One further attempt was planned by the dauntless Canadian cavalrymen but was mercifully abandoned on the insistence of the local brigadier of the 32nd Division. The Whippet tanks were also tried, with equally disastrous results.

General Kavanagh, commanding the Cavalry Corps, was under as serious a delusion to the strength of the opposition as to the nature of the country. Some good troops had arrived, among them the Alpine Corps, and they made the Canadians fight their hardest for possession of the villages of Fouquescourt, Chilly and Hallu, from which they had to ward off some stiff counter-attacks when they had won them. The famous 1st Australian Division on their left could make even less progress and spent the day battling ferociously for a copse half a mile in advance of their positions on the Lihons ridge. They gained it at heavy cost and had another costly fight to retain it against strong counter-attack. On the other side of the river, III Corps by contrast attempted less and had less tribulation, the Americans and Londoners working forward as far as the old Amiens line and the 37th Brigade of the 12th Division making another successful evening attack along the plateau beyond Morlancourt.

If the 10th was a grim day for the troops with closest experience of the enemy's re-found strength, they would have been cheered by knowledge of the stand made on their behalf by their Army Commander. The point at issue was whether a major lesson of the war should be applied, namely that in warfare on the scale of the Western Front it was easier for a defender to patch up a breach in his line than for the attacker to enlarge it and that instead of persisting, once the momentum of his attack had begun to decline, the latter should open fresh attacks at other points. It was easier to acknowledge this lesson than to observe it, because of the temptation always luring the attacker to squeeze the most from a penetration made. Ludendorff had fallen prey to it, and as a result each of his offensives had ended in awful losses and sown the demoralisation that was to make the collapse of his armies swift and sensational. Foch paid the lesson lip service at his 'turning point' conference by outlining the successive blows he planned to strike. But now, on this morning of the 10th, he showed himself just as vulnerable to temptation as Ludendorff. He arrived at Haig's advanced headquarters at Wiry with a directive to the effect that the British Fourth and French First Armies, supported by the French Third, were to press on towards the Somme Canal, with Ham named as Rawlinson's objective, from which preparations were to be made for a crossing.

Haig doubted they could do it. He more than anyone knew the cost of persisting with an offensive, and indeed he had already switched reserves from the Fourth Army sector for a fresh blow nearer Arras, which would in turn loosen the opposition for a resumption of the offensive by the Fourth Army. While approving of this other attack, Foch insisted that the Fourth Army must not pause. Misinterpreting withdrawal for rout, he said that resistance had collapsed in front of the French First and Third Armies and that now was the time for bold action. Haig gave way. He drove off to pass on the directive.

He met Rawlinson at Demuin, where the headquarters of the Canadian Corps were dispersed among carefully camouflaged huts and dug-outs, belying the chateau image of former years. The atmosphere was tense. Rawlinson was convinced that he could achieve no more of importance and that the time had come to switch the attack to another sector. The towering Currie was there, with facts to support this view. Haig produced Foch's directive, emphasised the progress made by the French, and said that the orders had to be carried out. At this, according to the Official History (which tapped liberally on private sources), Rawlinson "became almost subordinate and replied, 'Are you commanding the British Army or is Maréchal Foch?' " (Foch had just been made Marshal.) The remark touched Haig at his point of highest sensitivity and must have stung. It was a shock to find the loyal and urbane Rawlinson react so sharply. Haig, it seems certain, made gruff defence of Foch, but in the long-run Rawlinson would win.

It was while this discussion was raging that the Cavalry Corps had their vision of a breakthrough, and the news was at once passed to the ruffled generals. Foch, it seemed, was right after all. Haig drove off to hear more about it from Kavanagh, and not finding much evidence there to support the high expectations, he went on to the headquarters of the 32nd Division, which were at Le Quesnel. Here, around 6 p.m., he heard the chastening truth about the attempted breakthrough. None the less Rawlinson dutifully issued written orders in compliance with Foch's directive, naming the Somme Canal as the objective for the 11th, which meant an advance of eight miles from that part of the line nearest it. Verbally, Rawlinson made it clear to Currie that caution would not be censured.

An interesting experiment was carried out by Monash during the night. After all the trouble his troops had suffered from enemy positions on the other side of the river he had obtained permission for his boundary to be extended to include the northern bank. The next spur on this side ran southwards between the village of Etinehem on the west and the little town of Bray on the east, and Monash decided that he would cut its neck with an attack by the 4th Division's 13th Brigade (who had held the line for the Canadians) while a brigade of his 3rd Division made a conforming attack along the south bank. Tanks were used in the light of a rising moon and the mere noise of them as they roared up and down the Bray road put such terror into the Germans on the north bank that the 13th Brigade met hardly any resistance. But on the south bank the noise had the opposite effect. The column was caught on the main road by guns and aircraft, its commander was killed, two tanks were set alight and every subsequent move was scotched by shelling.

At dawn next day the other brigades of the 3rd Division redeemed this failure, and at the same time the 1st Division resumed their assault under cover of mist and quickly won the whole of the Lihons feature, together with the village, from which they repelled heavy counter-attacks made by two fresh divisions. The Canadians on their right were less successful. An enlarged brigade of the 32nd received little help from a too distant barrage and suffered heavy losses, nine tanks included, for a gain of half a mile towards Roye, and the 4th Canadian on their left found themselves attacked and forced out of the village of Hallu. Shortly after 10 a.m. a message arrived that put a stop to further attacks by the 32nd, even to a counter-attack by the 4th. Enough had happened to prove Foch wrong. Rawlinson had decided that, if he had to go on, he must halt to prepare a fresh, fully co-ordinated assault, timed for the 15th. Haig supported his decision, and the Battle of Amiens was ended, with only minimal squandering of the great gains made.

As the troops turned their attention to improving their defences and stocking up for the next move, their generals occupy the limelight, and there was a fine array of them at Villers Bretonneux on this sunny afternoon of Sunday, August 11th. Rawlinson had summoned his corps commanders, Currie, Monash, Kavanagh and the debonair Irishman Sir Alexander Godley, who had left his XXII Corps temporarily to take over III Corps while Butler went on sick leave to recover from the insomnia that had worn him to a shred. They met in the open, sitting under a mangled beech, and listened to Rawlinson explain his plans. Haig, who had already been consulted, had a few words to say as he stopped with Lawrence on his way to pass personal congratulation, with stiff, unsmiling yet manifest gratitude, on troops of the Australian Corps. Then Wilson, the C.I.G.S., turned up out of the blue, followed immediately and even more surprisingly by Clemenceau and his Finance Minister, Klotz. They had come to see the ruins, to congratulate the victorious generals, and to revel in the chance to stroll and chat on ground so recently freed from the crunch of shell and the slur of gas.

Next day the King arrived, showing once again that he regarded his post of Commander-in-Chief as by no means a purely nominal one. Rawlinson showed him the gaping holes blown by the railway guns in the still deserted streets of Amiens and took him inside the great cathedral, which mercifully had not needed the protective jacket of sandbags that encased its walls. Nearer the front line a hundred picked men from each division paraded in their corps areas for informal inspection by His Majesty and the bestowal of decorations. Pershing was with his Americans and he received the Grand Cross of the Bath together with some words on a very delicate subject, expressing the hope that some of his divisions might remain with Haig's army, where they had been trained and cared for, instead of joining the army of his own that Pershing was at last assembling for battle. Currie and Monash were appointed to the lesser order of Knight Commander of the Bath, and for Monash at any rate it was a great thrill to be dubbed by the King before his men in the battle zone. Debeney was also made a K.C.B. at a concourse of the great at Flixécourt. Foch and Weygand, Haig and Lawrence, Pétain, Fayolle, all were there, and a fine group for photography they made as they posed on either side of the King outside Rawlinson's headquarters, with senior members of the Fourth Army staff behind them and more junior brethren goggling from the wings.

But behind the splendid façade the cracks of disagreement were becoming more jagged. They were very proud, at Army Headquarters, of the fact that with thirteen infantry and three cavalry divisions and one American regiment they had destroyed or drawn into battle twenty-five German divisions and could produce the prisoners to prove it. And these divisions of theirs that had achieved all this were still in fighting shape. But there was a strong feeling that the Fourth had done enough for the time being and that other armies should spring into action to reap the benefit of this great suction of enemy reserves to the Santerre plain. Such moves were, of course, being planned, but Foch saw them as subsidiary and still wanted the British Fourth Army and their French neighbours to drive on towards the Somme with all speed. Meanwhile evidence steadily accumulated both of the strength of this old line the Germans had reactivated and of the quality of the troops holding it. The Australians and Canadians both made local improvement to their positions as a preliminary to the next big attack, which at the request of Debeney had now been postponed to the 16th. But they had to fight hard under heavy shelling and were sometimes dislodged by counter-attack; two more V.C.s were won by the Canadians (bringing their total to ten since zero hour on the 8th) and one by the Australians. Currie became increasingly apprehensive. Air photographs showed the labyrinthal nature of the enemy's defences and he used them to support a report stating that the attack "would be a very costly matter" and that he was "opposed to attempting it".

Armed with these, Rawlinson saw Haig at 10 a.m. on the

14th at Wiry and explained the difficulties. There was no cause for any insubordinate language now. In Rawlinson's words, "I suggested that it would be far better and cheaper to hold the enemy to his ground, on my front, by wire-cutting and bombardment until the Third Army is ready to put in a surprise attack, and then to press on simultaneously with that attack. This he entirely agreed with, and I left him the maps and photographs to show to Foch."

But Foch remained obdurate. A letter from Haig, sent by air, announced the postponement of the attack and received reply from Foch, "Very much to the contrary, the attack of the First and Fourth Armies should be hastened." It was on this day (the 14th) that the Kaiser presided over a conference of state at Spa at which Secretary of State Hintze was instructed or persuaded (versions differ) to open up peace negotiations through the medium of the Queen of the Netherlands. Much to the exasperation of his commanders and staff officers, Ludendorff regarded it as an essential complement to this policy that there should be no withdrawal back to prepared defence lines in rear; the German Army must stand where it was, retaining as much of France as it could. Nothing would have suited Ludendorff's purpose better than a rushed attack on that portion of his line where it was strongest, as urged by Foch.

Haig saw this, and next day he met Foch at Sarcus for a conference that in its way was just as much a turning point as the one on July 26th. The underlining in his diary, as much as the words, stress the emotion that Haig felt. He explained his plans for transferring reserves for an attack by Byng's Third Army, while keeping the enemy in expectation of an attack on the Rawlinson-Debeney front. Foch fired provocative questions at him, and then :

"I spoke to Foch quite straightly and let him understand that *I was responsible to my Government and fellow citizens for the handling of the British forces.* F.'s attitude changed at once and he said all he wanted was early information of my intentions so that he might co-ordinate the operations of the other Armies, and that he now thought I was quite correct in my decision not to attack the enemy in his prepared position."

Plans therefore went ahead for Byng to strike the next blow, with Rawlinson cast in supporting rôle and Debeney's army returned to Pétain's command under a prompt order from Foch, which none the less complimented Haig on his achievements with it and reaffirmed agreement with the change of plan.

For Rawlinson this victory over his superiors was as notable and almost as important as his success over the enemy. No one had previously achieved complete surprise in a big attack, nor succeeded in obtaining agreement for an offensive to be halted when the troops were still in good heart and the objective not yet reached. More might perhaps have been dared in between this great double event, but both the cavalry and the slow, lumbering tanks had paid heavily for their attempts at exploitation, and it is by no means certain that the rapier thrusts that can so easily be conjured in retrospect would have been either practicable or profitable. The most important thing was that the infantry felt that they had been skilfully and considerately handled. Confidence had been restored in command and staff, and with each carefully planned, methodical blow giving semblance of a master overall plan, so it would expand.

13

THE ATTACK WIDENED

(August 18–September 2)

August 21st was the earliest day Byng could accept for the start of his offensive. Foch pressed for the 20th "at latest" although in fact the preliminaries were ideally tuned to the 21st. The first was a surprise attack by a corps of Plumer's Second Army, launched at 11 a.m. on Sunday the 18th, just as Haig arrived at Amiens to receive the hero's Medaille Militaire from Clemenceau with imposing ceremony. Once again the battling Scots of the 9th Division were to the fore, and the whole of the Outersteene Ridge was won without great difficulty. It formed an obvious springboard for a leap towards Armentières or Kemmel.

Then on August 20th Mangin launched out with his French Tenth Army, striking on the right of Humbert's Third just beyond the Oise. Twelve divisions were employed on a twelve-mile frontage, and although the attack was not unexpected it gained two to three miles during the day and so shattered the defenders that Ludendorff described it as "another black day"; it fell on the German Ninth Army of the newly-formed von Boehn's Group, which also included the battered Eighteenth and Second Armies, freed from the command of Prince Rupprecht. In Jubilation Foch wrote Haig a line, which reached him at midnight, to say the enemy was shaken everywhere and must be kept reeling. He counted on "the attack of your Third Army, already postponed to the 21st, being launched that day *with violence*, carrying forward with it the neighbouring divisions of the First Army and the whole of the Fourth Army. After your brilliant successes of the 8th, 9th and 10th, any timidity on their part would hardly be justified in view of the enemy's situation and the moral ascendancy you have gained over him."

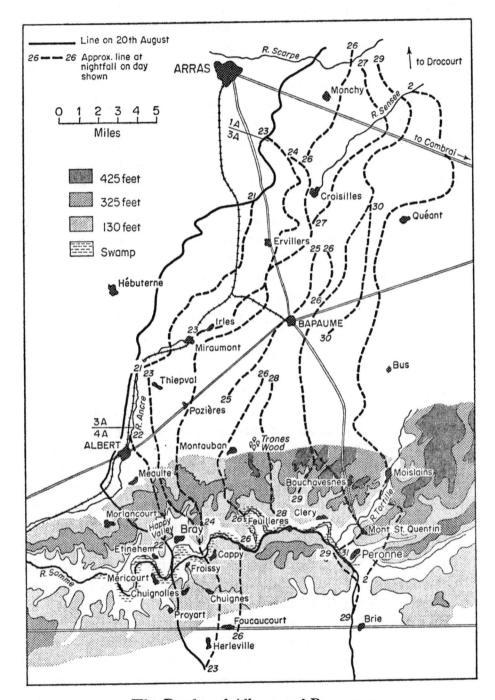

The Battles of Albert and Bapaume

The Third Army's plan was a replica, without quite such weight of fire support, of that on August 8th. Eight divisions made the main assault, of which three were in second line, and they had five battalions of tanks, of which one had the old Mark IVs and one Whippets. The frontage chosen was a twelve-mile stretch opposite Bapaume, which was to be extended by a subsidiary attack on the right across the Ancre. There had been a redistribution of guns, putting the Third Army on a par with the Fourth, and the Third now had the bulk of the Cavalry Corps. Once again the concentrations and dumping were made without detection by the enemy. The Fourth Army had shown that it could be done.

Even the fog co-operated in the attempt at emulation, and at 4.55 a.m. down went the barrage, quite unheralded, and three minutes later in came the men of five divisions—the 42nd (on the right), New Zealand, 37th, 2nd, and Guards—in most cases on a single brigade frontage, and with a few tanks blundering among them, others having lost their way. There was little opposition. The Germans had as a matter of policy thinned out their forward line and had their main defences on the Arras-Albert railway some three miles in rear. On the left the Guards and the 3rd Division (who passed through the 2nd) reached this railway line before 9 a.m., but now the fog lifted and neither tanks nor cavalry could get through to exploit. Further to the right the 5th Division gained a feature 1,000 yards beyond the railway, but the 63rd Royal Naval on their left were in difficulties and the 5th came back. Yet further to the right the Ancre in flood proved a forbidding obstacle. And it was hot, very hot, adding greatly to the strain of battle. Byng decided to suspend activities until the Fourth Army could apply leverage on the other side of Albert, as it had originally been agreed that he might. His troops had made a gain of three miles in places and had good reason to feel pleased.

Haig was not in the least pleased. He had told Byng before the attack that he did not think his plans ambitious enough and on the day following it he issued a curt order directing the Third Army to resume the offensive with the utmost vigour. He followed this up with a note to all army commanders—no doubt he had Rawlinson in mind as much as Byng—impressing on them in Foch-like style the "necessity for all ranks to act with the utmost boldness and resolution in order to get full advantage from the present favourable situation." That very day, he told them, a Bavarian division had fled in panic before the French Tenth Army. "The most resolute offensive is everywhere desirable. Risks which a month ago would have been criminal to incur, ought now to be incurred as a duty. It is no longer necessary to advance in regular lines step by step. . . . A vigorous offensive . . . will cost us much less than if we attempted to deal with the present situation in a half-hearted manner."

Appeals of this nature had been made before. Indeed, Allenby had issued one very similar in wording after his Third Army had successfully broken into the Hindenburg Line at the opening of the Battle of Arras. It had caused death and derision, little else. But now at last there was real justification for a more daring approach, as had been manifested by the events of the previous fortnight. The enemy's morale was low and his defences were shoddy, and Haig had the guns and the tanks to spread his offensive over a wide frontage, thus enabling him to retain the initiative by making frequent switches of pressure. The French could further extend the frontage of attack and keep fully occupied the picked German divisions that had been rushed to the defence of Roye, where they were no longer confronted by the Canadians, who had, to their joy, been spirited away for another surprise assault. This was a sound way of exploiting the victory of Amiens, and if Haig provided the impetus, Rawlinson had given the lead.

The only attack made by the British this day, August 22nd, was by Rawlinson's left corps, the IIIrd, together with one Australian division north of the Somme, the 3rd. It gained the sentimental and valuable prize of Albert, which fell to the 18th Division, with aid from a flanking attack along the ridge further south by the 3rd Australian (on the right), 47th, and 12th Divisions, the last-named capturing the village of Méaulte after projecting 50 drums of burning oil into a troublesome trench nearby. The 11th Royal Fusiliers and 6th Northamptonshire, of 18 Division, made a bold night crossing of the swollen Ancre, having pushed trestle bridge-floats across, sometimes by swimming, under fire that destroyed the great majority of them. This gained them lodgement, at heavy cost, on a spur round the right flank of Albert. At dawn the 7th East Surrey began the eerie task of clearing the pulped, corpse-strewn town whose famous cathedral was a mere shell of red brick, shorn of the golden Virgin and Babe that had dangled so long from its spire. The Surreys soon ferreted the Germans out of their cellars and rubble holes, and the 7th Buffs passed through to fight a prolonged battle for their objective on the slopes beyond, which they gained at 2.30 next morning.

Elsewhere the Germans had been attempting counter-attacks, but with none of the cohesion intended by their commanders. They had some success against the right wing of III Corps, driving the 47th Londoners back from their objective north of Bray, out of an oft-smitten valley that had the ludicrous title of Happy. But on the Third Army front they were easily dispersed. One attempt ended in the capture of a complete assault group, 242 strong, by two men of the 1st Devonshire (5 Division), Lance-Corporal Onions and Private Eades, who bumped into them in a trench they were exploring and fooled them into surrender. There was a V.C. for Onions, a D.C.M. for Eades.

On the 23rd, Haig's ginger produced the results required. The Third Army swept across the Arras-Albert railway and made deep penetration across the flowing undulations north-west of Bapaume, with 5,000 prisoners as proof of success, and the Fourth dealt what Monash described as "a smashing blow" just to the south of the Somme. Thus on the Albert sector, where the decay and devastation were at their most terrible, the Germans were in danger of envelopment, and the only attack here was a combined one by the flanking divisions of the two armies, the 18th and the 38th, which gained more high ground overlooking the town. The Germans had brought up fresh divisions, and their histories pay unwitting compliment to the British by telling of "overwhelming numbers" and "superior force", whereas in fact the Germans had the greater number of divisions engaged.

Behind a barrage consisting largely of shrapnel and with twelve tanks unhindered, and unshrouded, by mist, the 3rd Division made the first thrust across the railway just before daylight. They eased open a great, catacombed cutting for assault by the

37th Division on their right and formed a base for the 2nd Division to pass quickly through and advance in painful partnership with the Whippets as far as Ervillers, on the Arras-Bapaume road. The Guards on their left showed awareness of Haig's message by their brave disdain for that traditional brake on British progress, strict alignment, and on their left two newly-committed Territorial divisions thumped stoically forward, each with a fresh battalion of tanks, the 56th London, who had marched eleven miles during the night under torment by gas, and the 52nd Lowland, recently arrived from Palestine. The German riflemen put up a poor fight against their resolute, if rather cumbersome, foe, but their machine and anti-tank guns were manned by braver men and, making best use of some splendid fields of fire, they took increasing toll as the British outstripped their fixed artillery programmes and spilled blood and sweat—for it was again very hot—in response to some wild demands by divisional and brigade commanders.

As for Monash's "smashing blow", this was delivered by his 1st Australian Division with aid from the 32nd British. The latter were now under his command because the Canadians had been returned to the First Army, having handed half their sector over to the French, as demanded by Haig in exchange for the loss of three American divisions, and the other half to the Australians, who thus held a huge frontage on either side of the Somme. Their line south of the river was short of the badly-devastated zone and there were four German divisions on the frontage of attack, concentrated well forward in steep valleys for their comfort and fooled into complacence by their propaganda service's inept translation of an appeal for recruits Monash had made for consumption in Australia.

The 32nd Division had the task of protecting the right flank of the 1st Australian, and they did this by storming the village of Herleville, south of the main St. Quentin road. The Australians then ran amok through the wooded gulleys on a frontage of as much as five miles, capturing the villages of Chuignolles and Chuignes and Froissy Beacon in a three-mile advance admirably supported by their tanks. There were some extraordinary exploits. Lieutenant L. D. McCarthy, of the 16th Battalion, tunnelled himself into a covered machine-gun post, slew its occupants, and then made a lone advance down a trench 700 yards long, killing twenty more Germans, sometimes by the return of their stick grenades, wounding thirteen, and sending a further thirty-seven back as prisoners. When his men came up he grabbed a Lewis gun and did further execution at longer range. He won the V.C., and so too did Lieutenant W. D. Joynt, of the 8th Battalion, whose staggering audacity completely transformed a very daunting situation at Herleville Wood. The opposition was strong in places, but an outflanking attack was always forthcoming by tanks or infantry and the artillery also co-operated nimbly with a swift move forward of the guns for the assault on the final objective. 3,100 prisoners were taken—and this by men not exactly prompt in accepting surrenders—and twenty-one guns, among them a tormentor of Amiens, a 15-inch naval gun.

Such was the eagerness to get on that the attack was resumed next morning at the eccentric hour of 1 a.m., when the moonlight was at its brightest, and the front was ablaze all along a thirty-mile stretch from the left extremity of the Third Army, three miles south of Arras, to the Somme, where the success of the Australians on the south bank enabled those on the north to occupy Bray. The most brilliant feat was achieved even earlier when a brigade of the indomitable 21st Division, having crossed the Ancre, set off into the night at shortest notice and made a bold advance over the hills in square formation. This led to the speedy capture of two rubble redoubts that had in the past caused their attackers prolonged anguish, Thiepval and Pozières.

Again most progress was made in the early hours when the German vision was limited and the British gunners had a pre-arranged programme to fire. Later, cleverly sited machine-gun posts, lying ahead of the main line and therefore missed by the barrage, caused tribulation. Still the cavalry waited vainly for their chance, hopefully treading the heels of the infantry, and every day tanks were being disabled which could not be replaced. The pattern was repeated on the 25th. The day began well with a pre-dawn attack by the 2nd Division north of Bapaume, which was effectively exploited by the 62nd, but further northwards there was marked stiffening of the opposition as the old German defence line was bumped, and on the right flank III Corps ran into three fresh German divisions just as they were experimenting with advanced guard formations in response to urging by Rawlinson. This was the fifth day of the offensive, and there was a feeling in the Third Army in particular, as previously there had been in the Fourth, that the burden should be shifted elsewhere. With thirteen divisions they had eliminiated eight of the enemy and drawn a further eleven into the battle, severely mauling a number of them.

They had not long to wait. Haig had decided that the time had come to extend the attack yet further north and strike out with Horne's First Army, aiming to turn the flank of the Hindenburg Line by smashing through the reserve line known as the Drocourt-Quéant switch, where the Arras offensive had been halted. The Canadians returned to the fray, determined to prove their repatriation to the Arras sector justified. With only nine tanks each and on a frontage of almost five miles, their 2nd and 3rd Divisions attacked in darkness behind a most effective barrage, and when the sun set on this glowing Monday, August 26th, they had regained all the ground along the south bank of the Scarpe, four miles long, lost by the British since March 21st, including the battered pinnacle of Monchy Le Preux with its view deep into the plain of Douai.

Ludendorff was compelled to sanction another limited withdrawal, back behind the Somme Canal south of Peronne and from there along the high ground through Le Transloy, but abandoning Bapaume, where the New Zealanders in particular had met tough opposition. The troops were required to hold on long enough to allow supply dumps to be evacuated and thorough demolitions made, a task bedevilled by the incessant activities of the Royal Air Force and by long-range shelling, which was specially damaging from the heavy guns of the Fourth Army formed into mobile sections well to the fore.

There was as yet no serious shortage of troops in the German Army, and when the 18th Division, having captured Montauban, drew near their scene of former glory, the valley across which lay the stumps and brambles of Trones Wood, they were confronted by hefty guardsmen of the Kaiser Franz Grenadier Regiment of the 2nd Guard Division, who had just come forward against a stream of milling, leaderless masses. And not only did they hold the wood itself, but the high ground to the north, which the 18th understood to have been reached by their Third Army neighbours, the 38th Welsh. The 7th Royal West Kent and the 8th Royal Berkshire attacked, without tanks, at about 5 a.m. on August 27th, and the poor Berkshires, being on the left, came under devastating enfilade fire. The Germans counter-attacked and regained the whole wood. The two battalions were ordered to try again, reinforced by two companies of the 10th Essex, and to give time for adequate artillery preparations zero hour was fixed for 8 p.m. The bombardment, carefully planned by the brigadier, shook and rent the defences, and the assault companies took full advantage of it, creeping daringly close to the crashing shells and dashing in among the dazed Prussians on the instant of lift. The wood was soon retaken, with fifty Germans lying dead inside it amid forty machine-guns, and a stocky, youthful Cockney private gleefully marched back a squad of seventy towering but docile Prussian guardsmen.

A monument stands today in twice-won Trones Wood to the glory of the 18th Division. Captain Nichols, the divisional historian, rightly reminds readers that the men "knew it chiefly as a place of ugliness and horror, blasted with fire, echoing with curses, reeking with pain and death." The horror was the greater on the first occasion, when five battalions grappled all through a terrible night in July 1916, and finally cleared the wood at a cost of 1,500 casualties, and the second is of interest mainly for the comparison it invites and for the example it affords of the attacks that were being made in such abundance by the divisions of three armies. Forming part of the victorious right wing of Rawlinson's army in the Somme offensive of July 1916, the 18th was then at its peak in training, morale, and most of all the quality of its all-volunteer manpower. In August 1918 it consisted predominantly of untrained, hastily drafted, and often conscripted youngsters. Many had to be returned as being of too poor physique, and the former adjutant of one battalion has vivid memories of the pathetic letters he received from mothers drawing attention to frailties in their young that too often were found to exist. Yet when all allowances are made for the greater strength and determination displayed by the Germans in 1916, it would still appear that the 18th Division at any rate had shown improvement not only in planning, which one would expect, but in execution too—and as for morale, there can be no better test than to call on troops for a second attempt after their first has failed.

One obvious reason for this is that the youngsters had been well reared. Their indoctrination in the trenches had seldom been too horrific, and although the casualties had been steadily mounting since the start of the great offensive they had rarely reached harrowing proportions and always the troops had the satisfaction of seeing objectives captured and opposition overcome. The boys were keen to prove themselves, and there were just sufficient men of courage and experience left to respond to the challenge of leading them—and experience could be quickly gained; survival of two attacks was sufficient to turn boy into veteran. Brigade and battalion commanders of course by now had a wealth of experience, and the gunners, having fewer casualties, had a greater supply of it than the infantrymen. They had more guns too than in 1916 and better ammunition, and it was in the sphere of gunner-infantry co-operation that the greatest strides had been made. Trones Wood affords a good example. In 1916 the men were rushed in without any close supporting fire and were vulnerable to the enemy's fire because they were accustomed to tight formations. They cleared the wood not because of their density but because of their guts. In 1918 they worked in close harmony with their gunners and were well rewarded for allowing them the time they needed. The shells guided the infantry forward, in looser, wider formation than of old, though no doubt there was plenty of bunching behind trusted leaders, and it was accepted that all depended on the speed with which bayonet replaced crump. It was to such a method, common to every successful attack, that the British owed their mastery over the Germans. They might be clumsy and slow when conditions were fluid, and the Official History claims that they were, but so long as the infantry retained confidence in their gunners the steady crumbling of the German position was bound to continue.

Winston Churchill, as Minister of Munitions, had made an important contribution to this situation, and Haig expressed gratitude to him "for the immense vigour with which you set

15—A

about providing us with the munitions of war." Less obvious, and unacknowledged by the military, is the part played by Lloyd George, but it was on his insistence that the reduction in infantry was unaccompanied by any corresponding reduction in the support weapons, and it was as a result of this policy that the infantry could be deployed over wider frontages, backed by tanks, machine-guns, aeroplanes and guns of all calibres on a scale never previously envisaged. But there could never be sufficient infantry. Even with his tank battalions so weak that they had all to be withdrawn for retraining and re-equipping, Rawlinson, that pioneer of the wider frontages movement, wrote to Wilson on August 29th : "All you have to do is to keep our infantry up to strength and not waste man-power in tanks and aviation." This is a revealing view from the man reputed to have won the B.E.F.'s greatest victory by throwing 400 tanks into the attack.

Meanwhile the Canadians, with hardly any tanks at their disposal, continued to make great progress. On August 27th they became the first to penetrate the old pre-March front-line as they closed on the Drocourt-Quéant switch, with other corps in attendance to right and left. On this same day the French First Army at last took the town of Roye and joined in a general advance to the Somme Canal.

The Australian Corps reached the line of the canal and its adjacent swamps early on the 29th, and at once Monash planned a daring leap upon the nodal point of the defence line which a great motley of German divisions, in various stages of disarray, were busy fortifying : a leap upon Mont St. Quentin. The remains of this village stood above Peronne, a mile to the north of it, on the end of a long spur from the north-east, and the Australians would have to make deep penetration across a number of obstacles to get there. Rawlinson, who had in mind a wider turning movement by III Corps, although it lagged behind the Australian, raised his eyebrows when Monash told him of his project, but none the less gave it his blessing.

The 2nd Australian Division were to make the assault by a left hook round Peronne, while others made offensive gestures across the canal south of the town so as to distract the enemy. The 5th Brigade were assigned the spearhead rôle. Early on the

30th they tried to cross near Clery, three miles downstream from Peronne, but encountered heavy shelling and machine-gun fire and therefore marched two miles further down the river bank and crossed at a village secured on the northern bank by the 3rd Australian Division after some hard fighting. They then passed through the 3rd Division along the much excavated slopes by the river and with their Lewis guns, bayonets and grenades winkled the Germans out of the village of Clery, which was not strongly held, the main defences being on the higher ground to the north, the objective of the 3rd Division and III Corps. Leaving these enemy positions on their left behind them, the 5th Brigade gained a gentle ridge east of the village around midnight, and here they were joined by the fourth battalion of the brigade, who crossed by a nearby footbridge previously denied.

These tireless and intrepid Australians were now within two miles of Mont St. Quetin, which lay due east, and at 5 a.m. on the 31st, in the gloom of a dull dawn, they began their attack, three battalions in line, each little more than 300-strong, as shells from 120 guns smote the hillside in hastily arranged concentrations. The Tortille river, which runs into the Somme from the north, was no obstacle, and the men strode across it and mounted the wide, gradual and desolate slope on which their shells were falling. It was strewn with old wire entanglements and entrenchments, and there were Germans everywhere, blazing away with their machine-guns as they recovered from the initial shock, hurling stick grenades, putting their hands up or running away from the fearsome crump of grenade, stutter of Lewis gun and the yowl and scream that accompanied the thrust and receipt of a bayonet. By 7 a.m. the 17th Battalion in the centre had captured the wreckage of the village and the knoll above it and gained the line of a road beyond. The 2nd Guard Division were summoned to counter-attack. With powerful aid from artillery they regained the greater part of the village, but the 5th Brigade held on to most of the narrow wedge they had thrust into the German vitals, against prolonged and persistent counter-attack.

In the afternoon the 6th Brigade were fed forward, and next

day they continued the attack through Mont St. Quentin eastwards along the spur, but with little help from artillery because
no one knew where pockets of the 5th Brigade still lurked—the
17th Battalion limped away on relief only seventy-eight soldiers
strong. Meanwhile the 14th Brigade of the 5th Division, having
their first big fight of the offensive, began the assault on Peronne
—and with such verve that three V.C.s were won out of a total
of eight awarded to Australians for this three-day battle that
cost the three divisions involved all but 3,000 casualties. The
Germans fought hard, their troops being especially picked to
hold this prop of their new defensive line, and not until near
midday on September 2nd was the whole of Peronne cleared.
The 2nd Division were by now two miles along the spur beyond
Mont St. Quentin, with trails of dead Germans behind them,
and on their left the 74th and 47th Divisions of III Corps were
grimly struggling to come up alongside them, having pinched
out the 3rd Australian. The 74th were composed of ex-
Yeomanry regiments newly arrived from Palestine, and this was
their first attack in France. They had the misfortune to run into
the Alpine Corps and a weight of shellfire far beyond anything
they had previously experienced. It was not easy for newcomers.

On this same day, September 2nd, the Canadian Corps burst
through the elaborately fortified Drocourt-Quéant switch. The
1st and 4th Canadian Divisions made the attack with a brigade
of the 4th British on their left, and each were led by some thirty
tanks that carved paths through the massive wire entanglements.
The first objectives were speedily taken, in parts with wholesale
surrender of Germans cowering in dug-outs, but the tanks did
not go on and as usual the infantry found the going tougher the
further they went. Even so, an advance of up to four miles was
made, which completely broke the back of the Drocourt-Quéant
switch.

The two Colonial Corps had gored the German line like the
horns of a bull, while the various British divisions, and one New
Zealand, gave plenty of weight to the thrust of the forehead.
Ludendorff had to sanction another withdrawal back to the
Hindenburg position around St. Quentin and further northwards
along a prepared emergency line in front of Cambrai, running
through the swamps of the Sensee river. To conserve divisions, a

withdrawal was also ordered from the remains of the salient by
the Lys. Thirty-six had been thrown in in the attempt to stay
the British advance since its reopening on August 21st, and with
those already committed the total came to sixty-six (as claimed
by the British Official History). Haig had used only thirty-four
divisions to throw this number into retreat. Yet Ludendorff still
had large numerical advantage in the matter of reserves and,
granted a respite, his troops might yet hold out long enough to
achieve a negotiated peace.

Haig had received no message of congratulation from the
War Cabinet for his wonderful achievements during the month
of August. Indeed very little of importance had come from
London until a telegram from Wilson on September 1st. "Just
a word of caution," it ran, "in regard to incurring heavy losses
in attacks on Hindenburg Line . . . I know the War Cabinet
would become anxious if we receive heavy punishment." This
was a fine stimulant to receive on the day before the first
attack on that line was to be made (by the Canadians). Haig
was furious. "The Cabinet are ready to meddle and interfere
in my plans in an underhand way," he fumed somewhat inco-
herently to his diary, "but do not dare openly to say that they
mean to take the responsibility for any failure though ready
to take the credit for every success!" It was obvious enough to
him that, with his opponent groggy, now was the time to go for
the kill, and he was amazed that others could not see it too.
"What a wretched lot of weaklings we have in high places at
the present time!"

But with his operation chief, Marshal Foch, his relationship
was flowering into full bloom. Foch had, on August 25th, sent
Haig a personal letter couched in very complimentary terms,
praising his "progressive widening of the offensive" and assuring
him somewhat apologetically that "General Pétain's Armies are
about to continue their advance in the same manner."

This did not prove to be so. Debeney, as related, entered
Roye on the 27th, and on the 29th Humbert's army painfully
regained Noyon, but a fresh attack by Mangin failed, and
Fayolle's group, still lagging behind, lapsed into a policy of
awaiting developments. Apart from Mangin's attacks on
August 21st and 22nd there had been little sting in the blows

delivered by these three armies. Yet they had none the less captured 31,453 prisoners and 80 guns during August, in what they termed the Third Battle of Picardy, and it had cost them 85,396 casualties.

Rawlinson's army had taken 30,436 prisoners in the same period and at a cost of 50,996 casualties, spread over only fourteen infantry divisions and twelve battalions of tanks and including the much smaller loss (887) suffered by the Cavalry Corps. The Third and First Armies, with rather more divisions but over a shorter period, had captured 33,827 prisoners at a loss of 55,716 casualties. There could be no awaiting developments for these hard-fought divisions; they had still to shape them.

Haig accepted, with pride rather than grudge, that his troops must continue to bear the greater burden. He had always been sceptical of the French capacity for the offensive, but knew that the Americans did not lack it and was eager that they should put it to quickest use. Since early August Pershing had been proudly assembling his scattered divisions on his own newly-assigned operational sector east of Verdun, where they were conveniently placed for supply from the Atlantic ports. He planned an assault to eliminate the deep, two-year-old salient at St. Mihiel. It had grievously hurt Haig to send away his best three American divisions for this purpose, although he had been allowed to keep two immature ones. "What will History say," he irately and egotistically asked his diary, "regarding this action of the Americans leaving the British zone of operations when *the decisive battle* of the war is at its height, and the decision is still in doubt!" In reply to Foch's letter of the 25th, he urged him to spur Pershing into action and suggested that instead of striking eastwards against St. Mihiel as planned, his army should be used for a great blow westwards to converge with the assault Haig was planning on the main Hindenburg Line.

Although it was not admitted by Foch, it seems that this letter made him a convert to Haig's long-held but highly original view that the war could be won that year. Previously Foch's tireless offensive instinct had been directed to no more than chivvying the Germans back from salients which presented the greatest threats to communications, of which St. Mihiel was one. Now, at Haig's wooing, his mind turned to making his own salients, plunging from east and west into the very gizzards of the wounded German Army. At the cost of heated argument and the diluting influence of compromise, Foch prevailed on Pershing to adjust his plans and make two consecutive assaults, the one against St. Mihiel without exploitation eastwards, the other west of Verdun in conjunction with (but not, Pershing insisted, subordinate to) a French attack towards Mezières, which would immediately precede the main British assault a hundred miles further west. Then would every weary soldier all along the foetid line rise with the cry, *"Tout le monde á la battaille!"*

14

THE FORTRESS STORMED

(September 3–October 5)

The British pushed the Germans back to their famous bastion with typical deliberation. Having effectively applied the spur a fortnight earlier, Haig was concerned now about the need to conserve his overworked and irreplaceable divisions for the great task ahead and forbade large-scale attacks. Rawlinson and Byng on the other hand were more aware of a conflicting need. Remembering how grateful they had been for any easing of the pressure during the German offensive, they were determined to allow no easing themselves. The result was a compromise. The divisions plugged steadily away, led as usual by the infantry and well supported by their artillery. The prospect of victory, slowly dawning, was no stimulant to reckless daring. Even so, the 32nd Division made an enterprising crossing of the Somme Canal at first light on September 5th, and by the evening of the 7th the Fourth Army line was nine to ten miles further on, with behind it many filthy, stinking, hastily evacuated encampments and many gutted villages.

Ten days' rest was the most allotted to any of the 'shock' divisions (as they regarded themselves) that bore the brunt of the offensive. The mood of each was a characteristic blend of pride and self-pity, expressed in the claim that "poor old blankety umpteenth will always be first in and last out", in the suspicion that the high command had a personal grudge against them, and in the conviction that no other troops could be relied upon. A young captain, posted against his will as company commander from a regular battalion of his regiment, then with the Second Army, to a Kitchener battalion with the Fourth, felt he had stepped into a different world. His new

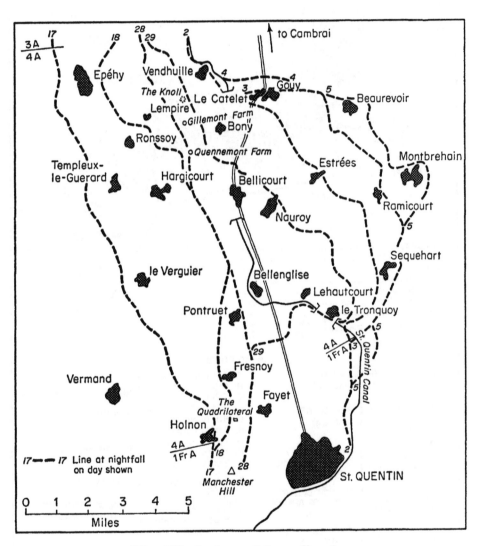

The Hindenburg Line offensive

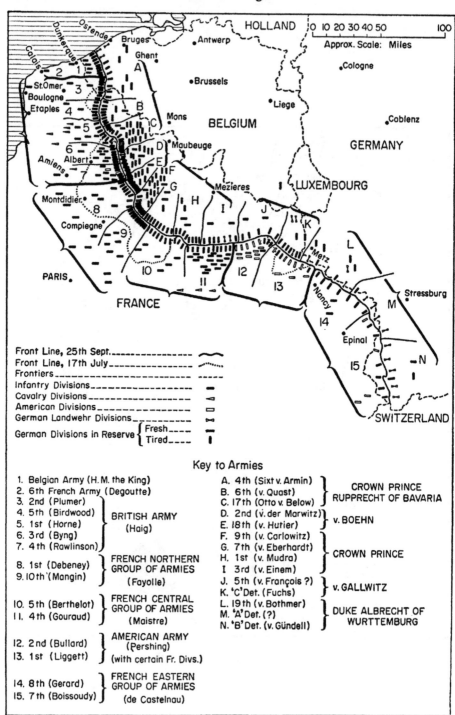

Front Line, 25th Sept. _ _ _ _ _ _ _ _ _ _
Front Line, 17th July _ _ _ _ _ _ _ _ _ _ _
Frontiers _ _ _ _ _ _ _ _ _ _ _ _ _ _ _ _ _
Infantry Divisions _ _ _ _ _ _ _ _ _ _ _ _
Cavalry Divisions _ _ _ _ _ _ _ _ _ _ _ _ _
American Divisions _ _ _ _ _ _ _ _ _ _ _ _
German Landwehr Divisions _ _ _ _ _ _ _
German Divisions in Reserve { Fresh _ _ _ _
                             { Tired _ _ _ _

Key to Armies

1. Belgian Army (H.M. the King)		A. 4th (Sixt v. Armin)	} CROWN PRINCE
2. 6th French Army (Degoutte)		B. 6th (v. Quast)	RUPPRECHT OF BAVARIA
3. 2nd (Plumer)		C. 17th (Otto v. Below)	
4. 5th (Birdwood)	BRITISH ARMY	D. 2nd (v. der Marwitz)	} v. BOEHN
5. 1st (Horne)	(Haig)	E. 18th (v. Hutier)	
6. 3rd (Byng)		F. 9th (v. Carlowitz)	
7. 4th (Rawlinson)		G. 7th (v. Eberhardt)	} CROWN PRINCE
8. 1st (Debeney)	FRENCH NORTHERN GROUP OF ARMIES (Fayolle)	H. 1st (v. Mudra)	
9. 10th (Mangin)		I. 3rd (v. Einem)	
		J. 5th (v. François ?)	} v. GALLWITZ
		K. 'C' Det. (Fuchs)	
10. 5th (Berthelot)	FRENCH CENTRAL GROUP OF ARMIES (Maistre)	L. 19th (v. Bothmer)	} DUKE ALBRECHT OF WURTTEMBURG
11. 4th (Gouraud)		M. 'A' Det. (?)	
		N. 'B' Det. (v. Gündell)	
12. 2nd (Bullard)	AMERICAN ARMY (Pershing) (with certain Fr. Divs.)		
13. 1st (Liggett)			
14. 8th (Gerard)	FRENCH EASTERN GROUP OF ARMIES (de Castelnau)		
15. 7th (Boissoudy)			

Haig's wall map on September 25th, showing magnetism of the
Amiens sector

commanding officer, who had been a sergeant in a different regiment at the outbreak of war, poured contempt on the regular battalion, saying they were too precious to take their share (although they were defending Ypres) and that the captain ought to be glad of the chance to serve with a fighting battalion. Next day the battalion had to advance five miles, under the direction of a brigadier who arrived mounted in full battle array and attended by a trooper carrying his penant on a lance—a romantic sight for a man from the squalid confinement of Ypres. Subsequent proceedings lacked such panache. The troops advanced warily, far spread by sections, and leapt for cover as soon as the enemy machine-guns opened up. Artillery fire called for and speedily brought down, and by dint of urging from the odd stalwart the advance jerked forward again and the battalion gained their objective, leaving behind thirty of their more rash, inexperienced, or unlucky members dead or wounded, with our captain among the latter. Such was the pattern of the advance.

Soon all would take their share, and even as this brash commanding officer rapped out his insults the regulars were on their way to the Fourth Army, not to replace the old divisions but to reinforce them. The 1st came from Horne's First Army, and apart from helping to defend Bethune in April and assisting the Canadians in their recent attacks they had not been involved in any severe fighting since Passchendaele. The 6th also came. They had been one of Byng's shock absorbers on March 21st and had since been under Plumer's command in front of Ypres, where gas had been their worst affliction; not since November 1917, in the Battle of Cambrai, had they launched an attack. While the offensive technique of these two divisions may have needed lubrication, a glance at their battalions on the march was sufficient to show that they had the will, and the material too, to uphold the traditions of the Regular Army.

They were followed by a fine representative of the Territorial Force, stocked with a much higher proportion of their original manpower than was to be found in most: the 46th North Midland Division. They came from the Fifth Army near

Bethune and, amazingly, had fought no major battle since the
First Army's attack on Hill 70 in August 1917.

Rawlinson now again had a third corps in which to place
these new divisions. The IXth, of Chemin des Dames fame, had
been reconstituted and the commander of the 62nd Division,
Sir Walter Braithwaite, formerly of the Somerset Light Infantry,
promoted to its command. Also taking the 32nd Division under
command, IX Corps came up on the right of the Australians
during the advance from the Somme Canal, with on their right
Debeney's First Army, mulish as ever in the face of shooing
by Foch under entreaty from Haig. The junction between
French and British was opposite the northern fringe of St.
Quentin, which was two miles south of its position before Haig
had grudgingly taken over the extra twenty-six miles in January.

By a sudden increase in shelling the Germans gave notice
that they intended to stand on the line that the British had
themselves been so busily fortifying around the turn of the year,
having won it during the spring offensive of 1917. Obviously,
mindful of Wilson's warning, of which he said no word to his
subordinates, Haig called on his army commanders to report on
their prospects of launching deliberate offensives. Rawlinson
was told in particular to consider breaching the main Hindenburg Line where its water barrier, the St. Quentin Canal, ran
underground for almost three miles beneath the villages of
Bellicourt and Bony. This open, commanding stretch of ground
was the key to the whole defence and communication system
between St. Quentin and Cambrai and therefore bristled with
old fortifications, a plan of which Rawlinson had captured
during his advance. It was ironic that the Fourth Army, having
been chosen to open the offensive because their ground was then
so suitable for an attack, should thereafter have to trudge across
the most forbidding terrain in front of any army (except perhaps
the Second): first the devastated Somme battlefields, then the
barrier of the Somme Canal and finally the miles of wired
entanglements, dug-outs and concrete emplacements constructed
in depth not just by one side but by both.

Rawlinson replied that he would not care to give an opinion
on the main Hindenburg Line until he had driven the Germans
from the line they held and that he would like to launch this

preliminary attack with the minimum delay. Byng also stressed the importance of speed. He was instructed to make a limited attack on the 12th, being now assigned the subsidiary rôle to Rawlinson, who was to chime in on the 18th. Ludendorff meanwhile was angrily resisting pressure for the initiation of a further, much larger withdrawal, back to the line of Antwerp and the Meuse, which was recommended by generals closely acquainted with the demoralisation of the troops and the dilapidation of the Siegfried (as they termed the Hindenburg) defences. The instinct of the British generals was right.

The left wing of Byng's army was already astride the Hindenburg Line, though with a number of water obstacles ahead, and his attack on the 12th merely extended the dent. It was launched by three divisions, the New Zealand, 37th, and 62nd, and the last-named, on the left, recaptured the village of Havrincourt, which they had won in the Battle of Cambrai. The German reaction was prompt and energetic, but their counterattacks, although by no means insipid, were broken up.

Almost simultaneously, starting at 5 a.m. on the 12th as opposed to 5.30, Pershing's First American Army made their first attack as such. Six huge divisions, in conjunction with four French ones, swept through the sides of the St. Mihiel salient after a brief, mighty roar from 2,971 guns, the majority of them French. The Germans, hopelessly outnumbered, were in process of withdrawing to shorten their line, but so rapid was the American advance near the shoulder of the salient that 15,000 prisoners and 443 guns were taken. But there was no eruption beyond the baseline, as Pershing had originally planned, and the Germans could occupy a prepared line without serious dwindling of their reserves, while the American generals chafed at an opportunity wasted.

For his attack on the 18th Rawlinson sent eight divisions against the various ridges and hillocks that had contained the battle positions of five of Gough's divisions on that grim day in March. There could be no alternative to a frontal attack and, in view of future needs, only twenty tanks were allotted, together with some dummies designed to spread alarm and draw fire. The artillery again had the main shepherding rôle, aided by a colossal peppering by massed machine-guns. At

5.20 a.m. 1,488 guns opened up and sent high explosive, shrapnel and smoke shells crashing, barking and fizzing along a twelve-mile line which slowly receded during a sustained programme of fury without pause in the first two hours. It was pouring with rain, and the mist lay thick, making the smoke shells unnecessary.

As usual the Australians, attacking in the centre with the 4th and 1st Divisions, made best progress. Although outnumbered by the Germans, of whom they captured no less than 4,243 during the day, they quickly nipped up the Le Verguier ridge, on which the 24th Division had fought so hard, and liquidated sixty machine-gun posts around the catacombed rubble village fortress, for their part in which a sergeant and a private were to win the V.C. Making good use of their few tanks, both divisions had stormed the multiple trench lines to a depth of almost three miles by nightfall, and the 4th resumed the assault in darkness and reached a spur a mile beyond the old British front line, which overlooked the southern entrance of the St. Quentin Canal into its tunnel at Bellicourt. Already Rawlinson had rung up Haig to tell him (as he himself recorded) that "the attack on the main Hindenburg Line was a feasible enterprise offering reasonable chances of success."

For the British 1st Division, on the immediate right of the Australians, the day had been less happy. It had started with casualties from their own barrage, because of complications in the programme not fully comprehended and although the left brigade redeemed this misfortune with a plucky advance, the right one was scourged, once the rain and mist lifted, by enfilade fire from Fresnoy, at the head of a valley they had to cross. This village stood within the 6th Division's sector, and it remained a scourge, partly because of the determination of its defenders and partly because the 6th were themselves sorely impeded by fire from their right flank. It came from that memorial to British heroism, Manchester Hill. The French had agreed to make a simultaneous attack on it. Their artillery fire came down, but nothing more; it was later explained that the weather was too bad.

Butler was back in command of III Corps, having returned from sick leave, and the 47th Division were gone, transferred to a quieter sector. The 74th went in on the right, and although they were bedevilled by gas shelling as they assembled for the attack, they showed that they had been learning from recent experience by keeping almost abreast of their redoubtable neighbours on their right, the 1st Australian. The 15th Suffolk in particular distinguished themselves in a skilfully executed flanking attack on Templeux le Guerard. The 74th gained a footing on one of the spurs jutting from the sprawling, commanding ridge on which further leftwards the joint villages of Ronssoy and Lempire lie and beyond them the bigger and tactically more important one of Epéhy, from which this battle takes its name. Epéhy was the objective of the 12th Division, with the 58th on their left assigned the adjoining hamlet of Pezière, while on their right the 18th tackled Ronssoy and Lempire. There was some very tough fighting for these villages. The whole of the Alpine Corps, twelve battalions strong, were committed to the defence of Epéhy alone, with orders to stay there to the last. The 12th gained a grip on the southern entrance, from which three battalions from Norfolk, Essex and Cambridgeshire slowly, painfully, methodically bombed sullen Germans out of stronghold after stronghold, unaided by their two tanks, both of which were disabled, and shot up at one stage by an over-zealous tank supporting the Londoners. As the sun set, the last of the defenders was found to be gone, and the 12th and 58th were in full possession of the many heaps of debris that was Epéhy. They were still far from their final objective.

The 18th meanwhile had had a rather easier passage into Ronssoy, thanks largely to more effective assistance from their tanks but found the going tougher as they battled on towards Lempire and were left far behind the corps barrage, as had been predicted without avail by their experienced commander, Major-General R. P. Lee. Showing dash that marked him as the newcomer that he was, young Lance-Corporal A. Lewis of the 6th Northamptonshire successfully assailed two machine-gun posts that were holding up his battalion, gaining a V.C. he did not live to receive. This tightened the 18th's hold on the ridge, but when a fresh brigade passed through they clashed with a counter-attack made by a fresh German division, and there was confused and breathless grappling amid a haphazard conglomeration of trenches, corpses, trees and ruined buildings. If it was weary, costly labour for the divisions of III Corps, they at least sent 2,300 prisoners to the rear during the day as proof of their perseverance.

Three divisions of the Third Army also joined in the attack and made good gains on the left of III Corps. The 21st were on the right. They had bravely held Epéhy on March 21st and now regained other ground they had held on the left of it. Further leftwards beyond the attacking divisions, on the sector around Havrincourt held by the 37th and 3rd Divisions, a violent bombardment by gas and explosive fell on the British trenches for over an hour during the late afternoon, followed by bombs and machine-gun bullets from aircraft. The infantry of three German divisions, one of them completely fresh, then swarmed into the attack with the old weaving tactics and made entry here and there. They had all been driven back or rounded up by midnight, and for their failure von der Marwitz was removed from the command of the Second Army and transferred to a quieter sector. It was the first breach in the ranks of the German high command.

Haig could now go ahead with his plans for a grand assault, based on successive blows by his armies, with Rawlinson reinforced with further fresh divisions and held back until last to obtain maximum dispersal of the enemy reserves opposite him. There had been some jockeying between Byng and Rawlinson, Haig noted, but when he announced his programme "all were quite pleased with my arrangements." It was synchronised with a much wider programme of death blows, the first of which was delivered on September 15th when General Franchet d'Espery at last justified the Allied presence in Macedonia by smashing through the Bulgarian line. Allenby followed on the 19th, striking at the tottering Turks with gleaming success, despite the draining westwards of so much of his strength. "The news is simply topping," wrote Rawlinson to Wilson. "Ferdinand must be feeling a bit of an ass, and Enver too." (Ferdinand being King of Bulgaria and Enver ruler of the Turks.) "Meantime, the Boche is going to get the biggest knock he has ever had."

For the men of his divisions there was more to it than one big knock. Many of them had been knocking away since August 8th, without more than a few days' pause between one attack and the next, and now they had to go on knocking to gain the ground still required, over two miles away in places, for the start of the assault on the main Hindenburg Line. For Butler's divisions this involved a further six days packed tight with assaults by brigades, battalions, companies, platoons or mere bombing parties. Their objectives were wired and fortified buildings or earthworks known by such names as Duncan, Doleful, Egg and Fleeceall, sounding so whimsical from a distance and so sickening from the lips of an officer briefing details for a fresh attack. And beyond them, defiant to the end, was a fiendish knoll known simply as The Knoll, the slopes of which had been strewn with British bodies in 1917 and now received another layer, felled by multiple machine-guns firing with intensity that staggered even the most grizzled veteran; they were ensconced in concrete emplacements entered by tunnel from the other side of the hill, a common enough amenity of the Hindenburg Line. These were the worst days experienced by the 18th, 58th and 12th Divisions in their long advance from beside the Somme. Two more German divisions had been rushed in to halt their laboured progress from Epéhy and Ronssoy, and they could be shifted from their labyrinthal redoubts only by a combination of guts and well-planned tactics. Spirits drooped at times, but they could revive with such speed that on two occasions men of the 18th Division leapt spontaneously from their trenches to turn the collapse of a counter-attack into rout.

Braithwaite's IX Corps encountered such opposition that a fresh corps attack had to be launched on September 24th, with the 46th Division making their début, squeezed in on the left of the 1st. They, too, had great difficulty in making headway and had a desperate fight for the village of Pontruet, just ahead of the old British line, for his part in which Lieutenant J. C. Barrett of the 5th Leicestershire was awarded the V.C. Not until the night of the 25th did the Germans here at last yield to pressure and withdraw to their main line, evacuating not only Pontruet but Manchester Hill and a redoubt known as the Quadrilateral which had been a great source of torment to the right wing of the 6th Division.

Haig had sixty-two divisions available for his greatest battle, which was three more than at the start of March 1918, such had been the scraping for men at home, some of whom were of medical category B, and the paring of British forces in Palestine, Macedonia and Italy. Of six divisions turned to scrap as a result of the German offensives, all but one had been reconstituted. Two divisions had arrived complete from Italy and two from Palestine, and the two Portuguese (who were still in France but no longer operationally engaged) were replaced by two American, an equal exchange only in the realms of finger counting. On the other sectors of the Western Front there appear to have been 136 operational divisions (97 French, 25 American, 12 Belgian and 2 Italian). The allied total was therefore 198 and the Germans, at any rate on paper, could put 197 against them, a drop of eleven since August 8th. Of these 197, 70 were opposite the British and many others were convalescing elsewhere after being mauled by them.

The American–French attack came first. Preceded by a three-hour bombardment, nine American divisions went into the attack at dawn on September 26th, stretched along a twenty-mile front with the Meuse on their right and the Aisne on their left. The French were to conform on the flanks, a familiar enough rôle and one they could claim as the privilege of veterans who had held the breach rather longer than is bearable. Ambition ran high among the Americans, but there were problems their staffs were too inexperienced even to recognise, no less than six of the nine assault divisions were new to battle, and the five against them, although convalescent, under strength, and at a hopeless disadvantage morally, could yet draw on a vast store of battle craft. Ardour was not enough. Accompanied by 189 light tanks, the Americans swarmed forward for two or three miles against hardly any opposition, and then the machine-guns, sited so cleverly, began to take a terrible toll. The Americans plugged gamely on, to a distance of almost five miles on the right, but the problem of regaining lost momentum, always so baffling, was beyond solution for the time being. No German reserves were moved from the British sector.

Next day, September 27th, it was the turn of Horne and Byng. The pattern of their recent operations was maintained. The Canadians, as the right corps of Horne's First Army, struck out across the half-dry Canal du Nord due east towards Cambrai with tremendous artillery support but with only eight tanks to each division. Once again they gained spectacular success. Bourlon Wood, highwater mark of the famous tank attack of the previous year (made from the south-west), was captured and an advance made beyond the final objectives, to a distance of four miles. The Third Army on their right attacked on a frontage of six divisions with five more in second line, their strength receding in succession from the left. They too gained great success, and on the 28th the left wing, led by the 57th and 63rd Royal Naval Divisions, reached the line of the St. Quentin Canal along the bulge that at the northern end is only two miles south-west of Cambrai. Two more lines of the Hindenburg defences had been overrun. Yet on the extreme right, where they trailed the Fourth Army, the Third were by design dormant.

On September 28th Plumer struck from Ypres together with the Belgian Army, and both were under command of King Albert of Belgium, whose eagerness to advance was a decisive factor in the choice of sector. He also had nine French divisions in reserve and a French chief of staff, General Degoutte. The plan was to free the whole of the Belgian coast and the general direction of attack was therefore divergent from the others. It was made from either side of Ypres, Plumer putting in four divisions with two more in second line, the Belgians seven and two. Despite heavy rain and differing views on the best form of artillery support—Plumer, as might be imagined, made his barrage sudden, violent and short—great success was achieved, and by the second day the Belgians were well beyond the Passchendaele ridge and Plumer once more held Messines. The Germans were outnumbered by almost two to one, thanks to the pressure elsewhere, and drew back once their deep-sited and concreted emplacements were lost. Such was the Fourth Battle of Ypres, a mere virgin beside her elders, but blood had been spilled all the same.

Rawlinson's day was Sunday, September 29th, the fourth in succession to open with a torrent of shells on a different portion of the German Army. His army had swollen and consisted now of sixteen infantry divisions, one cavalry brigade, and eleven battalions of tanks (out of fifteen with the B.E.F.), two of which had Whippets. There were five new divisions and two were gone, the faithful 58th London and the 74th having been transferred to quieter sectors. Three of these new ones came from the scrap heap, restocked with infantry from distant sources. The 25th Division, late of the Third and Second Armies, received nine battalions from Italy, unscarred by heavy fighting for almost a year, by the removal of the fourth battalions of the nine brigades over there. The 50th was similarly re-equipped, under its old commander, Major-General H. C. Jackson, mainly with battalions from Macedonia, only one of which was Northumbrian, the 2nd Northumberland Fusiliers; most of these battalions had been in India when the war began, reached the freezing trenches in France by January 1915, suffered appallingly at the Second Ypres and Loos, and since been emaciated by malaria, for which they had had two months' rehabilitation in France. The 66th East Lancashire, formerly of Watts's corps, had been used as a cadre for training Americans and been restored to strength with infantry from various theatres, of whom one third were indigenous Lancastrian, one third Irish, and one third South African, the last-named being transferred from the 9th Division to make room for more Scotsmen. Lieutenant-General Sir Thomas Morland and the headquarters of his XIII Corps were removed from the Fifth Army to take command of these divisions, and for the time being Rawlinson held them in reserve.

His other two new divisions were the 27th and 30th American, each consisting of twelve large battalions of infantry divided between two brigades of two regiments each. They had been prepared for battle under the fatherly guidance of Plumer, but had not as yet even held the line. It was part of Pershing's terms for their retention by Haig that they should be kept together under American command, that is as II Corps under Major-General G. W. Reed.

Unfortunately for Rawlinson, the Australians had reinforcement problems, and Monash had been promised that he could
soon withdraw his divisions and build them up for use again
next spring. It was in any case unfair to call on them to lead
the assault yet again, and the newest weapon of all was therefore
assigned the spearhead task, the American II Corps. They
were to link up with the Australians to form a combined
Colonial and ex-Colonial force. Monash was to nurse them and
pass through two of his own divisions to take the second
objective, a task which called for higher skills than the more
rigid opening attack. With the humility that still characterised
this eager army that had served such a long apprenticeship,
Read accepted subordination to Monash and moved his headquarters alongside his. He also accepted a large Australian
mission that supplied advisers down to company level; they
found they had a daunting task in teaching their pupils, at
such notice, the procedures, tactics and battle administration
that formed part of the routine for an attack by the Australian
Corps. The Americans had also to rely on the Australian Corps
for all their artillery support, for they had no guns of their own
—except for those mounted in one American-manned battalion
of British Mark V tanks.

They took over their line on September 25th, the 30th
Division on the right, the 27th on the left. It was that held by
the Australians, together with a part of the III Corps front,
and was opposite the all-important gap where the St. Quentin
Canal ran underground, the American first objective. Monash
held a big conference on the 26th at which the complicated
details of the artillery barrage, involving over a thousand guns
just on this corps front, were worked out. They were based on
the assumption that the start-line would be from the final
objectives for the attack on the 18th. In fact, III Corps had
not been able to reach this line. Three redoubts still held out:
Quennemont Farm (on the right), Gillemont Farm, and that
breaker of hearts and bodies, The Knoll. They were spread over
a frontage of two miles and covered spurs into the German
lines from which observation could be obtained of the northern
entrance to the tunnel. In preference to the seemingly untidy

alternative of altering the artillery plan, the Americans were called up to remove these prickly obstacles in a preliminary attack; Monash, who prided himself on leaving nothing to chance, was aware of the risk in such a course and claims that Rawlinson insisted on it. Haig was also opposed to it, but was persuaded by Rawlinson, in a lengthy submission, that all would be well. It turned out to be an occasion when Rawlinson was wrong, and all the friendliness he showed the Americans and his sympathetic consideration of their smallest problems—which both surprised and delighted them—were small compensation for the losses they suffered.

With twelve tanks in support, three battalions of the American 27th Division attacked these lethal redoubts at dawn on the 27th. They appeared to reach them, but then came the mighty, prolonged chatter of German machine-guns, and it dawned at last that any survivors still holding out were surrounded. One of the few definite accomplishments was the recovery from The Knoll of an incredibly tough subaltern of the 10th Essex who for three days had lain in a shell hole, his leg shattered, while shells from British guns crashed round him. Rather than submit American and other wounded to a similar fate a ban was placed on further shelling short of the prearranged start-line, and as compensation for this dire complication of their problems, the Americans were allotted extra tanks, the 27th Division having thirty-nine in all and the 30th thirty-three. All told there were seven battalions of tanks (Americans included) at Monash's disposal.

On the right of the Australian–American Corps, IX Corps were to make an assault crossing of the St. Quentin Canal with the 46th Division and push the 1st Division forward on their right along the high ground by the side of the canal, where it conveniently bent away from the direction of attack. The crossing was to be made just to the south of the start of the cutting into the Bellicourt tunnel, and although the canal was not very wide it was deep in places and its far bank was heavily wired and covered by fire from a chain of concrete emplacements. It was a desperate venture, justified by the need to create a diversion from the main, narrow-fronted American assault and to widen the frontage as enticement for the French First Army to join in. The Staffordshire Brigade—the 5th and 6th South Staffordshire and the 6th North Staffordshire—were to lead. They had first to advance almost a mile and then cross the canal, using equipment they could carry with them, such as rafts, ladders, mud-mats, collapsible boats and 3,000 life jackets hastily removed from Channel steamers. Their requirements had been attended to with all the imagination and energy that had gained the Fourth Army staff their reputation, and the men were keyed up by expectation of great happenings such as had not been experienced (rather ominously) since the unsullied eve of the Somme. The Staffordshires were under command of Brigadier-General J. V. Campbell, who had won the V.C. when in command of a battalion of the Coldstream with the Fourth Army on the Somme. Rawlinson came to his headquarters on the night before battle, discussed his plans at length and, in Campbell's words, "left us with 'our tails right up' ". "I don't mind saying now," Rawlinson told him when next they met, "that I never expected to see you again."

There could be chance of surprising the enemy after all the preliminary grappling, and for two days Budsworth's guns therefore belched forth their optimum in frightfulness. A million shells were fired, some with instantaneous fuses to blast holes in the acres and acres of barbed wire, some with delayed fuses in hope of penetrating the tunnelled shelters, and preceding them were thirty thousand shells bringing the first British-administered dose of mustard gas to the German gun lines, headquarters and rest areas and despatched with relish by those who had experienced the misery they could cause. As dawn approached on the Sunday the pattern gradually changed shape to conform to the well tried ritual. The aeroplanes came over, the tanks started up, and at 5.55, the final crunch came down on the forward positions, dutifully lifting after three minutes. The mist, just as dutifully, was lying thick.

To comply with the dictates of the barrage programme, the American 27th Division had for an hour already been battling against the three strongolds inside their start-line, though their tanks could not help them in the dark. They strove bravely and almost, but not quite, gained The Knoll; elsewhere they were repulsed. When the main attack began the tanks, of their own American battalion, suffered heavily, some being picked off at close quarters by gunners who did not panic at the sudden emergence of the monsters through the gloom, others being blown up by mines thought to have been laid by the British in 1917. But there were gaps between the strong points and probably two battalions of the 27th (out of a total of six in the attacking wave) strode on and made deep penetration. Reports reaching Monash sounded good. Bony was reported captured well before 10 a.m. and soon afterwards messages arrived from aircraft, now enjoying full visibility, that the Americans had reached Gouy, the final objective of the 27th and over two miles from their start-line. The 30th Division on the right were also reported to have reached their final objective, having captured Bellicourt. The 3rd (on the left) and the 5th Australian Divisions were already moving forward, with their own tanks, to pass through. Soon they were reporting that the way was not clear at all.

The Americans had been over-eager. They were well aware of the need to cling close to their barrage, but in the urge to get forward another need, which had been stressed by their Australian advisers, was forgotten : the need for thorough mopping up by a second wave. It had never been greater. The Germans were practically invulnerable to the bombardment in their deep shelters, and they remained down below as both the shells and assault troops passed over. Then they emerged through their multiple exits and as the mist gradually lifted rows of unsuspecting Americans were presented for slaughter in front and behind. It was sickening for their advisers (who included a few from the British 18th Division) to see these brave innocents drift into merciless enfilade fire and to lie piled in their rows like the dead on some battlefield of old. Their wounded were full of self-reproach for their folly, and it was in vain that the Germans might try to promote contempt for them, as by the note eventually found in one machine-gun post: "Dear Tommy, From this place I shot 60 American soldiers with my machine-gun; they came like sheep."

So far from speeding to the relief of the Americans at Bony and Gouy, the 3rd Australian had to fight their hardest to gain possession of those three redoubts which had caused both veteran British and fledgling American such anguish, largely through the failure of their commanders to appreciate how desperately the enemy would resist. Unsupported by artillery, with most of their tanks knocked out and with many delays to rescue wounded or stranded Americans, the Australians at last forced the Germans out of the two farms and off The Knoll, beating off fierce counter-attacks on the latter with confused assistance from the 18th Division, who with the 12th were responsible for carrying out the subordinate task allotted III Corps, that of conforming with the advance on their right. An attempt by the 3rd Australian to carry the advance further was brought to a swift and painful end. No more was heard of the Americans who had so bravely forged ahead.

The 5th Australian had a less forlorn task in following the 30th American and they fought their way into Bellicourt to find many of them holding out against Germans who had swarmed out of tunnels and other hideaways concealed by the mist. The tanks again suffered heavy losses as in full daylight the Australians pushed on towards Nauroy under heavy shell-fire, bringing parties of Americans with them. They reached this village, to find more Americans there, and set about clearing the adjacent trenches and dug-outs. Major B. A. Wark, commanding the 32nd Australian, won the V.C. here. He led his battalion from the front, capturing a battery of guns with the aid of a few men and driving the enemy from post after post.

Meanwhile marvels were being performed by the men on the right, the men of the 46th Territorial, the oak tree division from the very heart of England. Wearing life jackets, the Staffordshires swept down the spur towards the canal, jumping into trenches while Germans cowered in their shelters or blinked in the mist, and in the same continuous bound, regulated by the creep of their barrage, they swarmed across the canal before the defenders realised what was happening. The 6th South Staffordshire, crossing just to the north of the village of Bellenglise, laid planks and clambered over or plunged across with no more support than a cork float or paddle; they hurried into the village and sealed the exits of tunnels located from air photos, trapping hundreds of Germans inside. The other two battalions, on their left, found the water deeper and the banks steeper. Officers swam across with ropes which they secured as lifelines for the men who followed; rafts, ladders, and existing foot bridges were also used to bring the maximum thrust of bayonets upon the shell-torn, mist-shrouded emplacements along the far bank. One cart bridge was seized intact by a brave rush against a machine-gun as the German demolition party sheltered from the barrage.

Having secured their objectives, the gallant Staffordshires had the protection of a buttress of shells for three hours, while the other two brigades came up to pass through, a brigade of Sherwood Foresters on the right and a Lincolnshire-Leicestershire one on the left. They advanced up two convergent spurs and, under the inspiration of the famous start made for them, drove the Germans out of trench after trench. But soon the fog cleared, and so did the smoke laid by the gunners. The 6th Foresters on the right came under a fury of shellfire from their right flank, which made a crumpled smoking mess of the tanks that had come to their support through Bellicourt. Machine-gun bullets were flying too. The commanding officer of this battalion was the Reverend Lieutenant-Colonel B. W. Vann, the chaplain to a school in peacetime, but military in appearance with a long, lean face, clipped moustache and steadfast eye; he had already been wounded six times and held the M.C. and bar and Croix de Guerre. At once he was out in front among the shells and bullets, running from company to company and getting them moving again before they lost the barrage. Meanwhile a party had sneaked off to deal with the guns. They were firing from beyond the canal, where it flanked the line of advance; the Foresters made the crossing, put some infantrymen to flight and drove their bayonets into the gunners. Vann had now led his battalion on to their objective and reorganised them under continual fire. To round off proceedings he led a dash against the village of Lehautcourt, on his side of the canal to the right, where the Germans were bringing up horses to remove their guns. The Foresters won the race, and in the fight that ensued Vann personally liquidated five gunners with his revolver, boot and riding crop. He won the V.C.

It was now the turn of the 32nd Division, who were due to

pass through. They were not as prompt as they might have been, but one brigade gained best part of a mile with good aid from a few Whippets, bringing the total advance to nearly four miles, and another, branching right-handed, stormed the Le Tronquoy ridge, with the 15th H.L.I. leading, and took the ground above another tunnel here, which was barely a mile long. The 1st Division were due to link up with them at this point, from the other side of the canal, but they had found it slow work winkling Germans out of well-fortified positions while the bulk of the artillery concentrated on the main assault, and consequently the 32nd and 46th Divisions formed a wedge, far ahead of their neighbours on either side.

Sixteen tanks had made the detour through Bellicourt to support the advance of the 46th, and they all appear to have been put out of action. Although there had been some brave and useful contributions—most notably by a staff officer, Major F. E. Hotblack, who brought two tanks to the aid of the Australians near Quinnemont Farm, destroyed some strong-points and, with both tanks knocked out and himself badly wounded, still held the ground won—in spite of such deeds it had been a bad day for the Tank Corps. It had been shown that, now that the Germans knew what to expect, the tanks were vulnerable in the assault on carefully prepared positions, and once again the poor old infantry had nothing to lead them into wired and concreted emplacements except for their own bayonets and the crash of the shells. The tanks could be of greater aid once the enemy defences began to crumble, as was shown by the Whippets supporting the 32nd Division, but that they could not themselves force a breach was woefully brought home to a column of Whippets and armoured cars that set off on their allotted exploitation rôle in the mistaken belief that the Australians were on the final objective.

It was now a matter of applying the lever presented to Rawlinson by the fine advance of Braithwaite's corps. The 32nd bit deeper into the German defences on the 30th, on to high ground over a mile due east of Nauroy, overlooking much of the Australian line, and on their right the 1st Division duly linked up with them above the canal at Le Tronquoy. After a day of exhausting pressure the Australians felt the resistance slacken and on the morning of October 1st they advanced a mile all along their line. Bony was captured, together with the northern end of the tunnel, and further left the two sister divisions, the 18th and 12th, closed on the line of the canal, where their long partnership was to end. In the afternoon of the 1st the 32nd struck out again, making the first gash in the last highly developed line of defences the Germans had. The violence of the reaction showed how the blow hurt. The 5th/6th Royal Scots, on the extreme right, entered the village of Sequehart but were forced out by a double-pronged attack, and the 5th Border Regiment had a similar experience as Preselles. But the 2nd Manchester, leading the attack of another brigade with nine tanks in support, strode through yard upon yard of rusted wire and won nearly a mile of trench along a spur where it flanked, overlooked and was again ahead of the Australian line. Many counter-attacks were made during the night, but the Manchesters were not to be shifted.

To the left of the Manchesters a valley ran north-westwards between the troops of the Fourth Army and this last support line of the Hindenburg defences, known as the Beaurevoir Line. Its far stretching belts of wire, its shallow trenches, and its gun emplacements blended well with the scenery they had been part of so long, a scenery of grassy, open slopes and unscarred villages, the latter surrounded as a rule by green and leafy trees. Rawlinson decided that a fully co-ordinated attack must be made on this line with minimum delay. Fresh troops were brought up: the 46th Division took over most of the 32nd's frontage; the 2nd Australian relieved the 5th; and XIII Corps took over the frontage of both the 3rd Australian and the remains of III Corps, putting the 50th Division into the line. All these reliefs, together with reconnaissances, the preparation of fire plans, and the move forward of guns and tanks along roads strewn with half eradicated obstructions, were crammed into twenty-four hours, during which the only offensive venture was a second attempt by the 5th/6th Royal Scots to capture Sequehart. Again they broke into this village standing on a narrow ridge but were forced out.

The attack began at first light on October 3rd in the familiar Fourth Army manner—familiar, that is, to the veterans of the

2nd Australian in the centre, fast becoming familiar to the 46th on their right, but quite new to the 50th on the left, none of whose battalions had launched an attack on the Western Front since 1915. The 32nd also joined in. They had to capture Sequehart, and at their own request the 5th/6th Royal Scots once again took part in the attack. Having made their third entry into the newly battered village, they now held it against two counter-attacks made by different divisions. From this boulder on the right wing, won so dearly, Debeney's Frenchmen could be beckoned forward as they toiled warily along from St. Quentin—'debbing' along, to use a Fourth Army colloquialism.

The 46th attacked with the Staffordshire Brigade on the right and the Sherwood Foresters on the left and again made fine progress, having been led by tanks through the wire entanglements. The Foresters had a stiff fight to reach the village of Ramicourt, in the course of which Sergeant W. H. Johnson of the 5th Battalion won the V.C. for twice storming machine-gun posts although early wounded by a grenade. The 6th, on the left, were again led with great valour by Colonel Vann, but as he moved from section to section near the edge of the village, now forcing the pace, now restraining the impetuous, he went down with his seventh wound—and this time he was dead, shot through the head.

For a minute or two the 6th Foresters were stunned into inactivity. It was as though the whole battalion were at prayer, for the Colonel of course was a conspicuous figure and news that he had fallen travelled fast. Then a white flag was seen to be flying from where the worst of the fire had been coming. A platoon advanced to accept the surrender. They were met by a hail of machine-gun fire. The Germans had chosen the worst possible moment for such a trick. The Foresters came at them with taut, unshakable deliberation and slew them in the dust of Ramicourt. None the less 400 prisoners were rounded up, mainly by the less provoked 5th Battalion, and as they emerged from their cellars and redoubts so too did the village's inhabitants, singly and in great trepidation at first, and then in their scores. laughing and crying, oblivious of the danger, pathetically eager to hug their liberators in their joy at what

for the elderly majority was a second release from the Prussian
yoke. It was a new experience for the British to receive such a
welcome in a captured village; even administrative control was
slipping from the Germans' grasp.

There was trouble now from the left flank, where the
Australians, uncharacteristically, were lagging behind. Leaving
the 6th to intrude into their sector and refuse this flank, the
other Forester battalions made the assault on the final objective,
the straggly, orchard surrounded village of Montbrehain, standing on the final fortified ridge of the Hindenburg Line. It was
captured, with another good haul of prisoners, and beyond there
were scenes of wild confusion, opening visions of a glorious
breakthrough into wide, defenceless spaces. The tanks had been
a great help, one of them having demolished sixteen machine-
gun nests in a single redoubt, but all six were out of action now
and unable to take advantage of this great opportunity.

The 5th Cavalry Brigade came trotting up after an hour or
so, but perhaps fortunately for them they arrived too late to
be sent on. The scenes of confusion were delusive. A massed
counter-attack drove the Staffordshires off Mannequin Hill, on
the right of the Foresters, and another round the left flank of
the latter forced them out of Montbrehain. The Germans were
not beaten yet, as was emphasised by the weight of fire encountered by these sturdy Midlanders when they tried to regain
their final objectives and retrieve their wounded comrades. The
attempt soon had to be abandoned, but a number of wounded
were dragged back to safety with bullets whistling past them.
Lance-Corporal W. H. Coltman, a stretcher bearer of the North
Staffordshires, made three successful sorties on his own, winning
a V.C. to wear with his D.C.M., M.M. and bar.

The 2nd Australian Division, with six weak battalions opera-
ting on a frontage of almost three miles and with little assistance
from their tanks, made canny progress, forcing an entry into the
main trench line by skilled fieldcraft and good use of their guns.
There were six belts of wire to be crossed, each twenty feet
wide, and at one point, where fire was particularly heavy,
Lieutenant J. Maxwell of the 18th Battalion was the only one
who could crawl through. Some amazing feats, including escape

after being caught by a hoax surrender by twenty Germans, won him a V.C. He had already won the M.C. and D.C.M. On the left, the main trench line looped back round the side of a spur and ran in the direct line of the advance, and for the Germans inside it it was foolhardy to do anything else but run. But as the Australians approached Beaurevoir, the nodal village of the line, they met such opposition that they were obliged to make a small retirement and consolidate their line.

The 50th Division also provoked surprisingly vigorous reaction from the Germans after some early successes. The joint villages of Gouy and Le Catelet, which had been reached by the Americans five days earlier, were gained by 9 a.m. after a brief but tremendous pounding by the massed artillery. But at 1 p.m. a counter-attack, supported by volumes of machine-gun fire, came in and the Germans regained possession. However, the 1st King's Own Yorkshire Light Infantry still held a commanding ridge that overlooked Gouy from the east, and in the evening the 2nd Northumberland Fusiliers fought their way back through the streets to gain permanent custody at last of this much striven for village.

Further readjustment was needed for one last shove to complete the collapse of the Hindenburg Line. The 25th Division, of Morland's XIII corps, were brought in for the attack on Beaurevoir and the 2nd Australian were side-stepped so that they could attack Montbrehain and repay the 46th for the help they had given the Australian Corps by their splendid advance at the battle's start. Both attacks were made at first light on the 5th.

The Australians put in three battalions, one of which was the 2nd Pioneer Battalion, who were assigned the duty of protecting the right flank and had a very hard fight. There were twelve tanks and once in the village they wrought great destruction. Although jumbled remnants of at least four divisions—ten regiments were represented among the 600 prisoners taken—many Germans fought hard. One post, containing nine machine-guns and forty-two Germans, belched fire lethally until 2nd Lieutenant G. M. Ingram of the 24th Battalion reached it with a few men behind him. The Germans put their hands up when Ingram broke in among them but it did not save one of them his life. But this was only the start. Ingram next rushed a single machine-gun post, killing its six occupants, and he then led the remains of his company—thirty men out of ninety—against a heavily-wired quarry on the edge of the village, where his battalion had suffered many casualties. Having leapt into the quarry and turned it into a morgue, he scrambled out entirely on his own, shot some machine-gunners firing through the cellar ventilator of a house, and ejected sixty-two Germans from other parts of the house, whom he mercifully made prisoner. He then made a careful reconnaisance and disposed what was left of his company to meet a counter-attack that seemed to be in the offing but in fact amounted to no more than heavy shelling and machine-gunning. The Australians had won Montbrehain.

Ingram, who had already won the M.M., became the twentieth and last Australian to win the V.C. since the great advance began on August 8th. The Australians were relieved that night by the 30th American.

Suffering perhaps from lack of practice, the 25th Division had to labour long and hard for Beaurevoir. A pincer attack by two brigades was attempted, but was held up everywhere by a torrent of machine-gun fire. Five tanks rumbled into the village with the right pincer and let fly in all directions with their machine-guns and 6-pounders, but the infantry could not follow and the tanks had to come back, leaving one knocked out. A fresh attempt was made in the evening, with the 5th Gloucestershire, previously in reserve, attacking the village from the left flank, where some progress had been made, while the other two brigades made attacks along the flanks of the village on either side. Rushing in even before their barrage lifted, the Gloucesters gained complete surprise and took the village with little difficulty. Like Montbrehain, it had been defended by an amalgam of at least four divisions, and there were no troops now left to make a counter-attack.

In the course of seven days the Fourth Army had broken the back of the German defence system at the point where its structure was at its strongest. With twelve divisions they had decimated twenty and advanced across six miles of fortifications to which months of labour had been devoted. They had enabled the French First Army to reoccupy St. Quentin and given the British Third passage across the St. Quentin Canal through Le Catelet. They had captured 14,664 prisoners at a cost (including the Americans) of 15,000 casualties, slightly behind the ambitious target of one for one.

Ludendorff perhaps was not surprised. On the very day that Rawlinson's attack opened he had repeated his demand for an armistice at a Council of War held (not inappropriately) at the Hotel Britannique, Spa—"our situation admits of no delay, not an hour is to be lost." It had important political consequences: the Kaiser consented to bestow representative government to distract the people, and the liberally-minded Prince Max of Baden at length agreed, hesitantly and reluctantly, to accept the appointment of Chancellor and the rôle of harbinger of peace. Militarily, Ludendorff had virtually abandoned responsibility; it was left to the army group commanders to hold on as best they could.

Although delighted by the performance of his men, especially the 46th Division (whose captures amounted to 6,000 and losses to 2,500), Rawlinson was not deluded as to the cause of his victory. "Had the Boche morale," he wrote on the night of the 5th, "not shown marked signs of deterioration during the past month, I should never have contemplated attacking the Hindenburg Line. Had it been defended by the Germans of two years ago, it would certainly have been impregnable and, with my Fourth Army as it is now, I would gladly defend it against any number of German divisions."

If the Boche morale was understandably low—though in fact a stouter effort was made here than at any other time since the collapse of their own offensives—it must always be a source of marvel that that of the Fourth Army was so high, especially among those divisions that had been under heavy strain since the month of March. The Australians had set the pace and by their example inspired others. Since their arrival at Villers Bretonneux they had established a supremacy over the enemy which must be without equal for any such sustained period of fighting in the history of war. They were famous, of course, for

243

their initiative, audacity and superb fieldcraft, but Monash was well aware that they would not make full use of their skills without confidence in their commanders and that this in turn depended on thorough and imaginative planning. This above all else enabled him to abide by his maxim, "Feed your troops on victory," and certainly they found it sustaining.

The British were by nature less adventurous and were part conscript as opposed to all volunteer. Yet it is extraordinary how much had been cheerfully endured by the divisions of III Corps that had accompanied the Australians on the thirty-five mile journey into the Hindenburg Line. The Battalions of the 12th Division, for instance, had each made some twelve attacks during the course of fifty-two days and must have suffered at least 600 casualties (their approximate rifle strength at the start), for the total casualties in the division came to 6,229 and although the supporting arms had their share of gas and high explosive the infantry filled over ninety per cent of the graves and hospital beds. This figure is 2,000 more than the average suffered by the Australian divisions, despite their three extra battalions each, and except for their six weeks' fighting on the Somme in 1916 it was far in excess of anything previously suffered by the hard-fought 12th over a similar period. It is true that their progress was leisurely compared to the German onrush in March, but there is another big difference in that whereas the sting had gone from the German assault divisions at the end of a week, when their men were surrendering with the self-pitying excuse that they were being driven like pigs, the British were still in good heart even after seven weeks of steady grinding. Again it was a question of confidence, and tactful handling was needed to keep it alive. Rawlinson played his part here. He welcomed discussion, and Monash, Godley, and Braithwaite have all paid tribute to the patience and sympathy with which he listened to suggestions at his frequent conferences. He also made sure that whenever anything was achieved a message of appreciation from the Army Commander followed.

Now the Australian Corps, General Butler and the staff of his III Corps, and the 12th Division were all due for their farewell messages of appreciation. Except for their artillery, which remained to support the Americans, the Australians were now withdrawn from the battle zone—for them the war was over; Butler and his corps headquarters were transferred to Birdwood's command, to end the year as they had begun it, in the Fifth Army; and the 12th Division joined Horne's First Army. They were brought back into the line again on October 5th.

15

THE FINAL TRUDGE

(October 6–November 11)

The unfolding of the great plans that Foch had devised at such short notice had rather alarming consequences for a British officer, Colonel T. Bentley Mott, on his staff. Passing his chief in the street of Bombon one day in late September, he remarked that the Germans seemed to be getting more than they could stand. In place of spoken reply, Foch (in Mott's words) "came up close to me, took a firm hold of my belt with his left hand and with his right fist delivered a punch at my chin, a hook under my ribs and another drive at my ear; he then shouldered his stick and without a single word marched on to the chateau, his straight back and horseman's legs presenting as gallant a sight as one would wish to look upon."

With the coming of October Foch's jauntiness subsided. *"Tout le monde"* were not going into battle quite as intended. Pershing's First American Army by the Meuse had become clogged by depressing administrative failures which had brought not only his offensive to a halt but some of his divisions to the point of starvation; Pétain's armies remained characteristically unresponsive to renewed goading by Foch; and King Albert's had been unable to maintain their momentum in the face of hardening resistance, which had brought heavy casualties to the Belgians in particular. Only Haig pleased the Generalissimo, but there were still a daunting number of German divisions opposite him.

On the day after the fall of Beaurevoir and Montbrehain, that is on Sunday, October 6th, the headlines on the papers in France and Britain broke the news that Germany and Austria-Hungary had asked for an armistice based on President

Wilson's Fourteen Points, thereby indicating their readiness to withdraw from all territory they had invaded. The news also reached the German soldiers, in the sugared form of an order of the day from their Supreme Commander and Kaiser, the All-Highest. "Troops from every German province," it told them, "are doing their duty and, on foreign soil, are heroically defending the Fatherland . . . In the midst of the hardest fighting comes the collapse of the Macedonian front. Your front is unbroken and will remain so. In agreement with my Allies I have decided to offer peace once more to our enemies; but we will only stretch out our hands for an honourable peace."

For the men who had to remove these German troops from foreign soil, not by charade or diplomatic persuasion but with their bayonets, knowledge of the peace offer could hardly act as stimulant to greater daring. No great breakthrough had followed the piercing of the Hindenburg Line. Indeed, any attempt at exploitation wilted abruptly under the fire from machine-guns and artillery, and with their skill in siting these weapons, and with the best men creamed off to man them, the Germans could still make the march to the Rhine a long and heartbreaking affair for the British and their allies. Unlike Foch, whose attitude to the matter rather shocked him, Haig was no advocate of harsh peace terms, but he appreciated that the Germans might be merely playing for time and that any easing of the pressure could give them the break they needed. He was determined to crash through where he was strongest and the Germans most sensitive, on the front of his Fourth and Third Armies.

A combined attack was made on the 8th, the Fourth Army with five of their new divisions (from the right) the 6th, the American 30th, the 25th, 66th, and 50th, the Third Army, who had not yet penetrated the Beaurevoir Line, with five of their old and trusted ones, the 38th, 37th, New Zealand, 3rd, 2nd, and 63rd Royal Naval, the last named being charged with the envelopment of Cambrai, which was flanked on the north by the Canadians. A hundred tanks were produced, in varying stages of mechanical decrepitude. Now perhaps was the time to use them in mass, to break through *after* the infantry had enlarged the hole between Montbrehain and Beaurevoir, but this would be encroachment on the privilege of the cavalry. The tanks were distributed for support for the infantry, whom they had so often served so well, and although the Whippets were assigned a limited exploitation line, Kavanagh's Cavalry Corps were brought up in readiness to perform the honoured rôle of disrupting the enemy nervous system.

Only on the extreme right and left did the infantry encounter serious trouble. On the right the 6th Division again suffered from that endemic complaint, the absence of Frenchmen on their flank, but gained nearly all their objectives. On the left, near Cambrai, the Germans made three counter-attacks led by groups of four to five tanks, and as most of the latter were captured Mark IVs they were assumed to be British and caused shock and confusion when they opened fire, three British tanks being among their victims. However, they were soon disposed of, one by a captured anti-tank rifle—a nice case of tit-for-tat—and six by tanks, and the worst surprised division, the 63rd Royal Naval, regained the ground they had lost overlooking Cambrai.

An advance of four miles had been made and another 8,000 prisoners taken, of whom the American 30th Division contributed 1,500 together with thirty guns. But the attempts to pass through made by the cavalry met with their usual fate; indeed their chances were so forlorn that little was risked. The infantry were called from the shelters they had dug themselves for a further attack before daylight next morning. They found the enemy had gone from all along the line, including from the scarred but not flattened town of Cambrai, that Tantalus of a year ago. Again the cavalry rode up, having suffered disturbance and some casualties from air raids during the night. Rawlinson ordered Harman's 3rd Cavalry Division on to Le Cateau, some eight miles on. They made two charges to help the infantry drive out rearguards, the Canadian Cavalry Brigade capturing 230 prisoners in a brave but costly attack on Gattigny Wood and the 6th Cavalry Brigade taking two villages further on at rather lighter but by no means negligible loss. By nightfall the cavalry were within a mile of Le Cateau, but more in a scouting than destructive rôle.

The German Second and (on their right) Seventeenth Armies had pulled back just in time, with the former returned to the

Crown Prince Rupprecht's Group and the Eighteenth to Crown Prince Willie's, since the pessimistic von Boehn and his group headquarters had now been removed. Further northwards the right wing of the Seventeenth, the Sixth, and the Fourth Armies had gradually been pressed into an enormous bulge by Ludendorff's peeved reluctance to withdraw to a line, named and reconnoitred but barely fortified, that ran from Ghent along the River Schelde (or Escaut) and continued through Le Cateau; its name was the Hermann Line. Not until King Albert's group burst forth in a new attack on October 14th, with Plumer's Second Army reaching the outskirts of Menin and threatening Courtrai, was Crown Prince Rupprecht authorised to fall back on this line and to give up the whole of the Belgian coast. Poor Rupprecht was on the verge of despair, as is shown by a letter he wrote to Prince Max around this time complaining that his troops "surrender in hordes, whenever the enemy attacks, and thousands of plunderers infest the districts round the bases." None the less his armies retained some measure of cohesion, thanks to the devotion of their staffs and a few regimental officers. They would have been in desperate peril if Horne's First Army had struck northwards from Cambrai across the base of the bulge, but Haig needed to concentrate his strength for his direct drive towards Germany, aimed across the exits from the Ardennes, and his least endowed army, Birdwood's Fifth, were given the task of pushing the Germans back from their bulge, with flanking aid from the First and Second, through Lille and the black industrial wilderness stretching to the Schelde.

The old and solid town of Le Cateau lies on a tributary of the Schelde, the Selle. It should have been no great obstacle, but heavy rainfall and some industrious damming had raised its water level and made its adjacent marshes boggy. The approach of winter embittered the rawness of the evening mist and gave the young soldiers sharp taste of the new ordeal— of even greater misery on the impoverished German side— that the winter would bring. It was up this valley that the Germans had advanced, full of hope and ardour, in August 1914, to turn the flank of Smith-Dorrien's gasping but still lethal corps on the open plateau now held by Rawlinson's men.

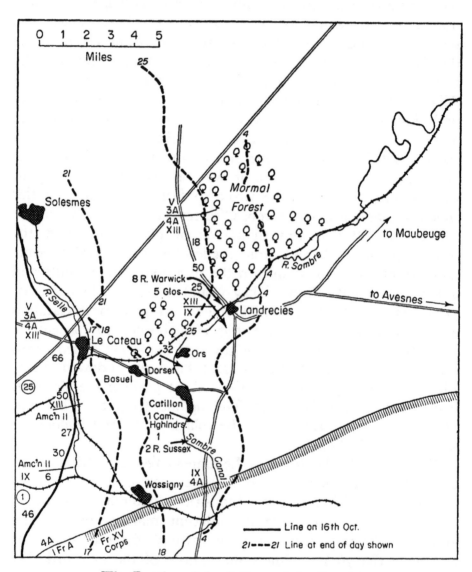

The Battles of the Selle and the Sambre

Beyond, on the eastern side, there was a marked change of scenery. The rolling sweeps, which had been the seldom broken pattern all the way from Amiens, gave way to choppier country, littered with trees, houses, and woods, and strewn with thick, closely spaced hedges beyond which reconnaissance became a matter of guesswork.

Having been the first to probe this new line, Rawlinson was the first to attack it. He needed seven days to bring up his guns and ammunition, partly because of delays in repairing demolitions on the one railway line available to him, partly because of the extra strain on the A.S.C. in having to feed the cavalry. The attack went in on October 17th—at 5.30 a.m. and in mist thicker than anything previously experienced by the most hardened connoisseur. It was made on a ten-mile front stretching southwards from Le Cateau, which the 66th Division were opposite. The 50th were on their right, and on theirs, with decreasing encumbrance from the river, the 27th and 30th American and the 6th and 46th with the 1st behind them ready to leapfrog. Lines of assault varied, as was the practice, to make best use of the lie of the land. There were forty-eight tanks in support, some equipped with cribs to help them over the water.

The capture of objectives four miles away at furthest took two days in place of the one planned. On the first the bridging was achieved without hitch despite gas shelling and complete lack of visibility; the assault troops of the 50th Division pushed across twelve duckboard bridges made from timber left in a nearby German dump, and the sappers of the 66th constructed 20-foot bridges by the northern outskirts of Le Cateau after the South African Brigade had made a stealthy crossing at dead of night and lain up the enemy wire. As the attack developed and visibility at last arrived the Germans made some strong counter-attacks. They drove battalions back here and there but could not withstand the counter counter-attacks delivered in co-ordination with the might of the British guns in the afternoon. Le Cateau was cleared by 6 p.m. thanks largely to a fine but costly enveloping movement by the South Africans. Next day the 50th Division in particular paid for the habit of the pre-dawn attack by being badly caught in shell fire as they were forming up, but the 1st gained complete surprise by attacking at 11 a.m. and the 1st Black Watch, having swept into Wassigny almost unopposed, had the satisfaction of capturing four officers at their dinner table. On the left wing the 25th Division entered the battle and captured Bazurel, two miles beyond Le Cateau on the main road.

Debeney's Frenchmen had this time more than kept up with their neighbours, and on the 19th the right wing of Rawlinson's army reached the line of the Sambre Canal, five miles beyond the Selle. Here they were halted. It was the turn of the Third and First Armies to make the main effort now, aiming rather more northwards than hitherto in order to assist the advance of King Albert's group on Brussels, in accordance with a new instruction from the mercurial Foch. The Fourth Army had taken another 5,000 prisoners, representing fourteen divisions. The enemy had if anything fought harder than in previous weeks; certainly there had been more sting in his counter-attacks.

Byng chose a night attack. It was made at 2 a.m. on the 20th in company with one division of the First Army, whose left were still in process of pursuing the Germans back to their new defence line. Tanks were used with some effect, although the moon was swaithed in mist. The problem of crossing the Selle was an increasingly hard one leftwards for the seven attacking divisions of the Third Army, but two months of mobile warfare had tuned the staff machinery to high pitch, without any diminishment of enthusiasm: the crossings were made, the bridges constructed and the tanks fed across with little confusion. But beyond the wire and jagged railway line on the far bank, some determined counter-attacks were made, especially just to the north of Le Cateau, and it was not until evening that all objectives had been gained, some two miles beyond the river. An average of rather more than fifty men from each attacking battalion had fallen, in exchange for a similar overall but less evenly spread number of prisoners.

They were not through yet, far from it. Much can be achieved in a fortnight, and the Germans had had at least a fortnight in which to build and wire-in their supporting, deep-sited lines beyond the Selle. It was incumbent on the Fourth, Third and First Armies to drive interminably on, and on October 23rd they together plunged deeper into the bewildering maze of hedges, houses and trees that stretched ahead of them. A steady advance of some six miles in two days was made. Resistance was still strong in places, and at Beaurain the 42nd Lancashire Division were involved in a fierce clash in which men on both sides were bayoneted. Heavily wired hedges were a source of delay and grief, but with the aid of the odd tank here and there and by local, persevering tactics the Germans were steadily thrown back or captured. On the 25th the Fourth and Third Armies paused to prepare yet another co-ordinated attack, while the First maintained slow, dogged pressure to envelop Valenciennes, having outflanked the Schelde at its bend from east to north.

Germany's request for an armistice had been made to President Wilson and he had taken it on himself to lay down his terms, demanding as preliminaries to negotiation the evacuation of occupied territory and "the immediate cessation of U-boat warfare, of wanton destruction and of other illegal and inhuman practices". Ludendorff, amazingly, was so enraged by this humiliating product of his own initiative and by Prince Max's inclination to accept it that on October 25th he issued an order of the day calling the terms "unacceptable to us soldiers" and urging "resistance to the utmost of our power". This was ludicrous insubordination to his Imperial Supreme Commander and Government, and on the 27th the Kaiser accepted his resignation at the end of a curt, sour, sad audience. It had, of course, been Ludendorff's hope that Germany would have been able to negotiate from a position of some apparent strength and, with one further, much shorter line to fall back on, he must have believed that his troops could still hold out long enough to avoid capitulation. Foch expected them to last until the following spring, according to the view expressed on his behalf on October 23rd (British Official History, p. 384). There can be little doubt that they would have done so, but for Haig's burning determination—which a year earlier had caused such suffering—to keep attacking his beaten enemy.

Hindenburg also tendered his resignation, but this the Kaiser could not accept. A patriot named General Gröner accepted the post of First Quartermaster-General; he was Chief of the

Field Railways and was the right man to organise the return journey to the Fatherland.

A further instalment of blows was delivered. On October 24th, after at least a month's instigation, the Italian Army struck out from the Vittorio-Veneto line, and with the aid of the three British divisions still there and some French ones they made such progress that by the 27th Austria had made a direct approach to Italy for an armistice. On the 31st King Albert's group began a new push, with the French Sixth Army now on the left of the British Second; their progress had been somewhat laboured, but now they achieved a spurt as far as the Schelde. On November 1st the American First Army—now under command of Lieutenant-General H. Liggett, since Pershing's command had expanded to an army group—and the French Fourth began another attack towards Mezières, and now, turning their past disappointments to advantage, these Americans broke through and kept going relentlessly, with the French responding to the challenge on their left. Also on November 1st the British First Army began the assault on Valenciennes, and despite restrictions on shelling, for the benefit of the population, some Canadians made an entry after crossing the Schelde. There was some tough fighting here; not until the 3rd did Valenciennes fall.

In the pre-dawn murk of Monday, November 4th, the guns opened up at varying intervals over a thirty-mile frontage and seventeen divisions of the Fourth, Third and First Armies went into the attack, followed by a further six in second line. It was the most extensive attack made by the British during the war, yet only thirty-seven tanks were in fit state to take part.

Rawlinson had a supporting rôle to Byng, but his troops had the most difficult task. He had only two corps left in the line, since the Americans had been withdrawn for rest after crossing the Selle. Braithwaite's IX Corps had to cross the Sambre Canal, which was wide and full and overlooked from the far side. He put in the 1st Division (on the right) and the 32nd, who had had a stiff fight in clearing the enemy from the western bank, with the 46th this time held back in reserve. Morland's XIII Corps on the left had to plunge into the great Forest of Mormal, a six-mile stretch of undergrowth, strewn with occasional clearings, bisected by many streams, and flanked by the Sambre

Canal. He attacked with the 25th Division, the 50th, and on the left those splendid old-stagers of the Fourth Army, late of the Fifth—indeed, the only one to remain with Rawlinson of the thirteen wrecks of divisions handed over to him by Gough— the 18th Division, who had returned to the line on October 22nd after three weeks' rest and had fought their way to their present positions.

It was presumably necessary to cross the Sambre at this point in order to sever communications with Avesnes and Maubeuge, and the Fourth Army had in any case shown themselves expert at this hazardous form of operation. They needed all their expertise now, and the determination to weather some desperate crises.

The 2nd Royal Sussex were the right-hand assault battalion of the 1st Division, and because the water here was only seventeen feet wide they chose to cross at a lock, which had its control house on the far bank. There was a dyke a hundred yards short of the canal bank and despite all the planning and rehearsal it was found that the planks the sappers carried to span it were not long enough. A few brave spirits plunged across, and one of them crossed the canal on his own over the lock-gate. His fate is not recorded. The remainder halted and inevitably there was contraction of the column, which consisted of two assault companies in their life-jackets and a company of sappers carrying four long bridges fitted with German runners. The barrage lifted, and there was nothing to protect the men on the wide open marsh except a transient compound of darkness, smoke and early mist. It was not enough. The shells whizzed in among them, singly at first and then in a hideous, terrifying stonk. Machine-gunners from the lock-house and the slopes beyond joined in the torture. The wounded called for help, officers for order.

The commanding officer of the Royal Sussex, Lieutenant-Colonel D. G. Johnson (from the South Wales Borderers) came up and restored order by energy and brave example, and Major G. de C. E. Findlay, of the 409 Field Company, R.E., finding himself the only officer of his company unwounded, set about repairing the damaged bridges and grabbing hold of infantrymen to take the place of fallen sappers. Johnson formed a scratch bridge and assault party and led them forward during a lull in the shelling, only to walk into a further stonk which (in the words of the unemotional battalion war diary) "landed right amongst them, literally blowing them back again on the rear waves". Johnson escaped being hit, again restored some sort of order out of the groaning confusion, and quickly got mixed groups going forward for a third attempt. Findlay had been hit, but he patched up bridges and bridge-carrying parties with undiminished energy. He got a bridge laid across the dyke. Another was lugged over it, brought to the canal bank, and laboriously launched, while under the inspiration of their colonel men of the Royal Sussex blazed away with all they had, the Lewis-gunners firing from the hip hose-pipe fashion. First to reach the far bank, to make fast the bridge, was the wounded Findlay. He was followed by a rush of infantry. The Germans gave up or ran away in the mist, allowing the remainder of the brigade to file past 140 prostrate bodies and cross in peace.

At the 1st Division's other point of crossing the 1st Cameron Highlanders encountered no obstruction and moved so swiftly that they were all on the far bank when the German defensive fire came down on the approaches. The 32nd Division had no such luck. They tried in the vicinity of Ors, but an attempt to float a span astride the remains of the road bridge failed and further north a torrent of shelling and machine-gun fire made the two bridges that were pushed across unusable. There were some great heroics here by members of the 16th Lancashire Fusiliers, 2nd Manchester, and 218th Field Company, R.E., and the attempt was not abandoned until the commanding officer of the Lancashire Fusiliers, Lieutenant-Colonel J. N. Marshall, who was a subaltern of the Irish Guards in the Army List, had been killed leading a dash across an already mutilated bridge and two hundred casualties suffered. However, the 1st Dorsetshire, who had made the attempt at Ors, managed to sneak a bridge floated by petrol cans across on the other, southern side of the village. They soon made this crossing safe, and with the 5th/6th Royal Scots following them, and then the battered Lancasehire Fusiliers and Manchesters, the opposition collapsed. There were 700 casualties in this division.

On the right of the 1st Division a corps of Debeny's army also attempted the crossing. They did not succeed.

The 25th Division, on the left of the 32nd but part of XIII Corps, had also to cross the canal in order to take the little town of Landrecies, where Haig had once thought himself in danger of capture. They had first to cross almost a mile of close, enemy-held country, and the task both of advance and crossing was entrusted in the main to two battalions, the 5th Gloucestershire and 8th Royal Warwickshire, who went about it with great eagerness. The Gloucesters, on the right, captured a bridge intact and swiftly grabbed a spur overlooking the town from the south. The Royal Warwicks had a stiff and long fight through the built-up approaches, in the course of which the main Landrecies bridge collapsed with a bang after a German officer had been seen galloping up to blow its charge. But the Warwicks persisted, rushed a subsidiary bridge intact, and won possession of Landrecies.

Elsewhere all was plain sailing—or so the overall result, one of complete success everywhere, suggests. The centre of the Third Army advanced over six miles, further than their intended objectives, and the total prisoners amounted to about 10,500, a much higher figure than the British casualties. 200 guns were captured, even though sited with retirement in mind. The remainder were wearily tugged back in headlong retreat, bombed all through a murky, rainy night by the R.A.F.

A change had come over the German prisoners. At last they seemed unashamedly glad to be captured, and there were cheers of greeting from the inmates of the Fourth Army cage on the arrival of each new batch. The advancing British soldiers also received greeting on a scale never previously encountered, for instead of being evacuated, each village seemed full of evacuees, and having emerged from their cellars very timidly the young and old soon displayed complete disregard for falling shells in their enthusiasm to hail their liberators or to rip the boots from dead Germans. Endearing though the British found their welcome, it could be embarrasing while enemy strongholds remained unquelled.

Yet, however complete the success, it was hard enough won in places. There were many fierce encounters all along the line, many plucky attacks by battalions that had little rest since mid-August and had sunk in strength to 400 men. The determination displayed at this late stage, when there was so little apparent incentive to risk, is staggering. In the Fourth Army, whose divisions admittedly were fresher than those of the Third, seven V.C.s were won, the highest number in this Army for any single day certainly of 1918 and probably of the whole war. The deeds of Colonel Johnson and Major Findlay have already been recorded; both already held the D.S.O. and M.C. Those of Colonel Marshall, who showed superb leadership under terrible fire before being killed at the head of his men on the broken bridge, are even more amazing because he had previously been wounded ten times. Second Lieutenant J. Kirk of the Manchesters, also won a posthumous V.C. here for paddling himself across the canal on a raft with a Lewis-gun, although under machine-gun fire from the opposite bank, and for keeping his gun in action long after being wounded, until at last he was killed. Major A. H. S. Waters, D.S.O., M.C., and Sapper A. Archibald, of the 32nd Divisional Engineers, were luckier, miraculously surviving repair work on a bridge first during a pounding at its launching and then in the canal itself, where they worked away with dead all round them and an enemy machine-gun firing at them from thirty yards. The seventh went to Lance-Corporal W. Amey, of the Royal Warwicks, for Australian-style exploits during the fight into Landrecies. A further four V.C.s were won for marvellous feats against machine-gun nests during the advance from the Selle, spread between the 50th Division (Sergeant H. A. Curtis of the 2nd Royal Dublin Fusiliers), the 25th (Private F. G. Miles of the 5th Gloucestershire), the 18th (Lieutenant F. W. Hedges, whose V.C. was the fourth won with the 6th Northamptonshire), and the 32nd Division (Sergeant J. Clarke, of the 15th Lancashire Fusiliers, who displayed great valour both on the 2nd and 4th of November). Obviously there would have been no call for these great deeds if plans had not gone awry here and there. On the other hand they express supreme confidence in the feasibility of tasks set, and there would have been no confidence without good generalship.

The German Army could, in the opinion of Ludendorff's

successor, Gröner, stand no more. On November 5th he told the Cabinet, "We can hold out long enough for negotiations." But by Wednesday the 6th he had changed his mind: "Even Monday will be too late; it must be Saturday at latest. . . . I have come to the conclusion that, painful as it is, we must take the step of asking Foch for terms and meanwhile retreat behind the Rhine." Desertion by her allies, mutiny in her fleet, the brewing of revolution, and one more resounding defeat at the front—these disasters had struck Germany in swift succession, and it was the last that gave such urgency to the crisis. The Allies had agreed on the terms Foch should ask, and since they were concerned with military matters the Commanders-in-Chief had been consulted. Haig alone had opposed demanding occupation of any part of Germany, because he feared the Germans might fight on rather than accept and did not wish to prolong the war merely to inflict humiliation. Even he, optimist that he was, had not realised the completeness of the German defeat.

General Debeney was deputed, somewhat ironically, to receive the German delegates, among whom, as a matter of prestige, there was no military representative. They were put on a train and taken to a forest rendezvous, where at 11 a.m. on Friday the 8th Foch presented them with the terms. They included withdrawal beyond the far banks of the Rhine, to allow the Allies bridgeheads over it. The delegates could not accept without reference to their Government. They were told that a reply was needed by 11 a.m. on the Monday, November 11th.

The British meanwhile trudged on, knowing nothing of these negotiations apart from rumours. Like all their previous attacks this last one had merely jerked the enemy back along his supply lines and once again pursuit was proving a laborious business; the weather was vile, and by extensive demolitions the Germans had presented the British with very serious problems of supply. Tiresome rearguard positions were continually encountered, and although cavalry patrols, armoured cars, or cyclists, suffering agonies on the bumpy roads, might locate them, the infantry nearly always had to remove them. At midday on November 8th two Scots battalions of the 32nd Division gained Avesnes after a brisk little battle; they were now sixteen miles beyond the Sambre. On the next day the 50th Division were subjected to a counter-attack on the road between Avesnes and Maubeuge, very hotly supported by artillery and machine-gun fire; it took them two hours to beat it off. On this same day, the 9th, Foch issued a ginger note making "appeal to the energy and the initiative of the commanders-in-chief to make the results obtained decisive", and in Berlin, Germany was proclaimed a Republic and government taken over by a Council of the People's Commissioners. The Kaiser, who was at Spa, took train at 5 a.m. next morning for Holland, closely followed by his son Willie, ex-Crown Prince, ex-commander of an army group.

All along the Allied line the laboured pursuit went on, with divisions dropping out in increasing number to speed the supply of those left ahead. Only the American First Army were able to produce the spurt Foch asked for—and this before the issue of his note and at the price of considerable pique among the French. For on the morning of the 9th the Americans, after a race between two divisions, reached the heights overlooking Sedan, an objective that the French could claim not only as a birthright but within the boundary vaguely assigned to them.

On the British sector, Birdwood's Fifth Army discovered on the night of the 8th that they could cross the Schelde unopposed instead of making the great attack planned for the 11th; the bulk of the Cavalry Corps was allotted this army, but the roads were too congested for many horsemen to get through to the front. Plumer's Second Army kept pace on the left, returned now to Haig's command after some lengthy agitation by him. At 2 a.m. on the 10th the old fortress town of Maubeuge fell to troops of Byng's Third Army, the 3rd Grenadiers, of the Guards Division, who had made a three-mile thrust assisted by pack mules; the Guards had come seventy miles since their attack began on August 21st, and the New Zealand, the 5th, 37th, 42nd and 62nd had accompanied them. Horne's First Army were now approaching that town of great emotional importance to the British, Mons. The German Seventeenth Army were not keen to let it go. The 2nd and 3rd Canadian Divisions battled all through the Sunday, November 10th, to drive stubborn groups out of the maze of orchards, canals and dreary houses around the town. In the evening there were signs of a withdrawal, but there was still plenty of machine-gun fire. At

2.30 a.m. on the 11th the Canadians pushed patrols across the main perimeter canal, followed by the whole of the 42nd Battalion (Royal Highlanders of Canada), and by dawn every German left in Mons had been killed or captured by these great experts at the infantryman's art.

The advance was resumed at daylight. The First, Fifth and Second Armies all made good progress against light opposition. On the Third Army front there was only probing against a riverline that appeared to be quite strongly held. The Fourth Army now had only the 66th Division in the line, covering a ten-mile frontage with the 5th Cavalry Brigade under command; the 18th King's and the 9th Manchester were on the right, just inside Belgium, and the South African Brigade on the left, still in France. The Lancashire men began their advance at 7 a.m. as usual and at first met no opposition, but the South Africans, who had had a tough fight for a village the day before, found the enemy active on their sector and the cavalry were unable to get round them. The shelling grew in volume, and the divisional artillery of the 66th made reply. They fired 1,800 rounds during the morning, which was a fair figure for a whole day's skirmishing, but of course the heavier guns of the Fourth Army, which had been in the habit of discharging some 7,500 rounds a day as a matter of routine, had been too far removed for any firing during the last three days. Then at 10.15 a staff officer arrived at the South African Brigade headquarters with a message that threw interesting light on the sudden increase in hostile shelling. An armistice had been signed—in fact, at 5.5 a.m., and the message had gone out from Haig's G.H.Q. at 6.50 to filter in the normal manner through the vine of command: "Hostilities will cease at 11.00 hours today, November 11th. Troops will stand fast on the line reached."

The Manchesters had now bumped the enemy and, like the South Africans, they kept their heads down, for the Germans were blazing away with all they had. Their fire rose to a crescendo a few minutes before eleven, stopped abruptly, and then reopened for one final crash. One machine-gun, which throughout had been maddeningly raucous, fired the longest burst anyone had heard, lasting two minutes and ending dead on eleven, as timed by a South African. A German soldier then stood up, removed his helmet, bowed to his audience, turned, picked up his machine-gun, and walked slowly away.

A strange quiet descended on the great battlefield, felt by the troops in reserve as much as by the few in the front line. There was champagne for some, to be drunk from enamel mugs, when the overworked horses arrived with the mess carts. But there was something spooky about that silence; it was hard to go to sleep.

16

AFTERMATH

The antipathy between Haig and Lloyd George, which had been stagnant while Haig was winning the war, frothed up again now it was over. Lloyd George made two advances which it is hard to believe he did not intend as slights: he offered Haig a viscountcy, which is what French had received when dismissed from command of the B.E.F. for incompetence, and he invited him to a ceremonial reception of Allied leaders, in procession to which Haig was to share the fifth coach with Wilson. Haig parried the one by refusing to take any title until adequate financial provision had been made for his officers and men—this undoubtedly would have been his response whatever the honour offered him—and he demolished the other by pointing out that the day chosen was a Sunday and stating flatly that he would not come unless ordered by the Army Council, while to his diary he gave the additional information that he had "no intention of taking part in any triumphal ride with Foch, or with any pack of foreigners, through the streets of London, mainly in order to add to L.G.'s importance and help him in his election campaign". Haig was the winner on both scores. He eventually received an earldom, with grant of £100,000, having delayed acceptance long enough at any rate to get the problem of pensions energetically tackled, and he was accorded a separate ceremonial reception for him and his army commanders, held at Buckingham Palace on December 19th. Haig's only complaint was that instead of being allowed to ride from the station they were taken by carriage "like a party of politicians or old women". The people gave them a tremendous welcome. Rawlinson, who on three previous occasions had accompanied a hero similarly honoured—Kitchener after

Omdurman in 1898, Roberts on return from South Africa in January 1901, and Kitchener again on his return in 1902—rated it "far the most enthusiastic".

Meanwhile the armies had been redeployed for the task of occupation. Plumer's was assigned the top honour of Army of the Rhine, and by the humanity they displayed his troops made some amends for the cruel continuation of the blockade. Rawlinson's was in Belgium and the others in France. Rawlinson had the 1st, 2nd and 4th Divisions among his thirteen. It was curious, he noted, how the traditions of the Regular Army clung to the old divisions. Although containing only a sprinkling of regulars, these three divisions fell rapidly into the rhythm of peacetime routine, with fine display of spit and polish, and when the King visited them on December 1st they received him (to quote Rawlinson) "stolidly". The 50th and 46th Divisions on the other hand "gave him a tremendous reception and cheered him to the echo".

But there was no cheering for the Government, despite its sweeping victory at the polls. The demobilisation scheme gave the needs of industry priority over equity and there was great unrest as men with long and honourable service glowered at the departure of colts who happened to be required for jobs at home. Base and transit depots on either side of the Channel erupted into mutiny, and at Calais, Byng had to deploy a division, with support weapons arrayed in deadly earnest, in order to force a particularly defiant cell into submission. Lloyd George called on Winston Churchill to meet the crisis, making him War Minister in place of Milner in the middle of January 1919, and Churchill's first discovery was "that Sir Douglas Haig forecasted accurately the state of indiscipline and disorganisation which would arise. . . . It is surprising that the Commander-in-Chief's prescient warnings were utterly ignored, and the Army left to be irritated and almost convulsed by a complicated artificial system open at every point to suspicion of jobbery and humbug." The remedy was now applied in Churchillian style.

There had been no breakdown of discipline among the fighting units. Officers who had led their men into the attack knew the value of tact, and by sympathy and explanation, as much as by firmness, they kept morale high to the end. The dissolution of divisions gained momentum. Those of the Territorial Force returned to England and those of the New Army disintegrated, senior battalions being awarded colours as a final gesture of Royal gratitude. The Fourth Army was disbanded on March 23rd. Its final score since the start of its great offensive on August 8th was 79,000 prisoners and 1,100 guns at a cost of 110,000 casualties. Looking back on the amazing events of the year Rawlinson attributed them to "three things: to the spirit of the troops—their recovery after the events of the spring is a glorious testimony to British grit; to the way old Foch pulled the operations of the Allies together; and to D.H.'s faith in victory this year—he believed in it long before I did."

Haig himself remained only until April 2nd, when his command was absorbed into Plumer's and he returned home to assume the appointment of Commander-in-Chief Home Forces. This job became redundant in January 1920 (with Lloyd George still Prime Minister) and the remainder of his life—until his sudden death in January 1928, aged sixty-six—he devoted wholeheartedly to the welfare of his Legion.

Alone of Haig's army commanders, Rawlinson made further advance in the military field. At the end of July 1919 he accepted a thankless task, the extrication from Archangel and Murmansk of the heterogeneous forces, of which some 18,000 were British, that had been trying to stay the collapse of the Russian Republican Army against the Bolsheviks. He set sail on August 4th, in the S.S. *Czarita,* and on an even more famous date (for him), August 8th, news reached him at sea that he had been created baron with a grant of £30,000. With him went some members of his old Fourth Army staff and (as a spare brigadier) the dashing Sadleir-Jackson, late of 18 Division, who had led the counter-attack at Baboeuf and later been shot through the knee during the attack on Albert. He turned out to be very useful, taking over the main withdrawal to Murmansk when the major-general in charge fell ill.

The task was achieved with gleaming sucess. The Bolsheviks were thrown into disarray by two brisk attacks and both the ports were evacuated without loss just before they were scheduled to become icebound. Rawlinson was back in England by October 13th, to be accorded the formal thanks of the Cabinet. After a year as G.O.C.-in-C. Aldershot Command he achieved his great ambition and set sail on November 2nd, 1920, to become Commander-in-Chief, India. He instituted bold measures of 'Indianisation' and built the foundations of a fully Indian Army by improving facilities for the education of Indian officer cadets. He took great interest in Dehra Dun College, the Sandhurst of India, and it gave him great joy to score twenty-one runs in a game of cricket against the boys soon after celebrating his sixty-first birthday, in February 1925, with a victorious game of polo. A few days later he was taken ill. He had an operation, which was not successful, and died on March 28th. "I have lost a tried and very true friend", wrote Hiag, "and the country has lost a great man."

As for the men who had inflicted that great defeat, few had found content. They had been promised a Land Fit for Heroes —as if the object of the war had been to raise their own standard of living—had waited naively for the plums to fall, and been treated instead to the bitter fruit of industrial strife, unemployment, and signs, scarcely believable, that the old enemy were preparing a further instalment of the war to end all war. Some were past caring about such matters, and not only because of bodily harm received. There could be no predicting the mental effects of the struggle on those who had long endured and apparently survived it. It is certain, as near as can be, that no mind escaped unscathed. Some had swift, complete breakdowns and recovered as swiftly. Others suffered from restlessness, which might not assert itself until four, five, or six years after the war's end and deteriorated into chronic inability to settle to any job, coupled often with a chronic sense of failure. Thousands and thousands of such cases, steadily accumulating until the next war came, have been brought to the notice of the Ex-Services Mental Welfare Society, London, and the bravest in battle have been among the worst sufferers. Fate perhaps did not treat such heroes as Bushell, Vann and Marshall so cruelly after all.

Yet whatever the torment at the time or its after effects, there is surely no veteran living who would want to forget those days. New Army and Territorial Force battalions still hold their annual dinners, and in very much larger number than functions commemorating service in the Second World War. It is enough for those that attend them that "they went through it together". Most would realise, without expressing it as such, that they come to celebrate a fellowship that sprang from the true spiritual source of reliance on each other and the subjugation of selfish motives, for war breeds love as prolifically as hate. They would take it for granted that their battalion was the best, in its spirit if not in prowess. And they could also claim, if it should ever occur to them, that the army they formed achieved something unique in British history by becoming, for those last three months of war, not only the best in the world but the most powerful.

INDEX

Note: Regiments, etc., appear under the name of arm or county, e.g., Artillery, Royal, and Shropshire Light Infantry, King's. Larger components of the B.E.F. are given under the headings Armies, Cavalry Corps, Corps and Divisions (infantry). Those of other armies are grouped under national headings.